EXPLORING STATISTICS
WITH MINITAB

EXPLORING STATISTICS WITH MINITAB

A WORKBOOK FOR THE BEHAVIOURAL SCIENCES

Andrew Monk
University of York, UK

JOHN WILEY & SONS
Chichester • New York • Brisbane • Toronto • Singapore

Copyright © 1991 by John Wiley & Sons Ltd,
Baffins Lane, Chichester,
West Sussex PO19 1UD, England

Other Wiley Editorial Offices

John Wiley & Sons, Inc., 605 Third Avenue,
New York, NY 10158-0012, USA

Jacaranda Wiley Ltd, G.P.O. Box 859, Brisbane,
Queensland 4001, Australia

John Wiley & Sons (Canada) Ltd, 22 Worcester Road,
Rexdale, Ontario M9W 1L1, Canada

John Wiley & Sons (SEA) Pte Ltd, 37 Jalan Pemimpin #05–04,
Block B, Union Industrial Building, Singapore 2057

Library of Congress Cataloging-in-Publication Data:

Monk, Andrew.
    Exploring statistics with minitab : a workbook for the behavioural
sciences / Andrew Monk.
        p.   cm.
    Includes bibliographical references and index.
    ISBN 0-471-92391-5 (paper/spiral bound)
    1. Minitab (Computer system)   2. Social sciences—Statistical
methods—Data processing.   3. Social sciences—Mathematics—Data
processing.   I. Title.
HA31.9.M66   1991
300'.28'55369—dc20   90–44615
                                                                    CIP

British Library Cataloguing in Publication Data:
Monk, Andrew
    Exploring statistics with Minitab : a workbook for the
    behavioural sciences.
    1. Statistical mathematics. Software packages
    I. Title
    519.5028553

    ISBN 0-471-92391-5

Printed by Courier International Ltd, Tiptree, Essex

CONTENTS

Preface xv

Quick reference xvii

Introduction:
How to use this book

    To the student 1

    To the instructor 2

    Instructions for systems administrators 3

Chapter 1
Experiments and variables

    Introduction 7

        An experiment 7

        Variables 7

        The independent and dependent variables 8

        Experimental control 9

        Subject variables 9

        Technical note—types of measurement 11

        Summary 11

    Work sheets 13

        Preliminary comments 13

    DCL 13

        Logging in to the computer 14

        Logging in for the first time ever 14

        Knowing you have been successful 15

        Logging out 15

        Logging in again 15

        Testing 15

        More about commands 16

Testing 16

Running Minitab 16

Mail 17

Leaving the system 17

MSDOS 18

'Booting' the system 18

Procedure when switching on the machine 18

Knowing you have been successful 18

Commands 18

The delete key 19

Testing 19

Running Minitab 19

Switching off 20

Assignment 21

Summary of DCL commands learned so far 22

Summary of MSDOS commands learned so far 22

Arrangements for using the computer 23

Chapter 2
Summary statistics

Introduction 25

Summarising nominal variables—contingency tables 25

Probability 26

The probability of something not happening 27

Measures of central tendency: mean 28

Measures of central tendency: median 28

Measures of central tendency: mode 29

Relationship between mean, median and mode 30

Measures of variation 32

Box-plots 33

The standard deviation 33

Populations and samples 35

The standard error of the mean 35

Practical considerations when sampling 37

Summary 38

Work sheets 39

Minitab 39

    Minitab 39

    Testing 40

    Columns of data 40

    Correcting mistakes in the data 41

    Testing 41

    Erasing and creating data 41

    Means and standard deviations 42

    Leaving Minitab and saving your data 43

    Entering more than one column at a time 44

    Frequency histograms 45

    Stem-and-leaf displays 45

    Box-plots 47

    Stop 48

    Answers 48

Assignment 49

Summary of DCL commands learned so far 51

Summary of MSDOS commands learned so far 51

Summary of Minitab commands learned so far 52

Chapter 3
Relationships between variables

Introduction 53

    Tables and graphs 53

    Tables, graphs and formulae 54

    Linear functions 56

    The scattergram 58

    'S' shaped curves 60

    Summary 62

Work sheets 63

DCL 63

    Files and directories 63

    Testing 64

    Manipulating files 65

    Testing 66

MSDOS 66

    Files and directories 66

    Testing 68

    Manipulating files 68

    Testing 69

Minitab 69

    Plotting graphs 69

    Testing 71

    Help 72

    Testing 74

Assignment 75

Summary of DCL commands learned so far 77

Summary of MSDOS commands learned so far 77

Summary of Minitab commands learned so far 78

Chapter 4
Goodness of fit

Introduction: 79

    Regression—the problem 79

    Deviations from a prediction and the deviance
    of a prediction 79

    The regression equation—the best fitting straight line 82

    The regression of X on Y and Y on X 82

    Deviance from the mean 83

    Correlation 85

    Interpreting r^2 88

    The correlation coefficient r 89

    Using r—the reliability of a psychometric test 89

    Summary 92

Work sheets 93

Minitab 93

    Three new Minitab commands 93

    Regress 94

    Testing 95

    Computing r^2 the hard way 95

Correlation command 96

Testing 97

DCL 97

Looking at files outside of your area 97

Testing 97

Wild cards in file specifications 97

Testing 98

MSDOS 98

Looking at files in another directory 98

Testing 98

Wild cards in file specifications 98

Testing 99

Assignment 100

Summary of DCL commands learned so far 103

Summary of MSDOS commands learned so far 103

Summary of Minitab commands learned so far 104

Chapter 5
Inference with statistics

Introduction 105

The problem 105

Statistical inference 109

Significance levels 110

The binomial test (sign test) 111

Technical note—what 'a result as extreme as' means in
this context 112

The t-test and other tests for comparing means 112

The significance of r 113

Critical values of r—Table A.1 113

Advanced note—how Minitab computes the p value for a
particular r^2 114

One- and two-tailed tests 115

How to report a correlation 115

How to report a binomial test 116

Summary 116

Work sheets 118

Minitab 118

    Using Table A.1 with the corr command 118

    Testing 120

    Finding the significance of a correlation using the
    regress command 120

    Testing 122

    Binomial test 122

    Testing 124

DCL 124

    The up arrow key 124

    Testing 125

    Control-A ($^\wedge$A) 125

    Testing 126

    Editing the command line in Minitab 126

    $^\wedge$S and $^\wedge$Q 126

    Testing 126

    Tidying up mail 127

MSDOS 127

    <F3> 127

    Testing 128

    <insert> 128

    Testing 128

    Editing the command line in Minitab 128

    $^\wedge$S 128

    Testing 129

Assignment 130

Summary of DCL commands 131

Summary of MSDOS commands 131

Summary of Minitab commands learned so far 132

Chapter 6
Comparing means

Introduction: 135

    The null hypothesis 136

    The normal distribution 136

    Parametric tests 138

When the assumptions are violated 138

Statistics using ranks 140

When to use the t-test and when the
Mann–Whitney U test 141

How to report the results of the t-test and the
Mann–Whitney U test 143

Summary 144

Work sheets 146

Minitab 146

Comparing two groups 146

t-test with the twot command 146

t-test with the twos command 147

Testing 147

The Mann–Whitney U test 147

Testing 148

Comparing the t-test and the Mann–Whitney U test 148

Assignment 152

Verbal reasoning test 153

Spatial manipulation task 153

Writing the report: 154

Summary of Minitab commands learned so far 155

Chapter 7
Two experimental designs

Introduction: 157

Within- and between-subjects designs..157

Other names..159

Matched samples designs...160

t-test for within-subjects designs 160

The Wilcoxon matched-pairs signed-ranks test.........................161

Designing your own experiments 161

Sampling bias and self selection 163

A test for use with nominal data—chi squared (χ^2)................163

Reporting the results of a within-subjects t-test and the
Wilcoxon test..166

Reporting the results of a chi squared test 167

Choosing a test—Figure 7.1 167

Summary 169

Work sheets 170

Minitab 170

Statistics for comparing means from within-subjects
(correlated samples) designs—ttest and wtest 170

Testing 173

Chi squared 173

Assignment 176

Summary of Minitab commands learned so far 179

Chapter 8
Multiple and stepwise regression

Introduction 181

Multiple regression—the problem 181

Simple regression 182

Extending the linear equation 183

Stepwise regression—linear equations as models 184

Degrees of freedom 185

The F ratio 186

Stepwise regression—statistical control 187

Partial correlation 188

Significance testing in stepwise regression—statistical
control 189

More complex hypotheses 190

Stepwise regression—descriptive use 190

The significance of a step in stepwise
regression—descriptive use 192

Other procedures for stepwise regression as a
descriptive technique 194

Reporting the results of multiple and stepwise regression 194

Summary 196

Work sheets 198

Minitab 198

Some data 198

Testing 198

Regression with more than one predictor 198

Testing 201

Significance of F from the cdf command 201

Stepwise regression—statistical control 201

Stepwise regression—descriptive use 205

Assignment 209

Summary of Minitab commands 211

Chapter 9
Putting it all together: analysis of covariance

Introduction 213

The problem and some data 213

Comparing means in a regression analysis 214

Analysis of covariance 216

Reporting an analysis of covariance 217

Comparing means with a correlation coefficient 218

Analyses with several continuous and nominal variables 218

Attributing causality 220

Summary 221

Work sheets 223

Minitab 223

Comparing means in a regression analysis 223

Testing 224

Analysis of covariance 225

Missing data 229

Selecting data with the copy command 230

Testing 230

Assignment 231

Summary of Minitab commands 233

Appendix A
Critical values of r 235

Appendix B
Data sets 237

Index 243

PREFACE

The availability of statistical packages for mainframe and micro computers has made what were previously considered quite advanced statistical techniques, such as multiple regression or the analysis of covariance, accessible to many more students taking courses in psychology and ergonomics. For the same reason these and simpler techniques such as correlation and significance testing are included in courses for students in other behavioural sciences such as sociology and linguistics. This book is for all those students. It is based on three assumptions: (i) that the reader has a practical interest in using statistical tests rather than a theoretical interest in their derivation, (ii) that statistical procedures are best learned by doing, and (iii) that the reader will use the book in conjunction with a statistical package.

In this connection the 'work sheets', where the reader explores the statistical concepts under consideration, are an important part of the book. The reader works through directions to perform computations and two-minute exercises to check that a point is understood before moving on to the next. By its nature a work sheet can only be effective if the commands required, and the responses from the computer which will result, are known by the author, i.e. the book has to be written for a particular statistics package. The package chosen has to be widely available and have all the functions and tests needed. Minitab meets these requirements; for example, it can compute probabilities from theoretical distributions. It is widely available on VAX VMS mainframe systems as well as the IBM-PC and many other micro computers running the MSDOS operating system.

Each chapter has four parts:

1. A short introduction where the statistical concepts covered in the chapter are explained by means of examples. The introductions also contain advice on how to report the results of the analyses discussed.

2. The work sheets. These are to be used with a computer. Minitab commands are introduced in these sections and used to illustrate how different statistics are computed. In addition the first five chapters contain further sections to introduce commands specific to the operating systems Minitab will be used with. Within the work sheets step by step procedures for computing statistical tests have been drawn out into 'boxes'. These provide instructions that readers can apply to their own data. They take one through from tabulating the data to forming a conclusion. Each step is illustrated by an example developed in parallel with the instructions.

3. An assignment for students to do in their own time. These assignments are an important part of the book. By completing them the student will become fluent with the techniques described.

4. A summary of the Minitab and operating system commands introduced so far. Developing the summary of commands incrementally in this way makes it more manageable as an aid to memory.

The traditional way to teach statistics is to make students perform calculations by hand in the hope that they gain some insight into the working of the test by doing so. This may work with stronger students but weaker students often become too embroiled in the mechanics of calculation for this to be effective. The approach taken in this book is to use the computer to illustrate basic concepts. Thus a standard deviation can be computed 'the hard way' using column arithmetic (the Minitab commands 'let' and 'sum'). At the same time that they are learning statistics students are becoming fluent in the use of a particular computer system. This experience will be a valuable base from which to learn new systems. The section 'How to use this book' elaborates further the purpose of the different sections of the book.

It is assumed that readers will have done some basic school mathematics. They will know how to plot a histogram. They will understand the concept of an average. Nevertheless, the book attempts to cover, sometimes necessarily briefly, all the concepts needed.

The book starts with the basic concepts of a variable and experimental control. Chapter 2 covers a variety of descriptive statistics. Chapter 3 reviews the use of graphs and functions. Most of the material in this chapter should be familiar to the reader but it is fundamental in understanding several other chapters. Experience shows that it is important to review this material thoroughly before going on to Chapter 4 which is concerned with correlation and regression. Significance testing is introduced in Chapter 5 through the binomial test and tests for the significance of a correlation. Tests for comparing means are introduced in Chapters 6 and 7. Chapter 8 introduces multiple regression and stepwise regression. Chapter 9 unifies much of the earlier material by showing how the t-test and analysis of variance can be viewed as model fitting in the same way as correlation and regression and how the two approaches can be used simultaneously in the analysis of covariance.

Three 'generations' of York students have used various drafts of this book and I am indebted to them for their undinting and constructive criticism. I would also like to thank my family, friends and colleagues who helped and supported me in this project.

Andrew Monk
Department of Psychology
University of York
York YO1 5DD
UK

QUICK REFERENCE

The following pages contain material which may be frequently referred to.

Arrangements for using the computer 23

Choosing a test—Figure 7.1 168

Box 5.6 Step by step procedure to compute a correlation matrix and assess
the significance of these correlations using Table A.1. 118

Box 5.7 Step by step procedure for determining a correlation and whether
it is significant using the regress command 120

Box 5.8 Step by step procedure for doing a binomial test 123

Box 6.1 Step by step procedure for comparing means (two groups) 149

Box 7.3 Step by step procedure for comparing means
(within-subjects design) 171

Box 7.4 Step by step procedure for evaluating a two by two
contingency table 174

Box 8.3 Step by step procedure for determining a multiple correlation and
whether it is significant using the regress command 199

Box 8.4 Step by step procedure for stepwise regression (statistical control) 201

Box 8.5 Step by step procedure for stepwise regression (descriptive use) 205

Box 9.1 Step by step procedure for the analysis of covariance 225

How to report a correlation [Chapter 5] 115

How to report a binomial test [Chapter 5] 116

How to report the results of the t-test (between-subjects) and
Mann–Whitney U test [Chapter 6] 143

Reporting the results of a within-subjects t-test or Wilcoxon matched-pairs
signed-ranks test [Chapter 7] 166

Reporting the results of a chi squared test [Chapter 7] 167

Reporting the results of multiple and stepwise regression [Chapter 8] 194

Reporting the results of an analysis of covariance [Chapter 9] 217

Summary of DCL operating system commands used in this book
[end of Chapter 5] 131

Summary of MSDOS commands used in this book [end of Chapter 5] 131

Summary of Minitab commands used in this book [end of Chapter 9] 233

INTRODUCTION:
HOW TO USE THIS BOOK

TO THE STUDENT

The nine chapters of this book present a complete course on statistics. The first three are concerned with basic concepts. Some of this material may be familiar, particularly in Chapter 3, but it is important to review it in order to understand what follows. The next four chapters cover basic statistical procedures for evaluating correlations and differences between means. The final two chapters describe some relatively advanced statistical techniques based on multiple regression.

Statistics is best learned by doing: exploring the techniques using the computer, and solving problems for yourself. To this end each chapter contains 'Work sheets'. These pages are designed for use with a computer. They lead you through various computations to illustrate some statistical technique. Initially in a chapter you will be told precisely what to do. As you progress through the work sheet the knowledge you have picked up following these instructions will be reinforced by giving you tasks where you must work out at least some of the procedure yourself. This is the purpose of the sections headed 'Testing'. Note that you will need a calculator for some of these exercises.

Minitab output is not included in the text, except where necessary. This is to encourage readers to take the information they need from the screen rather than from the book, as they will have to when using Minitab to analyse their own data. It is probably a good idea to look through the work sheet for a chapter briefly before you get to the computer. Try to get an overview of what you are going to do. Of course, without the computer displays some of what is said will not mean much to you at that point.

At the same time as you are learning about statistics you will be learning about computers. In Chapters 2 to 5 the work sheets are divided into three sections, Minitab, DCL and MSDOS. The latter two sections are concerned with working the computer itself rather than statistics. You will only need to read one of them. If you are working with a mainframe time sharing system (e.g. a VAX) then you should use the sections headed DCL and ignore those headed MSDOS. If you are not you should use the MSDOS sections and ignore the DCL section. This distinction is explained at the beginning of the work sheets for Chapter 1. If in doubt ask your instructor or systems manager which sections apply to you.

The computing skills you need to work Minitab may seem very different from those needed to use more modern software such as spreadsheets or word processors but many of the concepts you will learn are in fact very general (e.g. 'files', 'data and results' or 'commands'). Being fluent in the use of this system will make it easy to learn new systems.

Most readers will be using this book as part of a course; however at some point they will also need to use it for reference, for example, when analysing their own data. The 'Quick reference' page that follows the contents provides a list of material which may be useful from this point of view. Figure 7.1 (which is also reprinted inside the cover) should allow you to determine what sort of statistical test is needed. You can then move to one of the 'boxes' that contain step by step procedures for doing that test. The boxes take you through from tabulating the data to interpreting the Minitab output. Finally, the introductions to several chapters contain advice about reporting the results of tests.

Each chapter contains a summary of the commands learned so far. By building these summaries bit by bit in this way it is hoped to make them less intimidating and more useful as an aid to memory. When doing the assignments use these summaries, and the boxes, rather than the text of the work sheets. As you get more familiar with Minitab and statistics you will find the Minitab help facility useful. However, do not expect to be able to use this to learn about Minitab in the early stages.

Lastly, a note about the introductions to each chapter. These are intended to introduce the topics covered in the work sheets. They are deliberately brief and some students will want to supplement their reading elsewhere. There are many more wordy introductory texts that will serve this purpose. However, do concentrate on doing calculations as well as reading about them. As was stated earlier, you will only get a good understanding of statistics by working through examples and solving problems. Do not be dispirited if you do not understand everything in the introduction on first reading. When you have finished the work sheets return to the introduction. Review the concepts developed there and then review what you did with the work sheets.

TO THE INSTRUCTOR

The chapters in this book will be suitable for courses at various levels. At York the book is used as a single intensive course but the chapters could easily be used in separate courses. They can be divided into three sections. Chapters 1 to 3 cover basic concepts, some of which students will already be familiar with. Chapters 4 to 7 cover core statistical techniques. Chapters 8 and 9 describe the more advanced statistical techniques of stepwise regression and analysis of covariance, the latter within a multiple regression framework. The approach to correlation in Chapter 4, via the concept of deviations from a prediction, is unconventional but necessary to link with these later two chapters. Instructors who do not intend to use the last two chapters may prefer to substitute an alternative approach here. The work sheets will still apply.

For the work sheets to serve their purpose it is important that the machine behaves as stated in the text. The 'Instructions to systems administrators' following this section describe what is necessary to ensure this is the case. There will inevitably be some local variability, particularly in the case of systems running on MSDOS, but some care has been taken to write commands that will be generally applicable.

Solving problems is important to the learning process and so 'Assignments' are supplied at the end of each chapter. Tutors can obtain model answers in the form of a marking scheme by writing to the author at the address given at the end of the preface. Students respond to problems they can identify with and so data collection exercises are included in the assignments for Chapters 1 and 6. There may be some value in supplementing these with additional data collection exercises based on the courses students are taking alongside statistics.

The accompanying table shows the statistics, DCL, MSDOS and Minitab commands introduced in each chapter.

INSTRUCTIONS FOR SYSTEMS ADMINISTRATORS

Minitab is available for mainframes running the DCL operating system (VAXes) and PCs running the MSDOS operating system. The main differences from site to site will be: system prompts, arrangements for printing and the procedures for starting and finishing a session with the computer. These details, which the book can be least helpful about, are crucial to the procedures the students have to learn first, before they have any experience to draw on. For this reason it is important that they be given all the information they need in a digestible form. The following notes make some suggestions about what information needs to be provided.

Readers are encouraged to summarise the information they are given about local arrangements on the page headed 'Arrangements for using the computer' at the end of Chapter 1. The following notes use the headings from that page.

Starting a session with the computer

(See work sheets for Chapter 1)

Switching on and setting up:

Instructions of this kind are best presented as numbered steps. They should begin with switching on the equipment. DCL users may need instructions about where to find the switch (terminal manufacturers have a habit of hiding it). Chapter 1 cautions MSDOS users against switching off the machine, so rules should be given to users about this. Similarly, they should be given rules about the use of floppy disks, which ones to use, what to do with them and when.

Chapter	Minitab	DCL	MSDOS
1. Experiments and variables: continuous, nominal, dependent and independent variables; subject variables	None	Logging in, logout, help, delete key, minitab, mail, whois	Switching on and off, date, delete key, minitab
2. Summary statistics: contingency tables, probability, mean, median, mode, range, semi-interquartile range, standard deviation and variance, standard error of the mean	set, read, print, let, describe, mean, stdev, sum, table, histogram, boxplots, stem-and-leaf, erase, save, retrieve, stop		
3. Relationships between variables: Graphs, tables and equations, the linear function, scattergram, cumulative frequency plot, percentile points	plot, outfile, nooutfile, .MTW and .LIS files, help	directory, delete, rename, copy, type, print	dir, del, ren, copy, type, print
4. Goodness of fit: regression, deviation, deviance, correlation (r^2 and r), reliability	name, info, ssq, regress, corr	file names, * and % in file names, looking at a file outside of your area	file names, * in file names
5. Inference with statistics: the null hypothesis, p value, significance level, binomial test, F test in regression, significance of r	cdf for the bionomial test	editing a command line, ^S and ^Q	editing a command line, ^S
6. Comparing means: t-test (between subjects) Mann–Whitney U test	twot, twos, mann		
7. Two experimental designs: between- and within-subjects designs, t-test for correlated samples, Wilcoxon matched-pairs signed-ranks test; chi squared; choosing the appropriate test	ttest, wtest, chisq		
8. Multiple and stepwise regression: multiple regression, R, stepwise regression (descriptive and for statistical control) partial correlation	Stepwise regression using the regress command, cdf for an F ratio		
9. Putting it all together: analysis of covariance: comparing means in a regression analysis, analysis of covariance	Analysis of covariance using the regress command		

DCL login.com and MSDOS autoexec.bat files should be used to simplify file name specification for the user. The book assumes that the Minitab commands 'save', 'retrieve', and 'outfile' all operate on files in the current default directory and that the user can type 'minitab' or 'print' as operating system commands without changing directories.

Making the right connection:

It may be necessary to make physical connections with plugs. More likely it may be necessary to connect to the host computer via a pad. Step by step procedures for doing this should be given. Where possible procedures for invoking a network should be encapsulated in a .com file. Chapter 1 anticipates users of DCL systems being given an initial temporary password which must be changed the first time the system is used. It does not anticipate passwords with MSDOS systems.

How to know when the system is ready to use:

The book anticipates a $ prompt for DCL systems. It explains that the prompt for MSDOS systems will vary and refers them to the system administrator. The example used is 'A:\user>'.

Common problems and what to do:

Differences in keyboard design are anticipated in the book but there may still be problems here. Other problems that need to be mentioned will make themselves known through experience!

Finishing a session with the computer

(See work sheets for Chapter 1)

It is assumed that DCL users simply logout. Any additional procedures need to be specified here. MSDOS users are warned against switching off the machine and referred to the system administrator for instructions on what to do.

Printing

(See work sheets for Chapter 3)

Chapter 3 assumes that files can be printed simply by typing the command 'print' and then the file name. This section should detail any deviation from this and where the hard copy can be picked up.

Chapter 3 also explains the difference between .lis (ASCII) and .mtw (non ASCII) files but you should anticipate the odd student trying to print or type a .mtw file and provide instructions for recovering from such an error.

Other local details to watch out for

Chapter 4 introduces the concept of files outside of the default directory. It requires a file with the contents 'You have found this remote and uninteresting file'. The four data sets in Appendix B have spaces for the reader to write in file specifications if they are already available on the system.

CHAPTER 1
EXPERIMENTS AND VARIABLES

Statistical concepts introduced in this chapter: Continuous and nominal variables, independent variable, dependent variable, levels of an independent variable, random effect, fixed effect.

INTRODUCTION

An experiment

Psychologists and other behavioural scientists use statistics to test hypotheses. This section will discuss how an hypothesis is turned into an experiment. Consider the idea that, despite the claims of some manufacturers, people prefer butter to margarine. Now imagine you are devising an experiment to test such a hypothesis. Let us say that we are interested in measuring preference and that we have each taster put a mark on a 100 mm line as depicted in Figure 1.1. Measuring the distance of the mark from the 'very nasty' end gives us a preference rating, a measure of how much they like what they have tasted. We can then get two groups of tasters, one given margarine and the other butter. Our hypothesis will be supported if the average rating of the group having butter is consistently higher than that of the group having margarine.

Very nasty | _____ | Very nice

Figure 1.1 Preference rating scale

Variables

What could affect the results of this experiment? Temperature might be important. Perhaps people prefer margarine at room temperature and butter slightly chilled, or vice versa. In this experiment temperature can be described as a 'variable' which needs to be 'controlled'. One might decide to control the temperature at which the fats are tasted as 19°C (room temperature). This would be recorded in the report on the experiment. If someone suspected that different results might be obtained with cooler fats they could then repeat the experiment with that single change.

Temperature is a 'continuous variable'. It can take values 15°C, 19°C, 19.5°C and so on. Some of the other variables which may be important in determining the results of this experiment do not have values which are numbers; rather the values of the variable are categories or names. These are known as 'nominal variables'. Take, for example, the variable 'method of presentation'. This could take values such as, on-a-salty-biscuit, on-bread, on-its-own and so on.

Table 1.1 lists three variables to be controlled in the experiment; they are 'quantity of fat' in grams (continuous), 'presentation of fat' (nominal) and 'temperature of fat' (continuous). In addition Table 1.1 gives the 'independent' and 'dependent variables'. These terms are explained in the next section.

Table 1.1   Variables in an experiment

Quantity of fat in mouth—controlled: 2 gm
Presentation of fat—controlled: spread on white bread
Temperature of fat—controlled: 19°C
Kind of fat—independent variable:
                          level 1 'Koma Quality Margarine'
                          level 2 'Country Glow Slightly Salted Butter'
Preference rating—dependent variable (score between 0 and 100)

The independent and dependent variables

A good experiment seeks to control all the relevant variables in some way. Some, quantity, temperature and presentation here, will be held constant. Others will be manipulated, i.e. controlled at two or more values. In Table 1.1 kind of fat is the variable which has been chosen as the manipulation. Tasters will get 'Koma Quality Margarine' or 'Country Glow Slightly Salted Butter'. For somewhat obscure reasons this is called the *independent variable*. Notice that the independent variable is said to have levels. You may find it strange to think of kind of fat as a variable having levels 'Koma Quality Margarine' and 'Country Glow Slightly Salted Butter'. The analogy is with levels of a continuous variable. For example, Table 1.2 shows how temperature might be used as an independent variable. Here the levels of the independent variable are 15 and 19°C, while type of fat is controlled at a single level.

Table 1.2   An alternative experiment

Quantity of fat in mouth—controlled: 2 gm
Presentation of fat—controlled: spread on white bread
Temperature of fat—independent variable:
                          level 1   15°C
                          level 2   19°C
Kind of fat—controlled: 'Koma Quality Margarine'
Preference rating—dependent variable (score between 0 and 100)

The variable in which the result of the experiment is expressed is called the *dependent variable*. In this example the dependent variable is the preference rating.

The distance from the mark made by the taster on the 100 mm line, measured from the 'very nasty' end of the scale, gives a score from 0 to 100. 100 is a very positive preference and 0 a very negative preference.

Experimental control

This example is applied behavioural science so the values chosen for variables should be typical of the real situation we are trying to mimic. Accordingly we chose 19°C as the temperature and 2 gm as the quantity. These values will be recorded in the report of the experiment so that someone else repeating it can see how the variable was controlled. It is most important that none of these variables varies with the independent variable. Such a situation is known as 'confounding'. Quantity might, for example, inadvertently have varied with fat type. Perhaps the person running the experiment liked butter much more than margarine and gave everyone who tasted butter more than everyone who tasted margarine. Were this to be the case we can no longer interpret a difference in preference rating. Type of fat is confounded with quantity of fat. It may be that people prefer the margarine or it may be that they prefer being given less fat.

To summarise so far, we have seen three kinds of variable: (i) the most common kind of variable is controlled at a single level so as not to bias the results of the experiment; (ii) one variable is manipulated to two or more levels, this is the independent variable and forms the basis of the experiment; (iii) one variable is chosen to express the outcome of the experiment, this is the dependent variable. In the process of deciding how to control all these variables the original hypothesis has been refined quite considerably. We started off with 'people prefer butter to margarine'. Table 1.1 describes an experiment to ask the much more specific question—whether people give higher preference ratings to Koma Quality Margarine or Country Glow Slightly Salted Butter when both are presented on white bread at 19°C, there being 2 gm of fat in the mouth when tasting. This additional specificity is necessary to get a reasonably definitive conclusion from an experiment. It is a strength of the experimental method and also a weakness. The specificity makes it possible to answer the question, and it also forces the scientist to think clearly about the implicit assumptions being made. The weakness, the cost that has to be paid, is that the conclusions made are specific to the experimental situation. For example, the ingenuity required to control the amount of fat in the mouth of the taster may make the experiment rather atypical of real tasting situations.

Subject variables

Psychologists call the people who take part in their experiments 'subjects'. Table 1.3 contains a list of some of the variables on which subjects could vary and why they could affect the results of the experiment.

Recent eating history could conceivably be controlled at a single level by asking subjects not to eat or drink anything before they did the experiment. The other variables in Table 1.3 could only be controlled by selecting subjects. It would make sense to select people who were healthy, but what about long term eating history and attitude to food? Even if we could assess the values of these variables satisfactorily it would not be sensible to select subjects so as to control them at a single level as we want the results of the experiment to be generalisable. Ideally we would like our conclusions to apply to people in general, not just to 25 year olds who eat 150 gm of butter per week and who rate their attitude to food as 'positive'.

Table 1.3   Some subject variables

Recent eating history (Have they eaten anything with a strong flavour in the past hour?)

Long term eating history (Do they normally eat margarine?)

Age (the senses, including taste, dull with age)

Health (a blocked nose will interfere with smell which is intimately associated with taste)

Attitude to food (Do they care about the taste of food?)

The problem is finessed by specifying the population we wish to generalise to and then sampling at random from it. So, we might define our target population as psychology undergraduates at the University of York. We then sample at random from this population. The definition of a random sample is that each member of the population has an equal probability of being in it. This means that, within the limitations of chance, the proportion of subjects in the sample who have particular characteristics will be representative of the proportion of subjects having the same characteristics in the population. The procedure automatically assures that there will be a representative range of ages, attitudes to food and long term eating history. This is a clever solution to the problem of controlling subject variables as it even controls variables we don't know about. Let us say that, after we have completed our experiment some psycho-physiologist discovers an enzyme, found in the saliva of some people but not others, that strongly affects the ability to taste fats. We do not have to repeat the experiment selecting the appropriate proportions of subjects with and without this enzyme in their saliva. Because we sampled randomly the sample should already be representative.

Technically what we have done in randomly sampling from a population is to declare a new variable 'subjects'. This variable has the levels 'John Smith', 'Fred Jones', 'Jean Brown' and so on. This variable is called a 'random effect' as the levels chosen for the experiment are sampled randomly from the complete set of possible levels in a population. This can be contrasted with the independent variable in an experiment, such as type of fat, which is called a 'fixed effect' as the levels chosen are fixed for the experiment. Were we to repeat the experiment we would obtain a new random set of subjects but we would use the same brands of fat.

Random sampling presents certain practical problems which need not concern us at the moment. How these problems can be circumvented is discussed in Chapter 2 and Chapter 7.

Technical note—types of measurement

Variables may be classified in a number of ways. One of interest to statisticians concerns the kind of information given. At one end of the continuum there are nominal variables such as eye colour or sex. At the other end there are ratio variables which have numerical values, e.g. weight. Table 1.4 gives four types of variable ordered by the amount of information given. At the bottom of the table, a nominal variable only tells you whether two individuals are the same or different. At the top of the table, a ratio variable quantifies how much they differ; one can make statements such as individual A is twice the weight of individual B. An interval variable also takes a numerical quantity but does not have a meaningful zero point so one can only make statements about intervals rather than ratios (this is a rather fine statistical point without important practical implications in this book). Ordinal variables simply order individuals, so one cannot make statements about intervals or ratios.

Table 1.4 Types of variable

Type of variable	Example of use	Example of variable
Ratio	X is twice as big as Y	weight in gms
Interval	A – B = C – D	temperature in °F
Ordinal	X is greater than Y	ranking
Nominal	A is the same as B	marital status

For the purposes of this book we only need to distinguish between continuous variables (ratio and interval) and nominal variables. Strictly speaking a continuous variable can take any value within some range, e.g. 19.5638°C. A measure which can take only specific numerical values is said to be 'discontinuous', e.g. number-of-children can take only values which are whole numbers. In practice most of the measures used by psychologists are discontinuous, in the strict sense. If the number of possible values which the variable can take is not unduly restricted then they are normally treated as if they were continuous. We shall return to the issue of types of measurement in Chapter 6.

Summary

The chapter has shown how an initial hypothesis is made more concrete by thinking about the variables which need to be controlled in order to test it experimentally. 'People prefer butter to margarine' was progressively refined by defining an independent variable (what we mean by 'margarine' and 'butter') and a dependent variable (what we mean by 'prefer'). Other variables need to be controlled if the experiment is to be unambiguously interpretable. Some of these (e.g. temperature and quantity of fat) are fixed at a single sensible value. Others, subject variables, are controlled by sampling from a specified population. The concepts introduced are summarised in the following glossary:

Continuous variable: in theory a variable that can take any value, e.g. mass in gm. In practice variables which can take only some values, such as the number of words recalled in a memory test (you can only recall a whole number of words), are treated as continuous.

Nominal variable: a variable whose values are simply names, e.g. the variable eye colour with values: blue, grey, brown or the variable sex with the values: male or female.

Independent variable: the variable used to form the experimental question being asked, e.g. fat tasted (butter versus margarine), temperature (15°C versus 19°C) or sex (male versus female).

Levels of an independent variable: the different experimental conditions specified by an independent variable are known as its levels. In our example the independent variable was type of fat and the levels 'Koma Quality Margarine' and 'Country Glow Slightly Salted Butter'.

Dependent variable: the variable which is the 'output' of the experiment. In our example this was a preference rating. Most commonly the dependent variable is a continuous variable such as a score. Sometimes it is a nominal variable, e.g. 'succeeded' or 'failed'. Many people have difficulty remembering which is the independent variable and which is the dependent variable. The dependent variable is the one that is dependent on everything else that you do; for 'dependent variable' read 'result' or 'score'.

Subject: the person who takes part in an experiment, as distinct from the all-powerful experimenter who runs it.

WORK SHEETS

Preliminary comments

Work sheets are pages that you work through in front of the computer. The objective is to explore the use of statistics by doing your own calculations. If you have not read the introductory section 'How to use this book' you should do so now.

The work sheets for this chapter are divided into two sections. You should only use one of them—which one depends on the kind of computer system you have. You may be running Minitab on a microcomputer using the MSDOS operating system. In this case the 'processor' which does the calculations is part of the microcomputer you can see in front of you. The alternative is a 'time sharing system'. Here many users have access to the same central processor which shares its time amongst them. In this case the machine you see in front of you does not do the calculations itself. Its function is simply to transmit your commands to the central processor and to display the results coming back. For this reason the unit containing display and keyboard is often described as a 'terminal'. To confuse matters still further, the terminal to a time sharing system may be a visual display unit (VDU) or it may be a microcomputer running a program to make it behave like a VDU. Your instructor or systems manager will tell you which sort of system you are using.

This chapter is entirely concerned with working the computer. There is no Minitab section to the work sheets, though we do briefly use Minitab. Minitab is introduced more fully in Chapter 2. If you are using a time sharing system you need only concern yourself with the section headed DCL. DCL is the name of the 'operating system' for this kind of computer—it deals with the commands for starting a session and so on. If you are not using a time sharing system then you need only look at the section headed MSDOS.

The work sheets in this book tell you what to type and how to use the results displayed. Some effort has been expended to make these instructions as accurate as possible. Fortunately Minitab is very similar wherever you are. The main differences between one computer installation and another will be in the procedures for starting up and finishing a session at the computer, the very topic for the work sheets for this first chapter! You should obtain detailed information about local procedures from your systems manager before attempting this work sheet. This may be summarised by filling in the page headed 'Arrangements for using the computer' at the end of this chapter.

DCL
(SKIP TO THE SECTION *MSDOS* IF YOU ARE NOT USING A TIME SHARING SYSTEM)

DCL commands introduced in this chapter: Logging in, logging out, help, delete key, mail, whois

Logging in to the computer

The computer you will be using throughout this course is a 'time sharing system'. This means that many people can use it simultaneously. To use this computer you have to connect a VDU (sometimes known as a terminal) to it and 'log in'. Logging in tells the computer who you are. It gives you access to all its facilities and so it is important that only authorised users can log in. To prevent unauthorised use you have been given a password. To make doubly sure no one can 'break into' the system you may be asked to change this password every so often.

When you registered with the computing service you will have been given a 'user name', that is the name you will be known as whenever you use it, and an initial temporary password. You will be asked to change this to a permanent password of your own choosing the first time you use the computer.

Communication with this sort of computer system follows a set pattern. The computer gives you some sort of 'prompt'. Often with this system this takes the form of a '$'. You type some 'command' to that prompt and then press the <↵return> key. The computer does not do anything until you press <↵return> and you should wait for an appropriate prompt before typing anything else.

In these work sheets the commands will be typed in bold

like this

They will be on a line on their own. You will have to remember to put in the <↵return> yourself. The other convention, which I have already used, is to indicate single keys on the keyboard which have more than one letter engraved on them like so <↵return> (the key with '↵return' engraved on it).

Unfortunately what gets engraved on the <↵return> key depends on the whim of the manufacturer. It will be part of the main block of keys (the letters) and on the right hand side of that block. It will probably be larger than the other keys. The <↵return> key may be engraved '↵', 'return', 'ret' or sometimes 'enter' (there may also be an 'enter' key at the far right of the keyboard with the numbers; this is NOT the <↵return> key.

Before you go on check that you can find the <↵return> key and that you know your user name and your initial temporary password.

Logging in for the first time ever

1. Switch on.

Refer to the instructions given to you by the system administrator. You may find it convenient to summarise these by writing on the page 'Arrangements for using the computer' at the end of this chapter.

2. Press <↵return>

The computer should respond with a message of welcome and the prompt 'Username:'. If it does not you may need to make a further connection perhaps via a 'pad'. Again, refer to the instructions given to you by the system administrator or see the page 'Arrangements for using the computer' under the heading 'Making the right connection'.

3. Type your user name and then <⌐Jreturn>. It will then prompt you for a password.

4. Type your initial temporary password and then <⌐Jreturn>. You may find it somewhat disturbing that what you type does not appear on the screen. This is always the case when you are typing a password. There may be someone looking over your shoulder!

5. The machine will now take you through the procedure involved in setting up your proper permanent password. Points to note are:

(a) When asked for your old password give your initial temporary password

(b) Choose a password with at least six letters but not so long as to be cumbersome

(c) Be sure to remember your password.

Knowing you have been successful

You have successfully logged on when there is a dollar sign ('$') at the left hand side of the screen. This will be referred to as the 'dollar prompt'.

Logging out

There is a limit to the number of people who can use the system at any one time and you should ensure that you log out as soon as you have finished. Try the procedure; type

logout

The system will tell you how long you were logged on and other interesting facts. It may be possible to abbreviate 'logout' to 'log' or 'lo' on some systems.

Logging in again

Follow the procedure in the 'Summary of DCL commands learned so far' at the end of this chapter. You no longer need to establish your proper password so the procedure is as before except that you simply enter your permanent password when you are asked for it. You are successfully logged in when you get the '$' prompt.

Testing

Try the following commands, substituting the name of the person teaching you for my name and user name:

whois monk

whois AM1

whois smith

Try some other 'whois's.

Try the help facility; type

help

The system will give you a list of things it can tell you. When you finally get the prompt 'Topic?' type

whois

To 'get out of' help type <↵return> until you get the '$' prompt.

More about commands

Commands typed to the '$' prompt are called DCL commands. You can edit them, before you press <↵return> to send them off, by using the <←-del> key. This simply rubs out the last character you typed. The <←-del> key will be at the right hand end of the top row of the main part of the keyboard (there may be other keys labelled 'del' in other parts of the keyboard, ignore these). It may be engraved '←', 'del', 'delete', '⟨✕⟩ ' or some combination of these.

Testing

Hold down the 'G' key until you have twenty or so 'g's on the screen.

Rub them all out using the <←-del> key.

Type 'whooois', without pressing <↵return>, then correct it to 'whois smith', and then press <↵return>.

Running Minitab

The reason you are learning to use this computer is so as to be able to do statistical calculations with Minitab. The following sequence of commands gives you an idea of how this will work.

minitab

set c1

4 3 5 2 6 (there should be a space between each of these numbers)

end

print c1

describe c1

Your screen should now look like Box 2.1 in Chapter 2. The meaning of these statistics is also explained in that chapter. Notice that the prompt given you by the computer changed from '$' to 'MTB>' while you were 'in' Minitab. To return to the dollar prompt type

stop

Mail

The mail command allows you to send messages to other users. To send a message type

mail

to the dollar prompt and then

send

to the 'MAIL>' prompt.

Points to note:

(a) Remember there is likely to be more than one person with the surname you are sending to on the system. Always mail to a user name, e.g. AM1 not Monk.

(b) ^Z is typed by holding down the <Ctrl> key while you type 'Z'. It works a bit like a shift key.

(c) The VDU keys will repeat if you hold them down (not always when you want them to).

(d) IF YOU GET STUCK hold down the <Ctrl> key and press 'C' (^C). This will take you back to the dollar prompt whence you can logout.

To read your mail type

mail

You will then get a prompt 'MAIL>'. <↵return> will display the first message. Keep pressing <↵return> until there are no more messages.

exit

will return you to the dollar prompt. You can find out more about mail by typing help to the 'MAIL>' prompt.

Send yourself a message with mail and then read it.

Leaving the system

logout

Refer to your system administrator for instructions about switching off and disconnecting your terminal. You may find it convenient to summarise this information for future reference by writing on the page 'Arrangements for using the computer' under the heading 'Finishing a session with the computer'.

MSDOS
(THERE IS NO NEED TO READ THIS SECTION IF YOU ARE USING A TIME SHARING SYSTEM)

MSDOS commands introduced in this chapter: Switching on and off, delete key, date.

'Booting' the system

When you first switch on a microcomputer you have to wait a minute or so while it loads some of the software you will need from the disk drive into memory. Most of the programs and data in memory when you switch off a computer are simply 'forgotten'—this is why we save them on a disk. There is however some software, stored using a different sort of memory, which is not lost when the machine is switched off. In early minicomputers this was a very small program, just sophisticated enough to load another program which could then load the software required. The process was likened to pulling oneself up by the bootstraps and the program is known as a bootstrap. Switching on and waiting for the machine to ready itself has become known as 'bootstrapping' or 'booting' the system.

Procedure when switching on the machine

The machine may have been set up before you arrived. If it is already on, go on to the next section 'Knowing you have been successful'. If the machine is off refer to the instructions given to you by the system administrator. You may find it convenient to summarise these by writing on the page 'Arrangements for using the computer' at the end of this chapter.

DO NOT SWITCH THE MACHINE OFF IN ORDER TO TRY SWITCHING IT ON AGAIN.

Knowing you have been successful

When the system has been successfully booted you will get something of the form 'A:\user>' at the left hand side of the screen. This is known as the system prompt and will vary from system to system. In this book the prompt will be written 'A:\user>' even though what you see may be 'C:\stats\fred>' or whatever. Your systems administrator will tell you what the prompt will be. Write it on the form 'Arrangements for using the computer' under the heading 'How to know when the system is ready to use'.

Commands

Communication with this sort of computer system follows a set pattern. The computer gives you some sort of 'prompt', (e.g. 'A:\user>'). You type some 'command' to that prompt and then press the <↵return> key. The computer does not do anything until you press <↵return> and you should wait for an appropriate prompt before typing anything else.

In these work sheets the commands will be typed in bold

like this

They will be on a line on their own. You will have to remember to put in the <⏎return> yourself. The other convention, which I have already used, is to indicate single keys on the keyboard which have more than one letter engraved on them like so <⏎return> (the key with '⏎return' engraved on it).

Unfortunately what gets engraved on the <⏎return> key depends on the whim of the manufacturer. It will be part of the main block of keys (the letters) and on the right hand side of that part. It will probably be larger than the other keys. Find the <⏎return> key and then try the following command (don't forget to press <⏎return>).

date

This gives you the current date and then asks you to 'Enter new date:'. There is no need to enter a new date. Just press the <⏎return> key and you will get back to the 'A:\user>' prompt. Do not change the date if it is correct.

The delete key

Commands typed to the 'A:\user>' prompt are MSDOS commands. You can edit them before you press <⏎return> by using the <←del> key. This simply rubs out the last character you typed. The <←del> key will be at the right hand end of the top row of the main part of the keyboard (there may be other keys labelled 'del' in other parts of the keyboard, ignore these). It may be engraved '←', 'del', 'delete', '⊗ ' or some combination of these.

Testing

Hold down the 'G' key until you have twenty or so 'g's on the screen.

Rub them all out using the <←del> key.

Type 'daate', without pressing <⏎return>, then correct it, and then press <⏎return>.

Running Minitab

The reason you are learning to use this computer is so as to be able to do statistical calculations with Minitab. The following sequence of commands gives you an idea of how this will work.

minitab

set c1

4 3 5 2 6 (there should be a space between each of these numbers)

end

print c1

describe c1

Your screen should now look like Box 2.1 in Chapter 2. The meaning of these statistics is also explained in that chapter. Notice that the prompt given you by the computer changed from 'A:\user>' to 'MTB>' while you were 'in' Minitab. To return to the 'A:\user>' prompt type

    stop

Switching off

Switching off a microcomputer is a potentially dangerous operation. Often there is no need to switch off the machine when you leave it. Check what the house rules are for switching off the machine with your system administrator and write them down for future reference on the page 'Arrangements for using the computer' under the heading 'Finishing a session with the computer'.

Before switching off:

1. Check you should not be leaving it on!

2. Check you have the MSDOS prompt (e.g., 'A:\user>').

3. Remove all floppy disks from the machine and put them in their protective envelopes.

ASSIGNMENT

1. Indicate whether the following statements are true or false:

(a) The variable circumference-of-head is continuous—TRUE/FALSE

(b) The variable gender is nominal—TRUE/FALSE

(c) The variable marital status (married or single) is continuous—TRUE/FALSE

(d) An experiment to compare two designs of calculator involves measuring the time taken to perform ten sample calculations. The independent variable in this experiment is type-of-calculator—TRUE/FALSE

(e) In the experiment described in (d) the independent variable has two levels —TRUE/FALSE

(f) In the experiment described in (d) the dependent variable is accuracy—TRUE/FALSE

2. An experiment is performed to examine the effect of a powerful analgesic on memory. Ten people are given the drug and another ten a placebo (sugar pill). They are given a list of randomly chosen words to learn. 24 hours later they are asked to write down as many of the words as possible.

(a) What is the independent variable in this experiment?

(b) What are the levels of the independent variable?

(c) What is the dependent variable?

(d) List four variables, having to do with the test materials used and the way that the experiment is run, which should be controlled in this experiment.

3. Design an experiment to compare preference for two similar products as in the example used in this chapter. Find six volunteers to carry it out and then write up your results under the following headings:

METHOD

Divide up the method section using the following subheadings

      Subjects (age, sex and any other relevant details)

      Materials used (quantity brands etc.)

      Procedure (precise experimental procedure, timing etc.)

RESULTS

List the preference ratings obtained and write a one sentence conclusion.

DISCUSSION

Suggest how the experiment could have been improved, now you know the problems and if you had more time.

SUMMARY OF DCL COMMANDS LEARNED SO FAR

Logging in

1. Refer to the form 'Arrangements for using the computer', at the end of this chapter, in which you have summarised the procedure for switching on and connecting your terminal.

2. Press <⏎return>.

3. Enter your user name when prompted for it.

4. Enter your password.

You are successfully logged in when you get the '$' prompt.

DCL commands covered here

 logout (lo)

 whois

 help

 mail

Mail commands

 <⏎return> (show next message)

 send

 help

 exit

Start Minitab session

 minitab

SUMMARY OF MSDOS COMMANDS LEARNED SO FAR

Switching on and off

Refer to the page headed 'Arrangements for using the computer', at the end of this chapter, in which you have summarised the procedure for switching on and booting up your computer and for ending a session at the computer.

MSDOS commands covered here

 date

Start Minitab session

 minitab

ARRANGEMENTS FOR USING THE COMPUTER

Contacts

Who to see when you have trouble with the computer:

Who to see when you have trouble with statistics:

Other useful contacts:

Starting a session with the computer

Switching on and setting up:

1.

2.

3.

Making the right connection:

1.

2.

How to know when the system is ready to use:

Common problems and what to do:

Finishing a session with the computer

1.

2.

3.

Printing

1.

2.

Other local details to watch out for

CHAPTER 2

SUMMARY STATISTICS

Statistical concepts introduced in this chapter: Contingency tables, probability, mean, median, mode, range, semi-inter-quartile range, standard deviation and variance, standard error of the mean.

INTRODUCTION

Summarising nominal variables—contingency tables

Large quantities of data are difficult to take in. For this reason we normally compute summary statistics. The commonest of these is the humble average. First we will consider another way of summarising data, the contingency table

Some fictitious data about the patients passing through an acute psychiatric ward for depressives is presented in Table 2.1. This gives the number of days they were there before they were discharged, their sex and the treatment they received. ECT stands for electro-convulsive therapy.

Table 2.1   Abstracts from patient records (fictitious data)

	Number of days	Sex	Treatment
Patient 1	15	M	ECT
Patient 2	3	F	Anti-depressants
Patient 3	5	F	ECT
Patient 4	4	F	Anti-depressants
Patient 5	11	M	Anti-depressants
Patient 6	4	F	Anti-depressants
Patient 7	12	M	ECT
Patient 8	3	F	Anti-depressants
Patient 9	10	F	ECT
Patient 10	4	F	Anti-depressants

There are various ways we could tabulate these data. Let us concentrate on the sex of the patients and their treatment. We could count the number of male and female patients and put the answer in a table:

Number of patients

Male	Female
3	7

There are more females than males in this sample.

Similarly we could count the number of patients receiving the two kinds of treatment:

Number of patients

ECT	Anti-depressants
4	6

Finally we can count the number of males receiving ECT, the number of females receiving ECT and so on:

Number of patients

	ECT	Anti-depressants
Male	2	1
Female	2	5

This is known as a contingency table. It shows how one variable is contingent on the other. For example, the males are much more likely to be given ECT. (I should stress that all the examples used in this book are fictional!)

There are more females than males so an additional table giving the percentages of each sex having the two treatments would aid interpretation:

Percentage of patients of each sex receiving a particular treatment

	ECT	Anti-depressants
Male	67	33
Female	29	71

Probability

The above results could have been expressed as proportions. The proportion of males getting ECT in this study is 0.67. Proportions like this are sometimes referred to as 'a posteriori' (after the event) probabilities, or sometimes 'empirical probabilities'. The a posteriori probability of getting ECT if you are female is lower (0.29), i.e. the proportion of females being treated with ECT is .29.

Probabilities refer to events—in this case the occurrence of a patient who is female being treated with ECT. An a posteriori probability then is a number between 0 and 1 indicating how often an event has occurred. It is fairly rare to use a posteriori probabilities in this way as it is more straightforward to think of the result as a proportion.

'*A priori*', or theoretical, probabilities are much more important as we will see in later chapters. This is again a number between 0 and 1, but this time it expresses a prediction as to how likely some event is to happen. For example, if one is willing to assume that:

(a) it is equally likely a coin will come up heads or tails

(b) heads and tails are the only events possible (it never lands on its edge or falls down a crack in the floor for example) and

(c) it can't come up heads and tails at the same time, i.e. these are mutually exclusive events,

then one can compute the theoretical or *a priori* probability of one of these events occurring as 0.5. These are reasonable assumptions and empirical investigation with coins will prove it to be a good prediction in that the proportion of heads in a long sequence of coin tosses will be approximately 0.5. In Chapter 5, and the chapters which follow it, we will compute *a priori* probabilities where the event to be predicted is getting a particular result from an experiment. As with the coin example we will have to make assumptions though they are slightly more complex than (a) to (c) above.

The probability of something not happening

Readers who have learned how to manipulate probabilities in maths courses will know that if two events are mutually exclusive then their probabilities can be added to get the probability of one *or* the other happening. Let us say that we have computed the *a priori* probability that the next card in the deck is a king to be .10 and that the *a priori* probability it is a queen is .15. These events are mutually exclusive, the card cannot be a queen and a king at the same time. This means that we can add the probabilities. The *a priori* probability it is a king *or* a queen is .25 (.10 + .15).

You will only need to use this rule in one very specific situation, that is to work out the probability of something not happening. If we know that the probability of the next card being a queen is .15 then the probability it is not a queen is .85. This follows from the above rule because the card must be either a queen or not a queen. One of these events must happen, the probability of being 'a queen or not a queen' is 1.00, i.e. certainty. In addition, being a queen and not being a queen are mutually exclusive events. In summary:

Probability the card is a queen = .15

Probability the card is a queen + the probability the card is not a queen = 1.0 (must be true)

Therefore

Probability the card is not a queen = 1.00 − the probability it is a queen = 1.00 − .15 = .85

The same logic can be applied to *a posteriori* probabilities. Knowing that the probability of getting ECT if you are male is .67 and that everyone either got ECT or anti-depressants (but not both), it is possible to deduce that the probability of getting anti-depressants if you are male is

$1 - 0.67 = 0.33$

Measures of central tendency: mean

Now to return to the summary statistic you are all probably already familiar with, that is the idea of an average. An average summarises a set of numbers as some sort of 'central tendency'. Table 2.1 includes the number of days spent in the ward. Even though there are only ten data points it is difficult to see whether, say, patients receiving ECT tend to spend more time in hospital than those getting anti-depressants. With larger, more realistic, samples this is even more of a problem. What is needed is some statistic that summarises the 'central tendency' of a set of scores. The most commonly used is the *mean*. This is computed by summing the scores and then dividing by the number of scores summed:

Mean stay of patients receiving ECT $(15+5+12+10)/4 = 10.5$ days

Mean stay of patients receiving anti-depressants $(3+4+11+4+3+4)/6 = 4.8$ days

You may know the mean as the average of a set of numbers. The mean is a measure of central tendency. It gives a single value which is typical or central as a way of summarising a set of values. As we shall see there are other measures of central tendency that are sometimes also described as averages and so we shall always use the more precise statistical term, mean.

Measures of central tendency: median

Another measure of central tendency is the median. The *median* is a value having as many scores above it as it has below it. The median of the set of scores

41 53 37 31 64

is obtained by first putting the scores in order:

31 37 **41** 53 64

41 is the central value in this order so the median of this set of scores is 41 (no measure of central tendency is going to be very meaningful with samples as small as this but by using a small data set the procedures should be easier to follow). If there is an even number of scores in the set then the value with an equal number of scores either side of it will be somewhere in between the middle two scores. By convention it is set as the mean of these two values, i.e. half way between the two. So the median of the scores

34 52 46 75 60 61

which sorted are

   34 46 **52 60** 61 75

is (52+60)/2 = 56.

If some of the values are the same (ties in the ordering) we proceed just as above. The median stay of patients receiving anti-depressants (3 4 11 4 3 4) or sorted as (3 3 4 4 4 11) is (4+4)/2=4.

Measures of central tendency: mode

The mode is defined with respect to a frequency histogram such as Figure 2.1. It is only a meaningful measure of central tendency with large samples. The *mode* is the value, or range of values, which most frequently occurs.

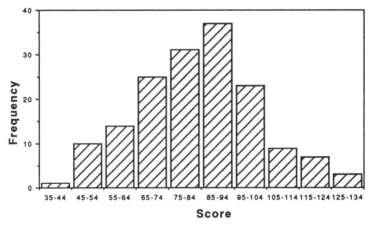

Figure 2.1 Frequency histogram for a population of scores—the modal range 85–94

You will have plotted frequency histograms in school maths courses. Figure 2.1 is such a histogram representing the data from 160 subjects. The horizontal axis is divided into ranges of scores. You might like to think of these as buckets. Any score between 35 and 44 is put into the first bucket, anything between 45 and 54 is put in the second, and so on. The vertical axis gives the number of scores falling into each bucket. So there is 1 score between 35 and 44 and 10 between 45 and 54. The fullest bucket, that is the range of scores within which scores most frequently occur, is the modal range, in this case 85–94.

Sometimes there is more than one peak in the histogram. In Figure 2.2 this happens because there are too few data points to make the use of a mode sensible. Most of the scores occur with a frequency of only 1 or 2. Increasing the size of the buckets would not help because one would end up with too few of them to be useful. In Figure 2.3 there are two modes, in the jargon a 'bimodal distribution'.

This may be the result of mixing two rather different populations of scores. The mode would not be a representative measure of central tendency for the data displayed in Figure 2.2 or Figure 2.3.

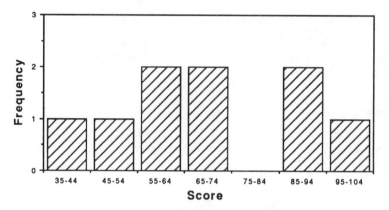

Figure 2.2   Frequency histogram—these data are not sensibly summarised by a mode as the size of the population is too small

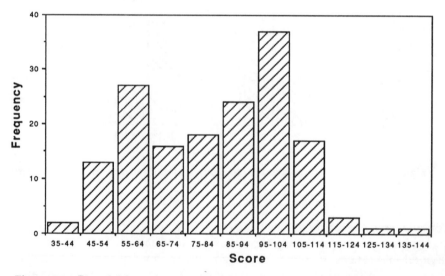

Figure 2.3   Bimodal frequency distribution—see text for explanation

Relationship between mean, median and mode

With a perfectly symmetrical distribution the mean will have an equal number of scores either side of it so it will correspond to the median. In many natural distributions the central values are the most common and the mean is the mode also. This state of simplicity is approximated in Figure 2.1. The mean for the data upon which it is based is 83.45, the median 84.0 and the modal range 85–94. Figure 2.4 is not symmetrical. There are more values at the lower end than at the higher end. This is often the case with small measurements of time. It is much harder to reduce one's reaction time from say .9 seconds to .5 than from 2.9 to 2.5. It is impossible to reduce it below 0 seconds! With asymmetrical distributions like this the mean, median and mode do not correspond. This distribution can be described as 'positively skewed'. It is as if a symmetrical distribution has been stretched at the higher or 'positive' end of the scale. This can be seen in the relationship between mean and median. The median is .50 and the mean .77. The median being less than the mean is a sign of a positively skewed distribution. Were the median to be greater than the mean that would indicate a negatively skewed distribution. Which measure of central tendency is most representative of a skewed distribution is debatable. Most people would probably take the median.

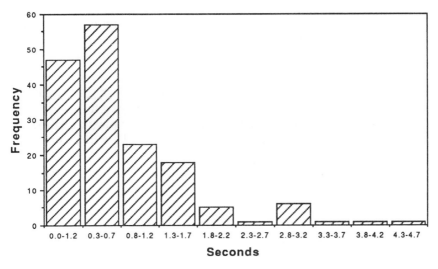

Figure 2.4 A positively skewed frequency distribution

In small samples the mean can differ from the median because of outliers. Outliers are values which are atypical because they are very much larger, or smaller, than all the others. Consider the following two sets of data:

(a) 3 5 7 5 4 5 6 7 7 4 29 Mean 7.45, Median 5.00

(b) 7 6 9 8 7 6 7 5 7 9 7 Mean 7.09, Median 7.00

Set (a) contains an outlier (29). All the other values are in the range 3 to 7. 29 is clearly aberrant as it is four times that range from the next highest value (a rule of thumb for identifying outliers is given in the section on box-plots below). Outliers distort the mean much more than they do the median. For this reason the median is generally considered to be a more representative measure of central tendency than the mean when there are outliers.

It is unusual for means and medians to give different conclusions (according to the means (a)>(b), according to the medians (b)>(a)). Where there are large differences between the mean and the median the validity of the data should be questioned and it may be possible to remove outliers, without biasing the results of the experiment, by applying some objective rule. The issue of outliers and skewed distributions will be reexamined in Chapter 6.

Measures of variation

The following two sets of data have means which are almost the same yet they differ in an important respect, the variation in scores.

(c) 42 41 50 59 46 63 74 35 75 42 46 Mean 52.09

(d) 31 34 5 99 56 87 63 57 40 25 61 Mean 50.73

Variation, sometimes known as dispersion, can be summarised in several ways; the simplest is the range. Data set (c) has a minimum value of 35 and a maximum of 75 so the *range* (i.e. maximum – minimum) is 40. Sample (d) has a minimum of 5 and a maximum of 99 so its range is larger at 94.

Sometimes the range may not be a very representative statistic because it is based on the two most extreme values and extreme values may be flukes in some way. The inter-quartile range is a related but slightly more sophisticated measure of variation devised to get round this problem. To explain how this works we need to look first at the concept of a 'quartile'.

The median is defined as the value having half the scores below it. On a similar basis the first quartile is defined as the value having one-quarter of the scores below it. The third quartile is the value having three-quarters of the scores below it (on this basis the median could be thought of as the second quartile). By taking the difference between the first and third quartiles we get a measure of variation which does not depend so heavily on the possibly aberrant minimum and maximum scores. Thus, the inter-quartile range is the difference between the first and the third quartiles. To find the inter-quartile range for data set (c) proceed as follows:

1. Find the first and the third quartile. Minitab will do this for you. To do it by hand rank the data and pick the scores with one- and three-quarters of the scores below them respectively:

     35   41   **42**   42   46   46   50   59   **63**   74   75

2. Compute the difference between the two quartiles. This is the inter-quartile range.

     Inter-quartile range = 63 – 42 = 21

It is easy to compute the first and third quartiles in this example because they are represented by actual scores (42 and 63). This will not always be the case. Just as the median of an even number of scores will always fall between two scores there will be occasions where quartiles fall between two scores. In such cases Minitab extrapolates. For example, if the first quartile should really be at rank 2.75 then it will work out the value three-quarters of the way between the score with rank 2 and the score with rank 3. Those who are interested may consult the Minitab reference manual for further details of how this is done.

Box-plots

The inter-quartile range is the basis of a box-plot. Figure 2.5 contains four box-plots, one for each of the data sets (a) to (d). The boundaries of the box are the two quartiles so it contains the central 50% of the data. The cross marks the median value. The lines going out from the box, known as whiskers, stretch to the minimum and maximum values. Where there are extreme outliers (conventionally 1.5 times the inter-quartile range above or below the relevant quartile) they are represented by individual points (see for example the '0' in the box plot for data set (a) in Figure 2.5).

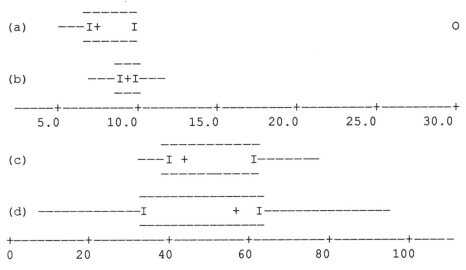

Figure 2.5   Box plots of data sets (a) to (d)

Box plots summarise central tendency and variation and so are useful for comparing data. Consider first the box plots for data sets (c) and (d). The minima and maxima of these data sets are not outliers by the above definition and so the whiskers contain all the data. The similarity of central tendency and the difference in variation between data sets (c) and (d) is apparent in Figure 2.5. Now consider the box plots for the data sets (a) and (b). The outlier in data set (a), 29, is plotted as a separate point ('0'). Otherwise the two data sets can be seen to be very similar in central tendency and variation.

The standard deviation

An alternative way of thinking about variation is in terms of the average deviation from the mean. The second column in Table 2.2 gives the deviation of each value in data set (c) from the mean of 52.09 Similarly the last column gives the deviation of each value in data set (d) from its mean of 50.73. The absolute size of these deviations is much larger in the case of data set (d).

If either of these sets of deviations from the mean is added up the negative deviations will balance the positive deviations and the net total will be zero. We need to average the absolute size of the deviations, i.e. ignoring whether they are positive or negative. For reasons too complicated to go into here it turns out that the most appropriate way of doing this mathematically is as follows:

(i) Square the deviations (this gets rid of all the negative values, e.g. $-10.09 \times -10.09 = 101.81$).

(ii) Sum the squared deviations.

(iii) Divide by $N - 1$, where N is the number of scores in the data set.

(iv) Square root the result.

The statistic thus computed is called the *standard deviation*. Its square, or what you get if you stop after step (iii), is called the *variance*. The sum of the squared deviations for data set (c) is 1868.9 and for (d) it is 7506.2, so the standard deviation is

$$\sqrt{1868.9/10} = \sqrt{186.89} = 13.67$$

in the case of (c) and

$$\sqrt{7506.2/10} = \sqrt{750.62} = 27.40$$

in the case of (d).

Table 2.2   Deviations from the mean, data sets (c) and (d)

(c)	Deviation	(d)	Deviation
42	−10.09	31	−19.73
41	−11.09	34	−16.73
50	−2.09	5	−45.73
59	6.91	99	48.27
46	−6.09	56	5.27
63	10.91	87	36.27
74	21.91	63	12.27
35	−17.09	57	6.27
75	22.91	40	−10.73
42	−10.09	25	−25.73
46	−6.09	61	10.27

This computation may seem complex but you will always have Minitab to do it for you. It may also seem very devious (statistical pun!) but the standard deviation is mathematically convenient and for that reason it is an important summary statistic. In general it will be approximately half the inter-quartile range and so to make the latter statistic imitate its more important cousin it is usual to quote the semi-inter-quartile range rather than the inter-quartile range calculated above.

You may be puzzled why we divide by N − 1 instead of N when computing the standard deviation. The explanation for this depends on the statistical concept of a sample to be described in the next section.

Populations and samples

Imagine it is required to measure the mean height of male students at some large university or college. Measuring all of them would be very time consuming and is beyond the resources available. The alternative is to choose at random, say, 200 and to take the mean of this sample as an estimate of the mean of the whole population of students. The accuracy of this estimate will depend on the size of the sample. Clearly a sample of 200 is likely to give a better estimate than a sample of, say, 10. It is also important that the sample is truly random and not biased in some way. For example, selecting the sample solely from the physical education department, where physique is an entrance requirement, may result in a poor estimate.

The mean of a sample is usually signified with the symbol $\overline{X}$ (capital X with a bar over it, which is said 'ex bar'). The standard deviation of a sample is usually signified by s (not capital) so the variance is written as s^2. For example, for set (c) one might write

$$\overline{X} = 52.09, s = 13.67, s^2 = 186.89.$$

For somewhat obscure mathematical reasons it turns out that computing the standard deviation by dividing by N − 1 rather than N gives an unbiased estimate of the population standard deviation. Dividing by the apparently more reasonable N gives, on average, an underestimate. Some calculators give you the choice of computing the standard deviation of a set of data using N or N − 1. Only use the former if you have measured the complete population (something you are very unlikely to do).

To summarise, the procedure for estimating population statistics using a sample is as follows:

(a) Define the population, (e.g. male students at a particular university of college).

(b) Sample at random from this population (at random means that each individual in the population has an equal probability of being included in the sample).

(c) Compute summary statistics for the sample. These are taken as estimates of the population statistics.

How well a sample statistic estimates the 'true' population statistic depends on the size of the sample. The standard error of the mean, explained below, is a way of quantifying how accurate the sample mean is as an estimate of the population mean.

The standard error of the mean

Let us say that instead of taking a sample of 200 students we were only able to sample ten. How accurate would the mean of this sample be as an estimate of the population mean compared with the 200 student sample? The problem is that it is always going to be impractical to measure the true population mean. However, we could measure the variation in the means derived from a number of 10- and 200-student samples. In this (hypothetical) evaluation of sample size we might take, say, 20 10-student samples, compute a mean for each of these samples and then compute the standard deviation of these means. Doing the same thing for, say, 20 200-student samples would allow us to compare the variation in sample means directly. This is a hypothetical exercise as it is unlikely to be practical to take 20 200-student samples. However, statisticians have shown that, if one makes certain reasonable assumptions about the data, the standard deviation hypothetically computed above can itself be estimated from the standard deviation of the sample. That is, the standard deviation of the means of a number of samples of size N is approximately s/√N where s is the standard deviation of one of the samples.

This mathematical finding gives rise to a measure of accuracy known as the standard error of the mean:

$$\text{standard error of the mean} = \frac{\text{standard deviation of the sample}}{\sqrt{N}}$$

For example, say the mean height of our sample of 200 is 1.65 metres and the standard deviation of the sample is .18 metres. Then the standard error of the mean is

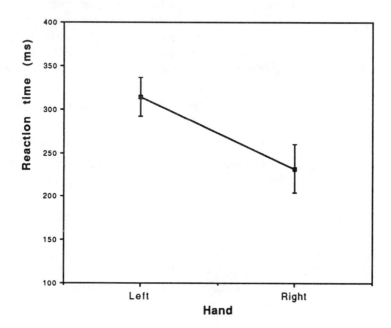

Figure 2.6   Graph of mean reaction time when responses are made with the left or right hand—the vertical 'error bars' are plus or minus one standard error of the mean

$$\frac{.18}{\sqrt{200}} = .013$$

If the sample had been of only 10 individuals the standard error of the mean would have been .057, that is over four times larger. The standard error of the mean is used to indicate precision of measurement. Unlike the standard deviation, which is independent of N, it gets smaller the more data points go into the mean.

Figure 2.6 has error bars of one standard error of the mean plotted above and below the mean value. This is a common way of showing how good the sample mean is as an estimate of some population mean. In this case reaction time is repeatedly measured for one individual using either the left or right hand. In such a case the population is the total set of responses the individual could have produced.

Practical considerations when sampling

The procedure for estimating population statistics described above is somewhat idealised because it is extremely difficult to get a truly random sample from an arbitrarily defined population. For example, psychologists depend on volunteers who are willing to take part in experiments. Although they would like to generalise their conclusions to humanity *in toto* they often sample from a population which should properly be defined as 'psychology students at the University of X who volunteer for experiments'. This is not usually a problem. Statistical arguments permit them to generalise from the results obtained from the sample to the limited population it is drawn from and then arguments based on psychological knowledge of how these effects vary from individual to individual allow them to generalise from this population to a more general one.

Take for example an experiment on colour perception. An experimenter compares the ease with which text can be read when it is printed in blue as opposed to black ink. A consistent difference in reading speed is observed in all twenty of a sample of students. The standard error of this mean difference is small and so it is concluded that the mean difference observed in the sample is a good estimate of the population mean difference. The experimenter knows of no experiments which indicate that members of this population (undergraduates at his university who volunteer for experiments) differ in their colour perception from the population at large and so generalises the conclusion appropriately.

The problem faced by opinion pollsters cannot be solved in this way. People who readily answer questions as to who they will vote for in the next election probably do have systematically different opinions from those who are unwilling to answer such questions. However there is a solution and again it involves the use of arguments outside of statistics. Pollsters know what kind of subject variables affect peoples' intention to vote. They are the region they live in, their socio-economic status and so on. They also know what proportion of the population of the country falls into each possible combination of the levels of each of these variables. They can then adjust their sampling techniques to make sure that they get a representative number of each type of person. This is no longer random sampling but as long as they really do know all the most important factors having an effect on voting intentions it will have the same effect.

Summary

1. It is possible to summarise the characteristics of some set of data by computing certain statistics.

2. Nominal variables are summarised by constructing *contingency tables* giving the frequency, proportion or percentage of subjects falling into different classes or combinations of classes (e.g., males receiving ECT).

3. An *a priori or theoretical probability* expresses how likely some event is to occur. A probability is represented by a number between 0 (will never occur) and 1 (will always occur).

4. The *mean* (written $\overline{X}$) and *median* are measures of central tendency. The mean is computed by summing the scores and dividing by N (the number of scores). The median is the number having an equal number of scores above and below it. The median may be more representative when there are outliers (atypically high or low scores).

5. The *mode* is only meaningful with large data sets where a frequency histogram is computed. The mode is the most frequently occurring score or range of scores in the histogram.

6. The *variance*, s^2, is a measure of variation or dispersion. It is computed by summing the squared deviations of each score from the mean and then dividing by $N-1$.

7. The *standard deviation*, s, is the square root of the variance.

8. Other measures of dispersion are: the range, the difference between the largest and the smallest score; the inter-quartile range, the difference between the first and third quartile (these are the scores with one- and three-quarters of the scores below them respectively); and the semi-inter-quartile range which is half the inter-quartile range.

9. It is often convenient to assume that the set of scores obtained is a sample from some larger population. The sample mean and standard deviation are seen as estimates of some theoretical 'true' population mean and standard deviation.

10. The standard error of the mean is an estimate of the standard deviation of the sample mean. That is, although we have only a single sample of size N and standard deviation s, were we to take numerous samples from the same population and compute their means, the standard deviation of those means would be $s/\sqrt{N}$. This standard error of the mean is often quoted as a measure of how good the sample mean is as an estimate of the theoretical true population mean, i.e. how precise a measurement it is.

WORK SHEETS

MINITAB

Minitab commands introduced in this chapter: set, read, print, let, describe, mean, stdev, sum, table, histogram, box-plots, stem-and-leaf, erase, save, retrieve, stop.

Minitab

Most of the work you will be doing will use a statistical program called Minitab. The best way to get a feel for what it can do is to try it. Don't forget to press <⏎return> after each command.

1. Login or switch on (see the summary at the end of this chapter).

2. When you have the appropriate prompt start Minitab by typing:

minitab

3. Work through the following commands:

set c1

4 3 5 2 6 (there should be a space between each of these numbers)

end

print c1

describe c1

Your screen should now look like Box 2.1. The describe command (which can be abbreviated to desc) computes a variety of summary statistics. N (5) is the number of scores in the column. TRMEAN is not a widely used statistic, the 5% highest and 5% lowest scores are 'trimmed' from the data and the mean computed on the remaining 90%. STDEV is the standard deviation (1.581, square this to get the variance) and SEMEAN is the standard error of the mean (.707) Use your calculator to check that the standard error of the mean is indeed the standard deviation divided by the square root of N.

Q1 and Q3 are the first and third quartiles respectively. Minitab extrapolates where there is no one score which is the quartile value, e.g. the first quartile should be at position 1.5 so it gives a value half way between 2 and 3 (2.5). Check that you can compute the range (4) and the semi-inter-quartile range (1.5) from this display.

Box 2.1 If you have typed the commands given above correctly your screen will end up looking like this

```
MTB > set c1
DATA> 4 3 5 2 6
DATA> end
MTB > print c1

C1
    4    3    5    2    6

MTB > describe c1

                     N      MEAN    MEDIAN    TRMEAN    STDEV
SEMEAN
C1                   5     4.000     4.000     4.000    1.581
0.707

                   MIN       MAX        Q1        Q3
C1               2.000     6.000     2.500     5.500

MTB >
```

Testing

Using the example above as a model, give Minitab another set of numbers, c2, consisting of: 34 56 78 23 51. Check that Minitab gives the mean of these numbers to be 48.40. If it doesn't repeat the operation making sure that you specify c2 for the two commands and that you type accurately. Write down: the median, standard deviation, the standard error of the mean for these numbers. Use your calculator to compute the semi-inter-quartile range and the variance from the results given by Minitab. Check your answers (given at the end of this section) before you go on.

Columns of data

During a given session with Minitab the data you enter are stored in the computer's memory. You can see the two data sets entered so far by using the print command:

print c1 c2

c1 is said 'column 1' and c2 'column 2'. Although data are entered as a row when using the set command they are actually represented in Minitab as a column as this display shows. The idea of a column is fundamental to Minitab.

Correcting mistakes in the data

If you make a mistake before pressing <↵return> you can correct it with <←del>. Otherwise you will have to (a) repeat the whole command again or (b) use the let command. These two ways of correcting a data set are illustrated below. In both cases '99' is the deliberate mistake.

```
set c3
2 4 5 7 2 99 3 7
end
print c1 c2 c3
set c3
2 4 5 7 2 9 3 7
end
print c1 c2 c3
set c4
7 99 5 8 2 5 19 2 5 6 7
end
print c1 c2 c3 c4
let c4(2)=9
print c1 c2 c3 c4
```

c4(2) means the second row of column 4. To change the fifth row of column 1 one would type 'let c1(5)='

Testing

Change the 19 in c4 to 9 using the let command. Check you have succeeded in doing this by using the print command.

Erasing and creating data

A more realistically sized data set is required for the exercise in the next section. First we will erase the current four columns:

```
erase c1 c2 c3 c4
print c1 c2 c3 c4
```

The display should now look like Box 2.2. The print command shows that there is nothing there.

Put the following data set in c1 and check there are no typing mistakes. (Don't forget the 'end' to signal you have put in all the numbers.)

15 18 23 12 16 39 25 37 41 75 32 76 23 78 34 23 65 23 56 12

52 58 69 63 41 47 46 25 41 52

Box 2.2   The erase command has cleared the work space so the print command shows no data

```
MTB > erase c1 c2 c3 c4
MTB > print c1 c2 c3 c4

ROW    C1    C2    C3    C4

MTB >
```

As well as editing single data points, the let command can be used to create data by performing some arithmetical operation on all the numbers in a column. Try

let c2=c1-10
print c1 c2

This makes a new column of numbers c2 by subtracting 10 from each of the numbers in c1 (see Box 2.3).

Box 2.3   c2 is c1 − 10,, e.g. 5=15 − 10, 8=18 − 10 and so on (only the first few lines of the display are given)

```
MTB > let c2=c1-10
MTB > print c1 c2

ROW    C1    C2

   1    15     5
   2    18     8
   3    23    13
   4    12     2
   5    16     6
   6    39    29
   7    25    15
   8    37    27
   9    41    31
  10    75    65
```

Means and standard deviations

In this section we will calculate a mean and a standard deviation 'the hard way'. You will never need to do this again. The objective is to give you a better feeling for what a standard deviation is and at the same time give you an opportunity to explore some more of Minitab. First try the following Minitab commands:

```
sum c1
mean c1
stdev c1
```

Write down the sum, the mean and the standard deviation. The mean of a column is the sum of the column divided by the number of numbers in it (N). Divide the value given by the sum command by 30, using a calculator. You should get the value given by the mean command.

The next set of commands computes the standard deviation. There are four steps in this process: (a) a new column of deviations from the mean will be computed using the let command; (b) from these another column of squared deviations from the mean will be computed; (c) these will be summed and the sum divided by $(N - 1)$ to get the variance; finally (d) the variance will be square rooted to get the standard deviation.

```
erase c2
mean c1
let c2=c1-40.567      (this is the mean)
print c1 c2
let c3=c2*c2      (* means multiply)
print c1 c2 c3
sum c3
```

Now use a calculator to compute the variance and the standard deviation from the sum of c3. Divide by 29 $(N - 1)$ to get the variance. Square root the variance to get the standard deviation. It should be the same as Minitab gave with the stdev command.

Leaving Minitab and saving your data

When using Minitab you can imagine that you are filling in a large table or 'work space' with data. This work space consists of columns of data. Some of the assignments involve statistics from large data sets and they may take you more than one session with the computer. Normally the computer forgets all the data you have typed in when you leave Minitab. However, you can save your current work space using the save command. You can get it back again using the retrieve command. You have to give the saved material a name which is enclosed in single quotes. In this case the three columns we wish to save include the deviations from the mean that we computed with the let command, so we will call it 'deviations'. Having saved the work space you will then leave Minitab using the stop command. (Some computer systems will not allow you to use names as long as 'deviations', so if you get an error message along these lines use some suitable abbreviation.)

```
save 'deviations'
stop
```

If you have trouble getting this to work you are probably using the wrong quote character ('). The character is the same at both ends of the word and on most keyboards it is the key next to <⏎return>.

Now start Minitab again, and before retrieving 'deviations' use a print command; you will find that the work space is empty. Box 2.4 shows what the screen should look like.

Box 2.4 After the command stop Minitab has to be started again. The print command shows the work space is empty

```
MTB > save 'deviations'

Worksheet saved into file: deviations.MTW
MTB > stop
*** Minitab Release 6.1.1 *** Minitab, Inc. ***
Storage available 843053

$ minitab
MINITAB RELEASE 6.1.1 *** COPYRIGHT - MINITAB, INC. 1987
VAX/VMS version
U.S. FEDERAL GOVERNMENT USERS SEE HELP FGU
MAY 2, 1989 *** University of York - Vax Cluster
STORAGE AVAILABLE 843053

  Type NEWS for information on NEW FEATURES and a list of
KNOWN PROBLEMS.

MTB > print c1 c2 c3

  ROW    C1    C2    C3

MTB >
```

Now retrieve deviations and try the print command again:

retrieve 'deviations'

print c1 c2 c3

This time the print command shows that the work space has been restored to its original form.

Entering more than one column at a time

The read command is like the set command except that you use it to enter several variables at the same time. Consider the following data from the first work sheet.

	Number of days	Sex	Treatment
Patient 1	15	1	1
Patient 2	3	2	2
Patient 3	5	2	1
Patient 4	3	2	2
Patient 5	11	1	2
Patient 6	4	2	2
Patient 7	12	1	1
Patient 8	3	2	2
Patient 9	10	2	1
Patient 10	4	2	2

Sex: 1=male, 2=female; Treatment: 1=ECT, 2=Anti-depressants.

Create a new data set in columns 4 to 6 containing these data as follows:

```
read c4-c6
15   1   1
 3   2   2
 5   2   1
 3   2   2
11   1   2
 4   2   2
12   1   1
 3   2   2
10   2   1
 4   2   2
end
print c4 c5 c6
```

The read command is very similar to the set command except that each subject's data must start on a new line.

The table command can be used to construct a contingency table:

```
table c5 c6
```

Frequency histograms

Minitab will count the frequency with which some score occurs in a column and plot a histogram for you. We could plot the number of patients having ECT or anti-depressants using the histogram command:

```
histogram c6
```

Stem-and-leaf displays

A stem-and-leaf display is a form of frequency histogram. Put the following data in c7 using the set command:

90	90	75	109	109	91	126	79	102	131	40
73	59	57	69	100	115	88	84	43	108	84
34	63	75	135	69	115	101	54	68	66	88
62	102	68	106	85	49	189				

Now try the commands

histogram c7
stem-and-leaf display c7

The stem-and-leaf display is almost identical to the histogram. They are shown in Boxes 2.5 and 2.6 for comparison.

Box 2.5 Stem-and-leaf display (see text for explanation)

```
MTB >
stem-and-leaf display c7

Stem-and-leaf of C7          N  = 40
Leaf Unit = 1.0

     1     3 4
     4     4 039
     7     5 479
    14     6 2368899
    18     7 3559
    (5)    8 44588
    17     9 001
    14    10 01226899
     6    11 55
     4    12 6
     3    13 15
     1    14
     1    15
     1    16
     1    17
     1    18 9
```

Box 2.6 Histogram for the same data as displayed in Box 2.5—there are four values between 30 and 49 (mid point 40), there are 10 between 50 and 69 and so on

```
MTB > histogram c7

Histogram of C7    N = 40

Midpoint    Count
      40        4   ****
      60       10   **********
      80        9   *********
     100       11   ***********
     120        3   ***
     140        2   **
     160        0
     180        1   *

MTB >
```

The main part to the right uses one digit to represent each score. The central values are most common so they extend further to the right. You can read off each score from the display by looking at its 'stem' and 'leaf'. The stems are the second column. So the first stem is 3. There is one score beginning with 3, it is 34, 4 is its leaf. There are three beginning with 4: 40, 43 and 49. So the stem 4 has leaves 0, 3 and 9. There are no values beginning with 14, 15, 16 and 17 so those stems have no leaves.

Many people are perplexed by the first column in the stem-and-leaf display. It gives a cumulative frequency. In Box 2.5 there is one value less than 40, four values less than 50, seven values less than 60 and so on up to the column containing the median (80-89) which is in brackets (there are five values in this column). Below the median we accumulate frequencies in the opposite direction, i.e. 17 values greater than 89, 14 values greater than 99 and so on. These frequencies may be useful when looking for outliers like the value 189 in Box 2.5

Box-plots

A common reason for plotting a histogram or a stem-and-leaf display is to summarise the spread of data and the central tendency. In particular one may want to look for outliers, aberrant data points which are very much larger or smaller than the others such as the last data point in the set above (189). A popular way of summarising this in a single display is the box-plot. Generate a box-plot of c7 as follows:

boxplots c7

The screen should now look like Box 2.7. The '+' marks the median value (84.5). This central value is in a box which contains the central 50% of the data, i.e. the values between the first and third quartiles. You can think of the box as the range of typical values. The dashes are called 'whiskers', they run from the edge of the box (first or third quartile) to the most extreme data value which is still reasonable in each direction. This is taken to be one and a half times the width of the box from each edge of the box. Anything more extreme than this is an outlier and is printed as a '*' or a '0'. '*'s are possible outliers: they are less than three times the width of the box from its edge. '0's are probable outliers: they are more extreme than this. The usefulness of box-plots will become apparent in Chapter 6 when we come to consider how different sets of scores may be compared.

Box 2.7   Box-plot—see text for explanation

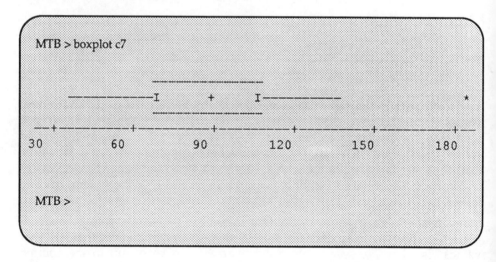

Stop

When you have finished leave Minitab and logout or switch off:

stop

lo (DCL only)

Answers

The median is 51, s=21.17, the standard error of the mean is 9.47. The semi-inter-quartile range is 19.25, s^2=448.17.

ASSIGNMENT

1. The *a priori* probability of throwing a six with one die is 0.1667. What is the probability of not throwing a six?

2. The *a posteriori* (empirical) probability of being female in a certain Psychology class of 43 students is .628.

(a) How many females were there in the class?

(b) What is the probability of being male?

3. The data listed below come from a memory experiment. The scores represent the number of words recalled from a story. Complete the following table to compute (by hand) the median, first and third quartiles etc. ((a) to (e) below).

The first step is to reorder the scores according to rank with the smallest at the bottom.

	Words recalled	Rank	Subject	Words recalled
Subject 1	45	11	...	...
Subject 2	60	10	...	...
Subject 3	74	9	...	...
Subject 4	82	8	...	...
Subject 5	21	7	...	...
Subject 6	65	6	...	...
Subject 7	54	5	...	...
Subject 8	93	4	...	...
Subject 9	108	3	...	...
Subject 10	80	2	...	...
Subject 11	69	1	...	...

(a) What is the median score? Subject No. .... Score ......

(b) What is the range of scores? Min. .... Max. .... Range ......

(c) What is the first quartile? Score ......

(d) What is the third quartile? Score ......

(e) What is the semi-inter-quartile range? Score ....

4. 70 pairs of students were observed during a five minute period of discussion. The scores below represent the number of times one of the students asked a question of the other. There is one score for each pair.

5 6 5 4 5 8 1 5 4 2 1 6 3 7 1 5 4 7 2 9 6 3 2 1 5 4 7 8 9 5 5 5 4 7 2 6 6 4 8

3 3 5 4 5 6 4 3 5 3 5 4 2 4 7 5 4 6 3 5 2 1 7 5 2 5 3 5 3 5 4

Use the histogram or stem-and-leaf commands in Minitab to compute the frequency of each of the scores 1 to 9. Copy the graph below and copy the histogram onto it.

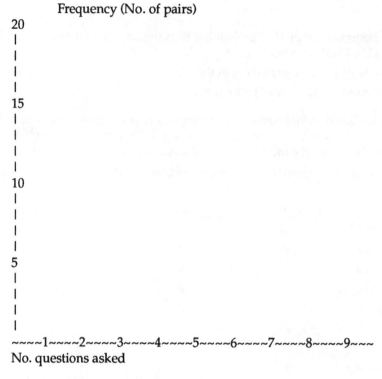

Frequency (No. of pairs)

What is the mode of this distribution?

5. The following data were obtained in an experiment on typing accuracy. The scores represent the number of errors made in typing a 100 word passage under noisy conditions.

23 36 33 33 31 23 34 26 26 30 43 28

28 28 40 26 33 23 31 29 28 32 27 37

24 26 26 32 31 30

Compute the following summary statistics using Minitab:

(a) Mean

(b) Median

(c) Minimum

(d) Maximum

(e) Range

(f) Semi-inter-quartile range

(g) Variance

(h) Standard deviation

SUMMARY OF DCL COMMANDS LEARNED SO FAR

Logging in

1. Refer to the form 'Arrangements for using the computer', at the end of Chapter 1, in which you have summarised the procedure for switching on and connecting your terminal.

2. Press <⏎return>.

3. Enter your user name when prompted for it.

4. Enter your password.

You are successfully logged in when you get the '$' prompt.

DCL commands
   logout (lo)
   whois
   help
   mail

Mail commands
   <⏎return> (show next message)
   send
   help
   exit

Start Minitab session
   minitab

SUMMARY OF MSDOS COMMANDS LEARNED SO FAR

Switching on and off

Refer to the page headed 'Arrangements for using the computer', at the end of Chapter 1, in which you have summarised the procedure for switching on and booting up your computer and for ending a session at the computer.

MSDOS commands
   date

Start Minitab session
   minitab

SUMMARY OF MINITAB COMMANDS LEARNED SO FAR

set   (indicate you have come to the end of the data with end)

read (ditto)   **erase**

print   **save**

let   **retrieve (retr)**

describe (desc)

mean

stdev

sum

table

histogram   (hist)

stem-and-leaf

boxplots

stop

CHAPTER 3
RELATIONSHIPS BETWEEN VARIABLES

Statistical concepts introduced in this chapter: Graphs, tables and equations, the linear function, scattergram, cumulative frequency plot, percentile points.

INTRODUCTION

Much of the material in the next four sections may be familiar to the reader. Nevertheless, it should be read as preparation for Chapter 4.

Tables and graphs

Tables and graphs can be used to supply essentially the same information. They make it possible to 'map' between one variable and another. Table 3.1 and Figure 3.1 both describe the relationship between search time and the number of stimuli that have to be searched. These fictitious data might have come from an experiment where subjects have to find a single letter 't' in an array of other letters. The density of the letters is manipulated so that there are between 20 and

Table 3.1 The relationship between search time and the number of stimuli to be searched

Number of stimuli	Time (seconds)
20	1.92
40	2.54
60	3.16
80	3.78
100	4.40
140	5.64
160	6.26
180	6.88
200	7.50

200 letters to search through on each page. Eight subjects each search 20 pages of each density and the mean time taken to find the 't', averaging across subjects and trials, is computed.

To use the table to map between number of stimuli and search time simply find the appropriate row. For example, to find out the search time when there are 100 stimuli the fifth row is consulted and the answer found to be 4.40 seconds. To map in the opposite direction, say to find out how many stimuli will take about 5 seconds to search, the same procedure is followed. Here the sixth row is consulted and the answer is just under 120.

Figure 3.1 does the same job. To find the time taken when there are 100 stimuli, using the graph, first find the value on the relevant axis (in this case the horizontal one) and then read off the corresponding value on the other axis. The same answer of 4.40 is obtained.

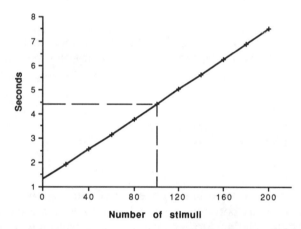

Figure 3.1   Search time plotted against number of stimuli, from Table 3.1

As they present equivalent information tables can be transformed into graphs and graphs into tables. To transform a graph to a table list values of one variable as the first column of the table and then read off the corresponding values for the second column from the graph. To transform a table to a graph plot a point for each pair of values in the table.

Tables, graphs and formulae

Some relationships commonly displayed as graphs or tables can also be described by a formula. Take for example the relationship between the two temperature scales Celsius and Fahrenheit. It is possible to map between these two scales using Figure 3.2 or Table 3.2, or alternatively the formula

$$°F = 32 + 1.8 \, °C$$

Let us say that it is required to find what 40 degrees Celsius is in degrees Fahrenheit. Table 3.2, row 7 shows that the answer is 104. Figure 3.2 gives the same answer (see dotted lines). To get this value from the formula the given value (40°C) is 'substituted into' the formula, i.e.

°F = 32 + 1.8 °C

°F = 32 + 1.8 × 40

°F = 32 + 72

°F = 104

Table 3.2 Table for converting degrees Celsius to degrees Fahrenheit

Degrees Celcius °C	Degrees Fahrenheit °C
−20	−4
−10	14
−10	14
0	32
10	50
20	68
30	86
40	104
50	122
60	140
70	158
80	176
90	194
100	212
110	230
120	248
130	266
140	284

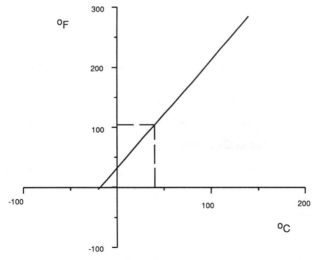

Figure 3.2 Plot for converting °F to °C and vice versa, corresponds to Table 3.2 and the formula °F = 32 + 1.8°C

The equation is written for converting Celsius to Fahrenheit but it can be used in the opposite direction as well, e.g.

$104 = 32 + 1.8\,°C$

$104 - 32 = 1.8\,°C$

$72/1.8 = °C$

$40 = °C$

As one can translate tables into graphs and graphs into tables one can also translate formulae into tables or graphs. A table can be constructed from a formula by putting some values into one column of the table and then working out the corresponding values to go into the other column using the formula. The table can then be transformed into a graph if necessary.

Linear functions

The formula for converting Celsius to Fahrenheit is of a particularly common type known as a linear function. This is because when two variables related by a linear function are plotted as a graph all the points fit on a straight line. Linear functions have the form

$y = c + mx$

y is conventionally the variable one wishes to compute or estimate from some given value of x. In the Celsius to Fahrenheit example the given variable is degrees Celsius and the variable to be computed degrees Fahrenheit. So for $°F = 32 + 1.8\,°C$

y is °F

x is °C

m is 1.8 and

c is 32

(When plotting a graph it is conventional, in the social sciences, to plot the given variable on the horizontal axis.)

There was a straight line relationship between number of stimuli to be searched and mean search time evident in Figure 3.1. The formula describing this line is

seconds = 1.3 + .031 number_of_stimuli

The graph was transformed into a formula as follows. In terms of the formula $y = c + mx$,

(a) y is the time in seconds.

(b) x is the number of stimuli.

(c) m is the slope of the line, i.e. how much it goes up for each unit along the horizontal axis (seconds per stimulus added to the page). It is determined by taking two arbitrary points on the line and dividing the change in seconds by the change in number of stimuli as one moves from one to the other. To minimise the error arising from reading the graph widely separate points are normally taken (see Figure 3.3). When there are 40 stimuli it takes 2.5 seconds, when there are 180, 6.9 seconds. So when the number of stimuli is increased by 140 the time is increased by 4.4:

$$m = \frac{6.9 - 2.5}{180 - 40} = \frac{4.4}{140} = .031$$

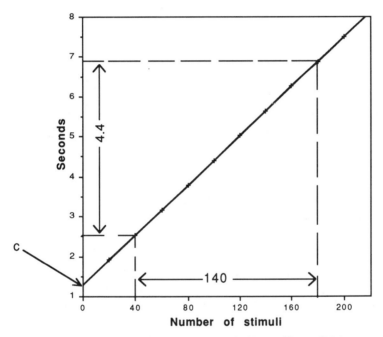

Figure 3.3   Deriving the linear function corresponding to Figure 3.1 (see text for explanation)

(d) c is called the intercept because it can be read from the graph as the y value where the line crosses the vertical axis. Every point on the vertical axis has an x value of zero (0 stimuli) so the intercept is the y value (seconds) when x is zero. In this case it is 1.3.

(e) Putting the above terms into an equation y = c + mx becomes

seconds = 1.3 + .031 number_of_stimuli

The slope and the intercept are psychologically meaningful in this example. The slope can be interpreted as the mean time it takes to scan each stimulus. The intercept can be interpreted as the time it takes to do all the things you need to which are independent of the number of stimuli present, e.g. starting to scan and making the response indicating that you have found the 't'.

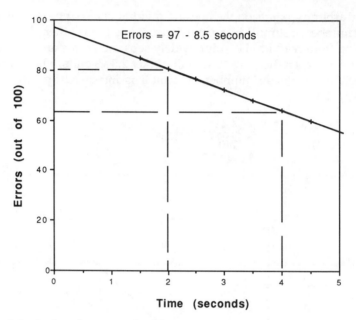

Figure 3.4 A plot of errors against time

Figure 3.4 has a negative slope; as one of the variables goes up the other goes down. The less time people have to solve an arithmetic problem the more errors they make (let us say that the subjects have a limited amount of time, varying from 1.5 to 4.5 seconds per problem, to solve 100 arithmetic problems).

Figure 3.4 is transformed into a formula in exactly the same way as Figure 3.3 was. Two arbitrary points are chosen to determine the slope (see dotted lines). As time changes from 2.0 to 4.0 the number of errors changes from 80.7 to 64.1, so

$$m = \frac{64 - 81}{4.0 - 2.0} = \frac{-17}{2.0} = -8.5$$

The intercept is 97 so the equation for this line is

errors = 97 − 8.5 seconds

The scattergram

This section considers a rather different kind of plot, the scatter diagram or scattergram. Figure 3.5 contains three plots of this kind. Each point on these graphs represents an individual. For example, Figure 3.5(a) plots one point for each of 12 children according to their score on a measure of arithmetic ability (Scale A) and their mark on an exam at the end of an arithmetic course. As the designers of Scale A hoped, children who have high Scale A scores also tend to do well on the exam and children with low Scale A scores tend to do less well on the

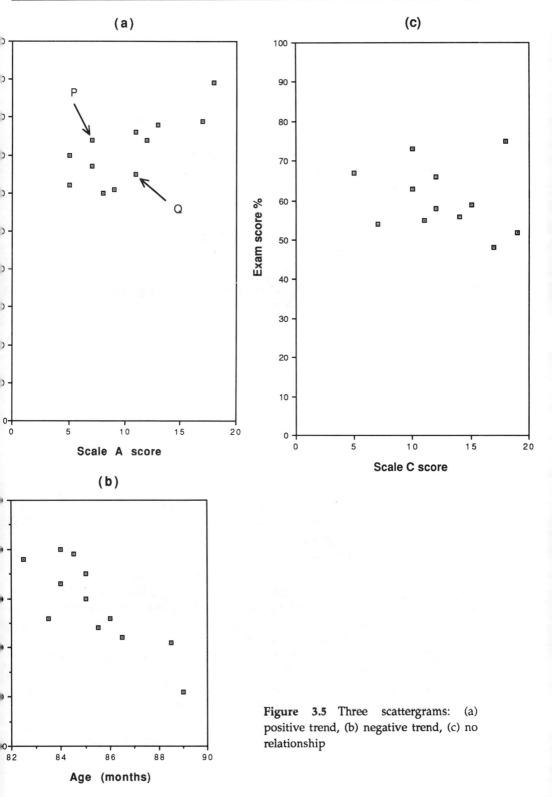

Figure 3.5 Three scattergrams: (a) positive trend, (b) negative trend, (c) no relationship

exam. There are exceptions to this trend however. The point marked P is a child who got a relatively low Scale A score but nonetheless did well on the exam. The point marked Q is a child who got a high Scale A score and did relatively poorly on the exam.

A scattergram differs from the other graphs considered in this chapter in that there is a 'cloud' of points which cannot be joined up to form a line. In Figure 3.5(a) the cloud of points shows a positive trend. In the next chapter we shall see how this trend can be described by thinking of it as a positively sloping linear relationship between Scale A and exam score plus some deviation from this idealised function.

Figure 3.5(b) is a scattergram showing a negative relationship. This plots the time it takes to solve a jigsaw puzzle against the age of the child in months. Here the trend is for the older children to solve the problem in less time. This can be thought of as an underlying linear trend, with a negative slope, plus some deviation from the trend.

Sometimes a scattergram will provide no evidence of an underlying trend. Figure 3.5(c) plots another measure of scholastic ability, Scale C, against exam score. Here there is no sign of a positive or a negative trend. There does not seem to be any relationship between Scale C and exam score.

'S' shaped curves

This far all the functions considered have been linear. Even in the case of a scattergram, where no simple function can be plotted through all the points, the trend in the data can be described as an *approximation* to a straight line (this is the topic of Chapter 4). Only one non-linear function will be considered in this book, that is the 'S' shaped curve derived from frequency distributions.

When a test of intelligence or whatever is constructed it is given to a large random sample from the population it will eventually be used on. The score of each person in this sample is obtained. When someone later uses the test to assess some individual the score obtained can then be related to the scores obtained by the people in the initial large sample to see whether it is good or bad. The procedure of testing a large sample is known as *standardising* a test. The sample is known as the *standardisation sample*.

A psychometric test was given to a standardisation sample of 1000 individuals. The number of individuals with scores between 8 and 11, 12 and 15 and so on are given in the second column of Table 3.3 under 'Frequency'. This column shows that the commonest scores are the central ones, 32 to 35. Those at the top and bottom ends of the scale are much less frequent. This would be apparent were a frequency histogram to be plotted as in Figure 2.1 in Chapter 2. Instead Figure 3.6 plots the cumulative frequency. This is obtained by summing the frequencies starting at the bottom of the table (see column 3 of Table 3.3). Thus 2 is added to 3 to get 5, then 2, 3 and 8 are added to get 13 and so on.

The cumulative frequency in column 3 of Table 3.3 shows how many people got some score *or less*. Two individuals got scores of 11 or less, five individuals got scores of 15 or less, 13 of 19 or less, and so on up to 55 which is the highest score recorded; so 1000 individuals (all of the standardisation sample) got 55 or less. The reason for doing this is that, when transformed to percentages, these cumulative frequencies give a score which can be compared across tests.

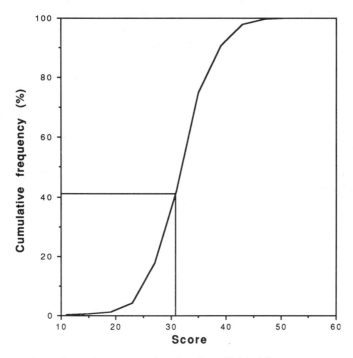

Figure 3.6   Cumulative frequency plot, data from Table 3.3

Table 3.3   Frequency data used in Figure 3.6

Class interval	Frequency	Cumulative frequency	Cumulative percentage frequency
52–55	1	1000	100.0
48–51	1	999	99.9
44–47	20	998	99.8
40–43	73	978	97.8
36–39	156	905	90.5
32–35	328	749	74.9
28–31	244	421	42.1
24–27	136	177	17.7
20–23	28	41	4.1
16–19	8	13	1.3
12–15	3	5	0.5
8–11	2	2	0.2

Rather than reporting a particular individual's score as 42, say, we can report that 97% of the standardisation sample got scores lower or equal to his. Without knowing anything about the test we can tell that this is a good score. If the score was reported as being one which only 27%, say, of the standardisation sample equalled or were lower than, then we would know that it was a moderate to poor score. This is known as reporting 'percentile points'. 42 is a score at the 97th percentile point. The median is the 50th percentile point and the first quartile the 25th percentile point. The 'S' shaped curve in Figure 3.6 can be used to extrapolate between values in the table. The lines show how a raw score of 31 is transformed to percentile points.

Summary

1. Tables, graphs and formulae can all be used to describe functions, that is the relationship between two variables.

2. The simplest functions considered in this chapter are linear functions. They take the general form

$$y = c + mx$$

c is the intercept and m the slope of the line.

3. A scattergram plots relationships between variables when no simple function can be plotted through all the points. The relationship between the two variables plotted in a scattergram may be positive, negative or non-existent. If there is a positive relationship then individuals high on one variable will tend to be high on the other. If there is a negative relationship then individuals with high scores on one variable will tend to have low scores on the other.

4. Cumulative frequency plots are usually 'S' shaped curves. They can be used to determine the percentile points corresponding to any raw score. The first quartile is the 25th percentile point, the median is the 50th percentile point and the third quartile is the 75th percentile point.

WORK SHEETS

DCL

DCL commands introduced in this chapter: directory (dir), delete (del), rename, copy, type, print (see Minitab work sheet).

Files and directories

Information that you do not wish to be lost when you leave the computer has to be stored in something called a 'file'. The last work sheet showed how to 'save' the current Minitab work space and how to 'retrieve' it at some later date (remind yourself about the save and retrieve commands introduced in the last chapter if you need to at this point). The Minitab command save creates a file. Retrieve then 'reads' this back into Minitab as if you had retyped all the data. A file has a name, usually concocted by you (e.g., deviations.mtw), and a contents (e.g., all the data you had typed into Minitab).

Apart from starting programs like Minitab and mail, DCL commands are used to manipulate these files, to create spare copies of files, to delete unwanted files or to rename them.

Log in (see summary of DCL commands at the end of this chapter) and when you have got the dollar prompt type

   dir

All the files you create will be stored in your 'area'. Each user is allocated an area for doing this. The dir command lists all the files in your area. Compare what is now on the screen with Box 3.1. The first line after the dir command is the name of my area for storing files on the computer. On your screen this will be replaced with the name of your area. It contains the name used to log on to the computer, in my case AM1, embedded in some other information. You will seldom need to use the name of your area. Whenever you use the save command in Minitab the resulting file automatically will be put here ready for you to 'retrieve' it at some later date.

Box 3.1   Example of display resulting from DCL directory command

```
$ dir

Directory DISK$PSYC:[AM1]

CH2ASS4.MTW;1   DEVIATIONS.MTW;1   LOGIN.COM;1

MAIL.MAI;1      RUBBISH.MTW;4

Total of 5 files.

$
```

Your area is a 'directory'. The dir command (full name 'directory') lists all the files in this directory. There are five files listed in Box 3.1. The first is

CH2ASS4.MTW;1

This file name has three parts. Let us consider the function of each of these in turn.

'*CH2ASS4*'—The first part of the file name identifies the file. Always try to use names that indicate what is in the files. In this case it is the data needed to complete Assignment 4 for Chapter 2. Spaces and punctuation are not allowed in a file name so that becomes CH2ASS4. TEST1 or DATA5 are not good file names as they do not provide any clues about what the file contains. If you are just testing something, and know you will never need the file you are creating again, use a file name that makes this clear such as RUBBISH.

'*.MTW*'—This is called a file extension. It indicates the type of file that it is, in this case a Minitab work space. The other file extensions in Box 3.1 are .MAI and .COM. Files with the extension .MAI have been created by the mail command. The .COM file, LOGIN.COM, automatically does useful things for you when you log in and should not be interfered with.

'*;1*'—This is the version number, it will normally be 1. If we were to create another file with the name CH2ASS4.MTW it would be given the version number 2, if we created another it would be given the version number 3 and so on. Thus the highest version number indicates the most recent version. In general we are only interested in the most recent version. If you do not specify a version number DCL will assume you mean the most recent version and fill in the highest version number for you. The only exception to this is the delete command (see below) where the version number has to be specified.

Examine the file names on your screen. There should be a file called 'deviations.mtw'. There may also be some .MAI files and a file called 'login.com'.

Testing

Type the following sequence of commands and then answer the questions below

```
minitab
set c1
1 2 3 4 5 6 7 8
end
save 'rubbish'
stop
minitab
print c1
retrieve 'rubbish'
print c1
let c1(8) = 100
```

print c1
save 'rubbish'
stop

(a) What new files have been created? Write down their full names including the extension and version number. Then use the directory command to see if you were correct.

(b) If you were to run Minitab and retrieve 'rubbish' would c1 contain the numbers

$\quad$ 1 2 3 4 5 6 7 8

or the numbers

$\quad$ 1 2 3 4 5 6 7 100?

Try it and see if you were right. (If you are unsure of the effect of let c1(8)=100 go back to Chapter 2 first and remind yourself how let works.)

(c) Using the first part of the command sequence above as a model create a work space with one column containing the numbers 1 to 20. Save it as 'onetotwenty' (no spaces). Leave Minitab and use the DCL command dir to view your new directory to check that the file onetotwenty.mtw is there.

Manipulating files

There are three basic operations you will want to do with files. You might want to make a copy of the contents of a file. To distinguish it from the original the copy will need to have a new name. You may just want to rename a file and you may want to delete (get rid of) a file. The DCL commands *copy*, *rename* and *delete* are there to perform these functions. Try the following sequence. After each manipulation look at the new directory to see what you have done.

```
copy
      onetotwenty.mtw
      1to20.mtw
dir
minitab
retrieve '1to20'
print c1
stop
ren
      1to20.mtw
      1through20.mtw
dir
delete onetotwenty.mtw;1
dir
```

Notice that only with the delete command do we have to specify the version number (';1').

Testing

Retrieve 1through20 (remember that Minitab commands require single quotes round a file name but DCL commands do not). Use the let command to create a second column containing the even numbers from 2 to 40 (let c2=c1*2). Save the new work space as 'even'.

Leave Minitab and rename the file you have created as 2to40.mtw

Enter Minitab and retrieve the data you saved:

print c1 c2

If you are successful c1 should contain the numbers 1 to 20 and c2 the even numbers 2 to 40.

Delete all the files created while working on this work sheet except for 2to40.mtw. Use the directory command and look for: 'rubbish', 'onetotwenty', '1to20', '1through20', 'even' and any other names you typed by mistake. ONLY DELETE FILES WITH THE EXTENSION .MTW

MSDOS

MSDOS commands introduced in this chapter: dir, del, ren, copy, type, print (see Minitab work sheet).

Files and directories

The last work sheet showed how to 'save' the current Minitab work space and how to 'retrieve' it at some later date (remind yourself about the save and retrieve commands introduced in the last chapter if you need to at this point). Information that you do not wish to be lost when you leave the computer has to be stored on disk. This disk may be a floppy disk which has been given to you for this purpose or it may be a hard disk or 'server', permanently attached to the machine used by several people. In either case, the Minitab command save creates a 'file' on the disk. Retrieve then 'reads' this back from the disk into Minitab as if you had retyped all the data. A file has a name, usually concocted by you (e.g., deviations.mtw), and a contents (e.g., all the data you had typed into Minitab).

In fact, you only have access to some part of the disk. This part is called a directory. The MSDOS prompt 'A:\user>' tells me that I currently have access to the directory '\user' on disk 'A: ' . The Minitab command save will create a file in this directory, retrieve will get it back from this directory. Your current directory is unlikely to have the same name and so the prompt will be different. In this book I will assume that your system manager has set things up so that you don't need to use the name of the directory. If this is not the case you will be given supplementary instructions.

Apart from starting programs like Minitab and mail, MSDOS commands are used to manipulate the files in a directory, to create spare copies of files, to delete unwanted files or to rename them. The files which are currently stored in the directory can be listed by using the MSDOS command dir.

Switch on (see the page 'Arrangements for using the computer' at the end of Chapter 1 if you have forgotten the procedure for doing this) and when you have got the 'A:\user>' prompt type

   dir

Compare what is now on the screen with Box 3.2. The first line after the dir command gives the full name of the disk, i.e. what 'A:' stands for. On your screen this will probably be different from that in Box 3.2.

Box 3.2 Example of display resulting from MSDOS dir command

```
A:\user> dir

Volume in drive A is DISK1.VOL3

Directory of A:\user

CH2ASS4        <MTW>      11-5-89      3:02p
DEVIATIONS     <MTW>       9-5-89      5.45p

2 File(s) 2605034 bytes free

A:\user>
```

The rest of the display is a list of the names of the files in the directory. There are two files listed in Box 3.2. The first is CH2ASS4. It has the extension MTW. The next two columns give the date and time it was created.

The display produced by dir separates the two parts of this file name into columns. Let us consider the function of each of these in turn.

'CH2ASS4'—The first part of the file name identifies the file. Always try to use names that indicate what is in the files. In this case it is the data needed to complete Assignment 4 for Chapter 2. Spaces and punctuation are not allowed in a file name so that becomes CH2ASS4. TEST1 or DATA5 are not good file names as they do not provide any clues about what the file contains. If you are just testing something, and know you will never need the file you are creating again, use a file name that makes this clear such as RUBBISH.

'<MTW>'—The file extension indicates the type of file that it is: in this case a Minitab work space. The other file extensions you may come across are <.>, <..>, <BAT>, <SYS>, <EXE>, and <COM>. DO NOT INTERFERE WITH ANY FILES WITH THESE EXTENSIONS. The '<' and '>' brackets are simply to indicate that these are extensions. They do not have to be typed when specifying a file. For example, when entering this file name as part of a MSDOS command, say to delete it, it would be typed ch2ass4.mtw.

Examine the file names on your screen. There should be a file called 'deviations.mtw'. The display finishes with a summary of how many files there are in the directory and how much space there is on the disk to store more files.

Testing

Type the following sequence of commands and then answer the questions below:

```
minitab
set c1
1 2 3 4 5 6 7 8
end
save 'rubbish'
stop
minitab
print c1
retrieve 'rubbish'
print c1
let c1(8) = 100
print c1
save 'rubbish'
stop
```

(a) What new file has been created? Write down its name including the extension. Then use the directory command to see if you were correct.

(b) If you were to run Minitab and retrieve 'rubbish' would c1 contain the numbers

1 2 3 4 5 6 7 8

or the numbers

1 2 3 4 5 6 7 100?

Try it and see if you were right. (If you are unsure of the effect of let c1(8)=100 go back to Chapter 2 first and remind yourself how let works.)

(c) Using the first part of the command sequence above as a model create a work space with one column containing the numbers 1 to 20. Save it as 'onetotwenty' (no spaces). Leave Minitab and use the MSDOS command dir to view your new directory to check that the file onetotwenty.mtw is there.

Manipulating files

There are three basic operations you will want to do with files. You might want to make a copy of the contents of a file. To distinguish it from the original the copy will need to have a new name. You may just want to rename a file and you may want to delete (get rid of) a file. The MSDOS commands *copy*, *ren* and *del* are there to perform these functions. Try the following sequence. After each manipulation look at the new directory to see what you have done.

```
copy          onetotwenty.mtw          1to20.mtw
dir
minitab
retrieve      '1to20'
print c1
stop
ren           1to20.mtw          1through20.mtw
dir
delete        onetotwenty.mtw
dir
```

Notice that with copy and ren the old file name is typed first and then the new name. Say to yourself 'from' as you type the first name and 'to' as you type the second.

Testing

Retrieve 1through20 (remember that Minitab commands require single quotes round a file name but MSDOS commands do not). Use the let command to create a second column containing the even numbers from 2 to 40 (let c2=c1*2). Save the new work space as 'even'.

Leave Minitab and rename the file you have created as 2to40.mtw

Enter Minitab and retrieve the data you saved:

```
print c1 c2
```

If you are successful c1 should contain the numbers 1 to 20 and c2 the even numbers 2 to 40.

Delete all the files you have created in this chapter except 2to40.mtw. Use the directory command and look for: 'rubbish', 'onetotwenty', '1to20', '1through20', 'even' and any other names you typed by mistake. ONLY DELETE FILES WITH THE EXTENSION .MTW

MINITAB

Minitab commands introduced in this chapter: Plot, outfile, nooutfile, help.

Plotting graphs

In the Introduction we considered the functions y=bx and y=bx+c. We can use

Minitab to plot these functions. Retrieve '2to40' into Minitab, erase column 2 and then use the let command to create two new columns computed from c1:

    c2=10*c1

    c3=10*c1 + 5

Print the resulting columns. The first three rows will be

    1 10 15

    2 20 25

    3 30 35

Save this work space as funcs:

    save 'funcs'

Now plot c2 as a function of c1:

    plot c2 c1

You will find that the graph is basically a straight line. The kinks are because the VDU can only put a point on one of its 24 lines and not in between two lines as it would like to.

Plot the other function against c1:

    plot c3 c1

You can get a printed version of your graph as follows. The Minitab command *outfile* puts the information appearing on your screen into a file. *nooutfile* 'closes' the file. You can then leave Minitab and look at it using the DCL or MSDOS command *type*.

    outfile 'times10'
    plot c2 c1
    nooutfile
    stop
    dir
    type times10.lis

There are several confusing things about what we have just done:

1. Although we have already plotted c2 against c1 we have to plot it again after the outfile command. Minitab does not try to guess what to do next on the basis of what you have done before, as a human would. It is best to think of the outfile command as a sort of switch. Once this switch has been set everything that appears on the screen also goes into the file. The switch is reset by the nooutfile command. Doing calculations and plots twice in this way is quite sensible. When you have put in your data you can check it using the screen output on a few commands and, only when you are satisfied, use the outfile command, repeating those commands, to record the results of your computation.

2. You have created two files: TIMES10.LIS and FUNCS.MTW. These are very different animals. TIMES10.LIS is a record of the screen output. The type command displays it on the screen and it can also be printed with the print command (see below). FUNCS.MTW is a Minitab work space—it contains the data you entered into Minitab. Minitab work spaces can only be viewed with Minitab. Using the type or print commands with one of these files will not produce anything useful and may temporarily put your terminal out of action or do something nasty to the printer. PLEASE MAKE EVERY ATTEMPT NOT TO TYPE OR PRINT FILES CREATED WITH THE SAVE COMMAND.

3. When using the save command we only specified the name 'funcs' and the file appears as FUNCS.MTW in the directory. Minitab puts in the .MTW to remind you the file is a Minitab work space and cannot be printed or typed. Again when using the outfile command we only specified 'times10'. Minitab put in the extension .LIS to indicate that it can be printed or typed ('listed'). Never specify an extension (.SOMETHING) when using save or outfile and then the files will always have the appropriate extension and you will be able to recognise them for what they are.

print times10.lis

See 'Arrangements for using the computer' at the end of Chapter 1 where you should have recorded local arrangements for getting files printed. If you have been successful DCL will come back with a message along the lines of:

Job times10(queue PR$CENTRAL, entry ...) started on PR$CENTRAL

or

Job times10(queue PR$CENTRAL, entry ...) queued

If it comes back with a message along the lines of:

%PRINT-E-OPENIN, error in opening .... file not found

then you have probably mis-typed the filename (check it with dir).

With MSDOS you should be able to see your graph being printed on the printer.

Note that you have now learned two print commands, an operating system command (MSDOS or DCL) and a Minitab command, and that they have quite different meanings. The Minitab command only works to the prompt 'MTB >', i.e. when Minitab is running. The operating system command only works to the prompt '$' (DCL) or 'A:\user>' (MSDOS). The operating system command sends a file to the printer to give you a hard copy. The Minitab command causes part of the work space to be displayed on the screen. You may care to speculate about the intelligence of people who design programs like this!

Testing

1. Box 3.3 summarises the difference between .MTW files and .LIS files. Read through it and make sure you can confidently answer the following questions. If you can't, go over the preceding section again.

(a) Which Minitab command records the data you have typed into Minitab in a file?

(b) Which command records the results of the calculations performed by Minitab in a file?

(c) Which files should never be printed or typed and what file extension will indicate a file is of this kind?

(d) Which files exist to be printed or typed and what file extension indicates a file is of this kind?

Box 3.3   The distinction between .LIS and .MTW files

Minitab has an implicit distinction between data and results. The Minitab work space contains the *data*. It consists of columns containing numbers. The columns can be given names with the name command. Having put in these data one can then compute a variety of *results*—means, graphs etc.

Commands for adding to or manipulating data in the work space include: set, read, erase, let.

Commands which produce results from the data in the work space include: desc, mean, sum, table, histogram, plot.

The Minitab command save creates a special kind of file containing the current Minitab work space. The only way the contents of this file can be inspected is by using the Minitab command retrieve and then the Minitab command print. Using the type or print operating system commands on files created with save is to be avoided. If an extension is not specified for the file given in the save command Minitab will assign these files the extension .MTW.

The Minitab commands outfile and nooutfile can be used to put the results of Minitab calculations into a file. After an outfile command everything that appears on the screen is also put in the file. The command nooutfile switches this off. If an extension is not specified for the file given in the outfile command Minitab will assign these files the extension .LIS.

2. The outfile command continues to put whatever appears on the screen into the file until a nooutfile command is issued. So, three graphs can be stored in one file by doing three plot commands between the outfile and the nooutfile. Print c2 and c3 as functions of c1 in this way. Use the one file 'graphs.lis' to do this.

Help

Minitab has a comprehensive facility for providing information about its commands. This can be used to remind yourself about how a command is used or to find out about additional commands you have not used before.

Enter Minitab and type

help set

There are three screenfuls of information on this topic. Press <⏎return> to the prompt 'More?' after you have looked at each of them. While much of this may be more than you bargained for there is useful information here.

Press <⏎return> until you get back to the 'MTB>' prompt and then type the command again to reveal the first screen.

help set

Your screen should now look like Box 3.4. The following points will help to interpret the information provided.

Box 3.4 The first screen of information on the set command

```
MTB > help set

SET data from 'FILENAME' into C
SET the  following data  into C

Subcommands:  FORMAT   NOBS

If FILENAME is not used, then data are entered from the
keyboard after the SET command.  Here is an example:

   SET INTO C1
   2 6 5.1  2.8
   7 6.1 5.2 8
   END

C1 now contains the numbers 2, 6, 5.1, 2.8, 7, 6.1, 5.2,
and 8.

More?
```

1. The first two lines describe how the command is to be used. Only the words in capitals should be typed. The other words are only by way of explanation. The 'C' in this general specification invites you to enter a column specification (e.g., 'c1'). Thus an example of the command actually entered is

set c1

2. There are two forms of the set command. One is the form we are familiar with. The other includes a filename. Do not concern yourself with the latter.

3. Subcommands will not be considered until Chapter 5.

4. Very often the examples given are the most useful part of this help information. The example at the bottom of Box 3.4 would give all the information needed to remind someone how this command is used.

Help can also be used as a reminder for the name of a command:

help commands

This gives a kind of contents page. One of these groups of commands can be chosen for display. For example, to get a list of the commands for 'Input and output of data' type

help commands 2

Testing

Find which category contains the desc command.

ASSIGNMENT

1. Plot the following straight line functions onto a graph (by hand):

$Y = 3X$

$Y = 3X+5$

$Y = 3X+9$

$Y = 1.5X+5$

$Y = -3X+5$

Use X values of 1, 3 and 5 and draw a line through the points.

2. Figure 3.7 plots the time it takes to write 1, 2, 3, 4 or 5 words under particularly difficult circumstances.

(a) What is the slope of the line in seconds per word?

(b) What is its intercept in seconds?

(c) Write a formula to predict seconds from words.

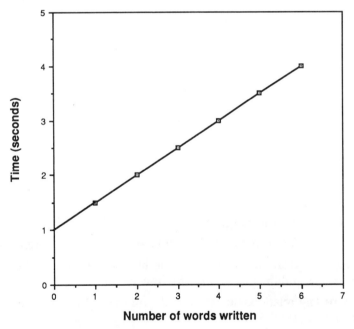

Figure 3.7 Plot for Assignment, Q2

3. The data given below were obtained in an experiment in which individuals were video-recorded in a group discussion. The total time they spent talking was assessed from this record. Before the discussion they were given a standard personality test which yields a score for extraversion. Use Minitab to plot a scattergram based on these data.

(a) Cut it out of the printout and stick it in your report.

(b) What name appears in your directory to refer to the file used to store the graph ready for printing?

Save the data for further analysis at a later time.

(c) What name appears in your directory to refer to the file in which these data are stored?

	Extraversion score	Minutes spent talking
Subject 1	22	10
Subject 2	12	6
Subject 3	15	8
Subject 4	25	12
Subject 5	20	11
Subject 6	10	8
Subject 7	25	15
Subject 8	13	6
Subject 9	17	5
Subject 10	16	11
Subject 11	21	9
Subject 12	14	5
Subject 13	18	12
Subject 14	20	11
Subject 15	16	6
Subject 16	14	4
Subject 17	23	16
Subject 18	15	4
Subject 19	18	8
Subject 20	19	9

4. Use Figure 3.6 to convert the following raw scores to percentile points:
(a) 23
(b) 33
(c) 41

5. Sketch three fictional scattergrams to illustrate:

(a) the (positive) relationship between height and weight in a sample of students;

(b) the (negative) relationship between the number of months they have been learning statistics and the time it takes to draw a graph;

(c) the lack of any relationship between the number of months they have been learning statistics and the time it takes to drink a pint of beer.

Label the axes and give each plot an appropriate title.

6. Use the set command to enter the numbers 1 to 10 into c1. The insert command allows one to add data to an existing column. Use the help command to find out how this works. What needs to be typed to add the numbers 11 to 20 to c1? (As well as reading the help you will probably need to experiment before you get this right.)

SUMMARY OF DCL COMMANDS LEARNED SO FAR

Logging in

1. Refer to the form 'Arrangements for using the computer', at the end of Chapter 1, in which you have summarised the procedure for switching on and connecting your terminal.

2. Press <⌐return>.

3. Enter your user name when prompted for it.

4. Enter your password.

You are successfully logged in when you get the '$' prompt.

DCL commands

logout (lo)	**rename (ren)**
whois	**copy**
help	**type**
directory (dir)	**print**
mail	**delete (del)**

Mail commands

    <⌐return> (show next message)

send

help

exit

Start Minitab session

minitab

SUMMARY OF MSDOS COMMANDS LEARNED SO FAR

Switching on and off

Refer to the page headed 'Arrangements for using the computer', at the end of Chapter 1, in which you have summarised the procedure for switching on and booting up your computer and for ending a session at the computer.

MSDOS commands

date

ren   (the first file name given is the 'from' file,

       the second the 'to' file)

copy (again 'from' 'to')

dir	**type**
del	**print**

Start Minitab session
   minitab

SUMMARY OF MINITAB COMMANDS LEARNED SO FAR

set   (indicate you have come to the end of the data with end)
read (ditto)   **erase**
name   **save** 'name'
info   **retrieve   (retr)** 'name'
print   **outfile** 'name'
let   **nooutfile**
describe
mean
stdev
sum
table
histogram   (hist)
stem-and-leaf
boxplots
plot

help commands
stop

CHAPTER 4
GOODNESS OF FIT

Statistical concepts introduced in this chapter: regression, deviation, deviance, correlation (r^2 and r), reliability.

INTRODUCTION

Regression—the problem

Chapter 3 contained a scattergram (Figure 3.5(a)) depicting the relationship between Scale A, a psychometric test for predicting a child's ability to learn arithmetic, and the child's mark in an examination following an arithmetic course. On the whole children who do well on Scale A also do well on the examination. This trend could be summarised by drawing a straight line through the points as in Figure 4.1. When all the points fall on or very close to a straight line it is simple enough to fit such a line 'by eye'. With a data set such as this, where there is some scatter in the points, this is not advisable as it is possible that you would draw a line different from the one someone else would choose. The solution to this problem is to use a statistical procedure known as regression by which one can compute the best fitting straight line. Minitab can always be trusted to do this in a sensible way and you will never need to do the calculations described in the next four sections. They are included because they are of theoretical rather than practical importance.

Deviations from a prediction and the deviance of a prediction

The line drawn onto Figure 4.1 can be thought of as a prediction. It allows us to predict an exam score from a Scale A score. For some individuals, the ones close to the line, this prediction is good, for others it is less good. Table 4.1 gives each individual's score on Scale A and the exam, and the predicted score on the exam using the formula. The difference between the prediction and the observed score is given in the column 'deviation'.

Take subject 1 for example. His score on Scale A was 11, so the formula for the line

predicted_exam_score = 55.4 + 1.55 Scale_A_score

predicts that his exam score should be

$$55.4 + 1.55 \times 11 = 72.45$$

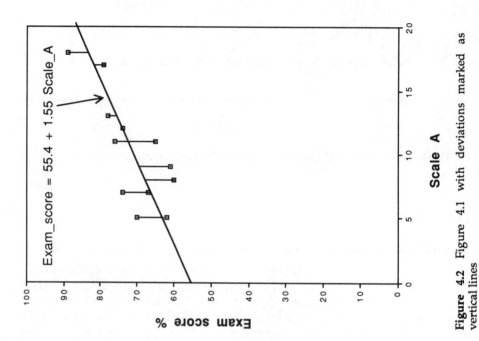

Figure 4.2 Figure 4.1 with deviations marked as vertical lines

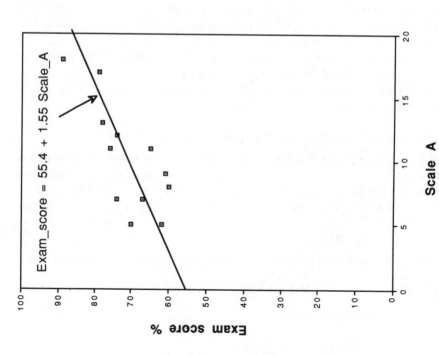

Figure 4.1 Scattergram depicting the relationship between exam_score and Scale_A-score

Table 4.1 Data for Figure 4.1

Subject	Scale_A	Exam score	Predicted exam score	Deviation	Squared deviation
1	11	76	72.45	3.55	12.60
2	8	60	67.80	−7.80	60.84
3	11	65	72.45	−7.45	55.50
4	9	61	69.35	−8.35	69.72
5	7	74	66.25	7.75	60.06
6	17	79	81.75	−2.75	7.56
7	7	67	66.25	0.75	0.56
8	18	89	83.30	5.70	32.49
9	12	74	74.00	0.00	0.00
10	5	62	63.15	−1.15	1.32
11	13	78	75.55	2.45	6.00
12	5	70	63.15	6.85	46.92
				Deviance	353.59

His actual 'observed' exam score was 76 so the difference, or deviation from prediction, is 3.55. Some of the differences are positive and some are negative. They are plotted onto Figure 4.2—the positive ones go up from the line, the negative ones go down.

The extent to which the observed values deviate from the predictions is summarised by summing the squared deviations. This is the purpose of the last column in Table 4.1. The sum of the squared deviations (353.59) is known as the *deviance*. It is a measure of how bad the fit is. Readers will recognise this calculation as being similar to that made when computing the variance. There the mean was subtracted from the observed score and the deviations squared and summed.

As we shall see later on in this introduction, and in Chapters 8 and 9, computing a deviance is the starting point of many of the calculations performed for you by Minitab. The procedure is summarised in Box 4.1.

Box 4.1 Summary of the procedure for obtaining the deviance of a prediction

1. Tabulate the observed and predicted scores. In this example we are comparing the predicted_exam_score with the subject's actual exam score. The subject's predicted_exam_score is obtained from his Scale_A_score using a linear equation (predicted_exam_score = 55.4 + 1.55 Scale_A_score).

2. Subtract each predicted score from each observed score to get the deviation of each subject from the prediction, e.g. the deviation of each subject is obtained by subtracting his predicted_exam_score from his actual exam score.

3. The deviance of the prediction is obtained by squaring all the deviations and then summing the squared deviations.

The regression equation—the best fitting straight line

We are now in a position to define what is meant by the best fitting straight line. It is the one with the least deviance. As the deviance, as defined above, is the sum of the squared deviations, this is sometimes known as the 'least squares solution'. The best fitting straight line could be determined by computing the deviance for a best guess, moving the line slightly, seeing if the deviance is better or worse, moving it again and so on. Fortunately, this kind of 'iterative' procedure is not necessary and the slope and intercept of the best fitting straight line can be computed using simple formulae. You will always use the computer to evaluate these formulae so they are not given here. In point of fact the best fitting straight line for the data in Table 4.1 is the one drawn on Figure 4.1:

predicted_exam_score = 55.4 + 1.55 Scale_A_score

This is known as the regression equation; more precisely it is the regression equation for predicting exam scores from Scale_A_scores or technically *the regression of exam score on Scale A.*

The regression of X on Y and Y on X

Notice that in order to define what we meant by 'best fitting line' we had to say what was being predicted from what. You may find it surprising to learn that the best fitting straight line for predicting Scale A from exam score is not the same line as the best fitting straight line for predicting exam score from Scale A. The best fitting straight line for predicting Score A from exam score is

predicted_Scale_A_score = –16.2 + 0.372 exam_score

Rewritten with exam score as the y variable, this is

exam_score = 43.55 + 2.69 predicted_Scale_A_score

which has a steeper slope and a lower intercept than the best fitting straight line for predicting in the other direction. The two lines are plotted in Figure 4.3.

To reiterate, the regression line for predicting exam score from Scale A is said to be the regression of exam score on Scale A. The regression line for predicting Scale A from exam score is said to be the regression of Scale A on exam score.

The two regression lines for a set of data will only coincide when all the points fall precisely on a straight line, i.e. when there is a perfect fit. When there is no real relationship between the two variables they will be at right angles to one another.

This follows from the form of the regression equation. We are predicting exam score with a formula of the form

predicted_exam_score = c + m Scale_A_score

If Scale_A_score has no bearing on exam score then m will be zero, i.e. the formula becomes

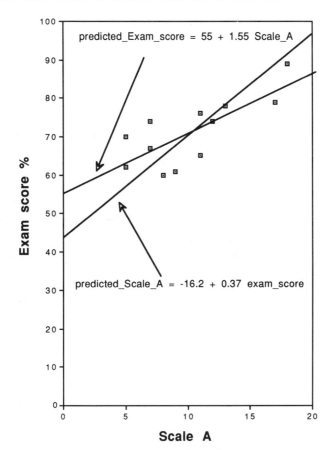

Figure 4.3   Figure 4.1 with both regression lines drawn

predicted_exam_score = c

Likewise the formula for predicting Scale A score will be of the general form

predicted_Scale_A_score = c

These two lines will always be at right angles to one another.

Deviance from the mean

The deviance of the best prediction that can be made of the form

predicted_exam_score = c_o

can be thought of as a baseline against which we can evaluate the regression equation

predicted_exam_score = c + m Scale_A_score

The regression equation is the linear equation that has the smallest deviance. If we compare that with the deviance of the equation

$$\text{predicted\_exam\_score} = c_o$$

which has the smallest deviance we can see how much we have gained by adding Scale_A_score to the equation.

It turns out that the least deviance is obtained if c_o is set to the mean exam score. So the baseline deviance we use to evaluate the deviance of the regression equation is the deviance from the mean. This is computed in Table 4.2.

Table 4.2 Computing the deviance from the mean for the exam scores from Figure 4.1. The deviation from the mean is computed by subtracting the mean exam score (71.25) from each subject's actual exam score

Exam Score	Deviation from mean	Squared deviation
76	4.75	22.56
60	−11.25	126.56
6	−6.25	39.06
61	−10.25	105.06
74	2.75	7.56
79	7.75	60.06
67	−4.25	18.06
89	17.75	315.06
74	2.75	7.56
62	−9.25	85.56
78	6.75	45.56
70	−1.25	1.56
	Deviance	834.25

So we know that the best prediction we can get of the form

$$\text{predicted\_exam\_score} = c_o$$

is when $c_o = 71.25$ and that this prediction has a deviance of 834.25.

The deviations going into this deviance are plotted in Figure 4.4. Compare these with the deviations from the regression equation in Figure 4.2. On the whole they are larger. This can be seen in the deviance computed when the deviations are squared and summed. The best prediction of the form

$$\text{predicted\_exam\_score} = c + m\,\text{Scale\_A\_score}$$

has c = 55.4 and m = 1.55 and a deviance of 353.59. Adding Scale_A_score has reduced the deviance from 834.25 to 353.59. This gives us a way of quantifying

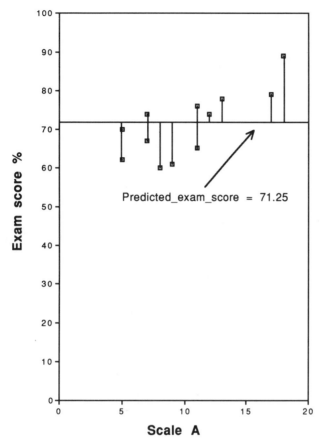

Figure 4.4 Figure 4.1 with deviations from the mean drawn

how strong the relationship between two variables is. This quantification is known as a correlation coefficient.

Correlation

Regression is a procedure for finding the best fitting straight line. Correlation is a way of quantifying how good this best fit is. Figures 4.5 and 4.6 illustrate two extreme cases. Figure 4.5 illustrates the somewhat unlikely case of a perfect fit. If someone's score on Scale B is known then their exam score is known also.

There is no apparent relationship between the scores plotted in Figure 4.6. Someone with a high Scale C score is just as likely to have a high exam score as a low one. The situation in Figure 4.1 is somewhere in between these two extremes. There is a relationship between Scale A and exam score but there is some deviation from a perfect fit.

The correlation coefficient r summarises the strength of the relationship. r is just one of the possible ways a correlation can be summarised. Its full name is

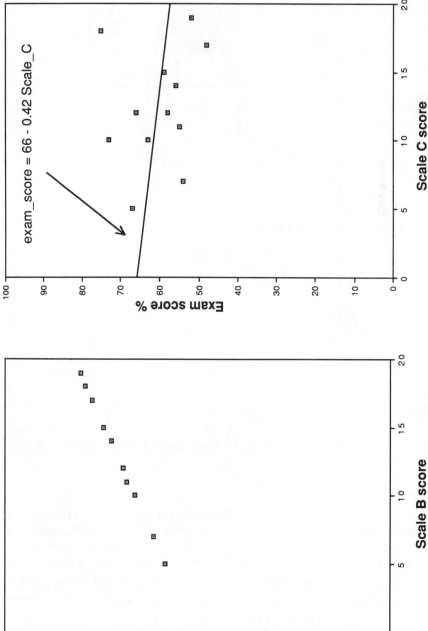

Figure 4.6 Scattergram depicting the relationship between exam_score and Scale_C_score. There is very little evidence of a relationship here∆86

Figure 4.5 Scattergram depicting the relationship between exam_score and Scale_A_score. These scores fall almost exactly on a straight line

Pearson's product-moment correlation coefficient. This book concentrates on r to the exclusion of other correlation coefficients because it can be interpreted in terms of deviance from a prediction. This will be important when we come to consider multiple regression in Chapters 8 and 9. We will start off by considering r^2, the square of r. This is a number between zero and one. The higher r^2 is the stronger the relationship between the variables.

For the data presented in Figure 4.5 $r^2 = 1.00$ (a perfect correlation). For the data presented in Figure 4.6 $r^2 = .047$ (nearly a zero correlation). For the data in Figure 4.1 $r^2 = .58$.

These values for r^2 can be obtained in the following way:

$$r^2 = \frac{\text{deviance of the mean} - \text{deviance of the regression equation}}{\text{deviance of the mean}}$$

So for the data presented in Table 4.1

$$r^2 = \frac{834.25 - 353.59}{J88} = .58$$

Adding Scale_A_score to the equation reduces the deviance from 834.25 to 353.59, i.e. by 480.66. r^2 is simply this figure expressed as a proportion of the baseline deviance (deviance of the mean).

When there is a perfect correlation between the two variables the deviance of the regression equation will be zero, so r^2 will be 1.00. For example, in Figure 4.5 the exam score predicted from Scale B is equal to the actual exam score for all the subjects. This means that the deviation from the prediction is zero for all subjects. Summing and squaring all these zeros gives zero as the deviance. The deviance from the mean exam score is 796.8 (this is a new set of subjects) so

$$r^2 = \frac{796.8 - 0.00}{796.8} = 1.00$$

For the data in Figure 4.6, where there is very little sign of a relationship, the deviance of the regression equation is very close to the deviance of the mean (see Table 4.3). There is very little reduction in deviance achieved by adding Scale C to the equation (36.43) so r^2 is close to zero:

$$r^2 = \frac{775.0 - 738.57}{775.0} = .047$$

The logic behind these calculations is summarised in Box 4.2.

Table 4.3   Data from Figure 4.6

Exam	Dev. from mean	Sq. Dev	Scale C	Prediction from Scale C	Dev.	Sq.Dev
63	2.5	6.25	10	61.56	1.44	2.07
56	−4.5	20.25	14	59.86	−3.86	14.93
52	−8.5	72.25	19	57.74	−5.74	32.99
54	−6.5	42.25	7	62.83	−8.83	78.00
73	12.5	156.25	10	61.56	11.44	130.87
48	−12.5	156.25	17	58.59	−10.59	112.19
66	5.5	30.25	12	60.71	5.28	27.96
55	−5.5	30.25	11	61.13	−6.13	37.65
58	−2.5	6.25	12	60.71	−2.71	7.35
67	6.5	42.25	5	63.68	3.32	11.02
59	−1.5	2.25	15	59.44	−0.44	0.19
75	14.5	210.25	18	58.16	16.83	283.31
Deviance of mean		775.0		Deviance of reg.		738.57

Box 4.2 r^2 as a measure of how good a linear model is

(a) We have a hypothesis or model to evaluate. In this case the model is that one score can be predicted from the other with a linear equation (the regression equation).

(b) The model is to be evaluated against a simpler model, in this case we take the baseline model of predicting each score from the mean score.

(c) The deviance of each of these two models is computed by summing the squared deviations of their predictions.

(d) The deviances are compared in a statistic reflecting their difference, in this case r^2.

(e) If the deviances are similar (r^2 close to 0) the first model can be said to be a poor one, it does not do much better than the baseline model.

(f) If the deviance of the first model is much smaller than that of the baseline model (r^2 close to 1) then it can be concluded to be a good one.

Interpreting r^2

r^2 can also be interpreted as the proportion of the variance in one score that can be accounted for by the variance in the other score. So we can say that .58 of the variance in examination scores can be accounted for by the variance in Scale A scores. r^2 is the same whatever direction you are predicting so we can also say that .58 of the variance in Scale A scores can be accounted for by the variance in exam scores.

This proportion is often reported as a percentage, i.e. 58% of the variance in examination scores can be accounted for by the variance in Scale A scores.

The correlation coefficient r

r, unsurprisingly, is the square root of r². r takes the sign of the slope of the regression equation. A positive r indicates a relationship where high values on one variable are associated with high values on the other as in our example (the r for Scale A and exam score is .76). A negative r indicates that high values on one score are associated with low values on the other. Figure 4.7 (based on Figure 3.11(b)) gives an example of such a relationship. The higher the age of a child in months the less time it takes to solve a jigsaw puzzle.

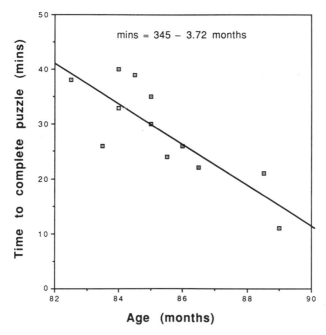

Figure 4.7 Scattergram depicting the relationship between age and time to complete a puzzle

Using r—the reliability of a psychometric test

Correlation coefficients, particularly r, are used extensively in behavioural science. One important example of this is the concept of the 'reliability' of a psychometric test. Any measuring instrument should give you the same answer if you measure the same thing twice. A tape measure which gave the length of some object as being 12 cm on one occasion and 13 cm on another would not be of much use. Unfortunately behavioural characteristics are difficult to measure with precision and so we need to assess how repeatable the measures obtained are. Technically this is known as assessing the 'reliability' of the test and is performed as part of the standardisation of the test.

The simplest way of assessing the reliability of a test is to apply it twice to the same set of individuals. If the test has a high reliability then, in general, people will get the same score on the second test as they do on the first. We can describe the strength of that relationship by computing r. This is known as the 'test–retest reliability' of the test. Figure 4.8 is a scattergram plotting each subject's score on Day 1 (first testing) with their score on Day 2 (second testing). On the whole the results obtained on the two days are similar, so the scattergram approximates to a straight line with slope of 1. r for these data is .95 which is a perfectly adequate reliability. Figure 4.9 depicts a much less satisfactory situation. Although people

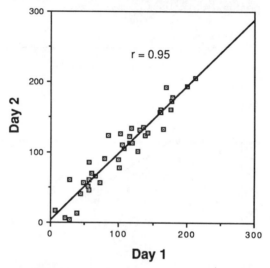

Figure 4.8   Scores obtained from the same test on two different days plotted as a scattergram—good reliability

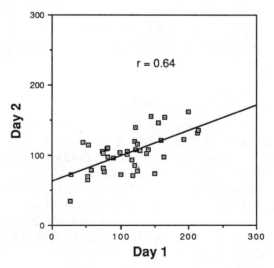

Figure 4.9   Scores obtained from the same test on two different days plotted as a scattergram—poor reliability

who do well on Day 1 also do well on Day 2 (as one would hope!) there are some quite large discrepancies. r for these data is .64. In general one is looking for a reliability of .8 or .9 in a psychometric test. This second test obviously needs further development before it can be used as a measuring instrument.

With many tests there are practical problems in interpreting a test–retest reliability. For example, a personality test may involve reading 40 statements (e.g., 'I enjoy noisy parties'). You have to say whether you agree or disagree with each statement. Let us say that you are given this test one day and then again the next day. On the second day it is quite likely you will be able to remember your responses from the first day. This may result in an artificially high estimate of the reliability of the test because you are trying to be consistent. More generally, the problem of using a test–retest reliability is that testing the sample on the first occasion may somehow affect their results when they are tested on the second occasion.

One solution to this problem is to have two versions of a test. Version 1 can then be used in the first testing session and Version 2 in the second. The correlation between the scores of each individual on two versions of a test is known as the 'alternate forms' reliability of the test. This also has its problems. The alternate forms reliability of a test may be an under-estimate if the two versions are not really equivalent. It is also extremely tedious to have to prepare two tests when one is only for testing reliability.

The most commonly used measure of reliability is 'split-half' reliability. This is similar to alternate forms reliability except that the two versions of the test are obtained by dividing the test into halves. Consider again the example of a personality test consisting of 40 statements. In the normal course of events a score would be obtained for the whole test by examining the subject's response (agree or disagree) for each of the 40 statements. To obtain a split-half reliability the test is administered in the normal way but scored as if it had been two 20-item tests. Perhaps the odd statements are treated as if they were from one test and the even items as if they were from another. We can then correlate the scores for the two halves. All the items in a test should be measuring the same thing so this correlation will reflect the reliability of the two halves of the test. If there is a high correlation the reliability is high. If not it is not.

The only problem with the procedure as stated this far is that the results from two 20-item tests have been correlated, whereas the final test contains 40 items. This will make the correlation computed an underestimate. Imagine an arithmetic test based on three addition problems. How would you expect its reliability to compare with one based on 100 addition problems? Other things being equal the more items you have the more reliable a test will be. So, we have estimated the reliability of a 40-item test by correlation of two 20-item tests. The resulting under-estimation is systematic and we can correct for it using a formula

$$r_{\text{split-half}} = \frac{2r}{1+r}$$

where r is the correlation between the two halves of the test. This is known as the Spearman–Brown formula.

Summary

1. The trend in a scattergram can be summarised by a straight line.

2. The best fitting such straight line is known as the regression equation.

3. 'Best fitting' is defined as follows:

(a) One variable, the predictor variable, is being used to predict the other, the predicted variable.

(b) A linear equation is used to compute a predicted value from the predictor variable.

(c) The deviation is the difference between the observed value of the predicted variable and its predicted value.

(d) The deviance is the sum of the squared deviations.

(e) The linear equation with the lowest deviance is the regression equation.

4. The regression equation for predicting A from B (the regression of A on B) is not the same line as that for predicting B from A (the regression of B on A) unless all the points fall on a straight line.

5. Correlation is a measure of how good the best fit is.

6. r^2 is used to compare the deviance of the regression equation with the deviance from the mean. (r is the Pearson product-moment correlation coefficient.)

7. $$r^2 = \frac{\text{deviance of the mean} - \text{deviance of the regression equation}}{\text{deviance of the mean}}$$

8. r^2 can be interpreted as the proportion of the variance in one score that can be accounted for by the variation in the other score.

9. r takes the sign of the slope of the regression equation. So a positive relationship has a positive r and a negative relationship has a negative r. No relationship is indicated by an r approaching zero.

10. The reliability of a psychometric test is measured by obtaining two estimates of each subject's score on it and then correlating these scores.

WORK SHEETS

MINITAB

Minitab commands introduced in this chapter: name, info, ssq, regress, correlation.

Three new Minitab commands

ssq computes the sum of squares for a column, e.g. $1^2 + 2^2 + 3^2 = 1 + 4 + 9 = 14$. Enter Minitab (you may need to login or switch on first) and try the following:

```
set c1
1 2 3
end
ssq c1
```

name specifies names for columns. Try the following:

```
name c1 'x'
desc c1
desc 'x'
```

If you have trouble getting this to work you are probably using the wrong quote character ('). It should be the same each side of x and, on most keyboards, it is the key next to <⏎return>.

```
let c2=c1*c1
let c3='x'*'x'*'x'
name c2 'square' c3 'cube'
desc 'cube'
desc c1-c3
desc c1 c2 c3
```

Notice that the last two commands were equivalent. '-' has two meanings in Minitab. In commands like let 'c1-c5' means subtract c5 from c1. In commands like desc it means c1, c2, c3, c4 and c5.

The name and the column number can be used interchangeably in commands. The results always give the name. Try

```
desc 'cube'
desc c3
```

info lists all the columns currently being used in your work sheet, how many numbers there are in each and any name you have assigned to that column. Try

```
info
```

Regress

Regress is a powerful Minitab command that can be used for many purposes. In this chapter we shall use it to compute a regression equation. In Chapters 8 and 9 we shall use it for multiple regression. Because it has these different uses the display it produces and the way you specify what is to be computed is somewhat complex. Say we want to predict the time it takes to complete some skilled task (in minutes) from the number of years experience of doing the job. The following commands read in this data and then compute the regression:

```
name c1 'Mins' c2 'Years'
read c1 c2
4.1    2.1
2.2    1.5
2.7    1.7
6      2.5
8.5    3
4.1    2.1
9      3.2
8      2.8
7.5    2.5
end
regress 'Mins' 1 'Years'
```

Before going on to look at the results this produces consider the form of the regress command. The first column specified is the variable to be predicted (Y, here 'mins'). Next the number of variables used in the prediction is given. In this chapter this will always be 1 (multiple regression considers the case of predicting one variable using several other variables). Finally the predictor is specified (X, here 'Years').

The regress command produces a bewilderingly large number of results. The important information is given in bold in Box 4.3 (it will not be in bold on your screen). This is the regression equation (intercept −4.67, slope 4.40) and R-sq (95.7%). R-sq is r^2 times 100, i.e. $r^2 = .957$ (one can only guess why it is written like this!).

Ignore R-sq(adj) and s. Similarly Stdev is not the standard deviation of anything useful to you. The table headed 'Analysis of variance' contains the deviances we considered when thinking about the theory behind correlation and which need not concern us until Chapter 8. Minitab refers to what we have called deviations as 'residuals'. Large residuals/deviations are reported after the analysis of variance table.

Box 4.3   Output from the regress command—emphasis (bold face) added

```
MTB > regress 'Mins' 1 'Years'

The regression equation is
Mins = - 4.67 + 4.40 Years

Predictor          Coef        Stdev       t-ratio          p
Constant        -4.6674       0.8572         -5.44      0.000
Years            4.3975       0.3514         12.51      0.000

s = 0.5727      R-sq = 95.7%      R-sq(adj) = 95.1%

Analysis of Variance

SOURCE               DF          SS        MS          F          p
Regression            1      51.353    51.353    156.56      0.000
Error                 7       2.296     0.328
Total                 8      53.649

Unusual Observations
Obs.    Years         Mins            Fit Stdev.Fit   Residual
St.Resid
   9     2.50        7.500          6.326      0.196      1.174
2.18R

R denotes an obs. with a large st. resid.

MTB >
```

Testing

Save the minutes and years data and make a new work space with the Scale A and exam scores from Table 4.1. Use the regress command to compute the best fitting regression line for predicting exam score from Scale A. Write it down and check it is the same as given in the Introduction. (You can either use the steps taken to analyse the Minutes/Years data as a model or follow the step by step procedure described in Chapter 5, Box 5.7, ignoring the last step).

Computing r^2 the hard way

In this section we will rehearse the procedure described in the Introduction for computing r^2 from deviances. First the regression equation is used to compute the fourth column in Table 4.1. and then the deviance. (You may have used different columns, if so adjust the name command accordingly.)

```
name c1 'ScaleA' c2 'Exam' c3 'PExam' c4 'Dev'
let 'PExam' = 55.4 + 1.55*'ScaleA'
let 'Dev' = 'Exam' - 'PExam'
print 'ScaleA' 'Exam' 'PExam' 'Dev'
ssq 'Dev'
```

ssq should give the deviance quoted in Table 4.1 (353.59).

Now we need to find the deviance of the mean:

```
name c5 'DMean'
mean 'Exam'
let 'DMean' = 'Exam' - 71.25
ssq 'DMean'
```

ssq gives the deviance of the mean as computed in Table 4.2 (834.25). Now use a calculator to compute

$$\frac{834.25 - 353.59}{834.25}$$

See if the answer you get agrees with that given by the regress command. Save these data.

Correlation command

Very often we are only interested in the correlation coefficient (r) and not the regression equation. The correlation command (corr for short) is very much simpler than the regress command. (Remember that the sign given to r denotes whether the relationship is negative or positive.) Retrieve the data used to introduce the regress command which indicate the minutes taken to perform a task as a function of the number of years experience of doing the job. Then try

```
corr 'Mins' 'Years'
```

corr can be given a list of columns and it will calculate the correlation between every pair of variables. The resulting table is called a correlation matrix. Try

```
read c3-c5
1 2 6
2 3 5
1 3 7
2 4 5
end
corr c3-c5
```

The correlation between c3 and c5 is −.905.

Testing

What is the correlation between c5 and c4?

Retrieve the exam and Scale A scores. Use a calculator to square root the r^2 computed above (.58). Now use the corr command to check your answer.

DCL

DCL commands introduced in this chapter: File names, * and % in filenames.

Looking at files outside of your area

The full file name of each of your files includes the name of your area. You will remember that this is printed when you use the dir command. The full name of one of my files is 'disk$psyc:[am1]deviations.mtw'. DCL commands assume the prefix 'disk$psyc:[am1]' if I don't specify some other.

The files in your area are 'protected' so that no-one else can look at them or change them. There are some files on the disk that anyone can have access to. You will sometimes want to use these files. To do this simply specify the full file name in the command.

Testing

Your system administrator will give you the name of a file in another directory containing the message 'You have found this remote and uninteresting file'. Write down the full name of the file in the space below

Full name of file ....

Use the type command to get this message onto your screen.

Wild cards in file specifications

Your directory may be beginning to get cluttered with files by now. It is a good idea to tidy it up after each major session with the computer, while you can still remember what all the files are.

So-called wild cards can be used to save typing when performing these 'housekeeping operations'. The wild cards '*' and '%' can be used in DCL commands to indicate that parts of a file name can be filled in by the system. For example:

    del ch2*.lis;*

will delete all versions of files in your area beginning with 'ch2' and ending '.lis'. If any of the following files were to be found in your area they would be deleted:

    ch2.lis;1 ch2ass1.lis;1 ch2ass1.lis;2 ch2a.lis;3

'%' is similar, but whereas '*' refers to any number of letters (including none) '%' refers to exactly one letter. Of the above files 'del ch2%.lis;*' will only delete:

　　ch2a.lis;3

Deleting files should of course be done with care. It is good practice to try the file specification you are going to type with del with dir first, e.g.

　　dir t*.r%%;*

before you type del t*.r%%;*

Testing

Use dir to list only those files that begin with 'd'. Use dir to list only those files which have the extension 'mtw'. Now delete all the files you no longer need. Leave any with the extension .MAI or .COM. The former are mail files. How to tidy up your mail files is described in Chapter 5.

MSDOS

MSDOS commands covered in this chapter: File names, * in file names.

Looking at files in another directory

The full file name of each of your files includes the current directory as specified in the MSDOS prompt. My MSDOS prompt is 'A:\user>' The full name of one of my files in this directory is 'A:\user\deviations.mtw'. MSDOS commands assume the prefix 'A:\user\' if I don't specify some other.

You will sometimes want to access files on other directories. To do this simply specify the full file name in the command.

Testing

Your system administrator will give you the name of a file in another directory containing the message 'You have found this remote and uninteresting file'. Write down the full name of the file in the space below

Full name of file ....
Use the type command to get this message onto your screen.

Wild cards in file specifications

Your directory may be beginning to get cluttered with files by now. It is a good idea to tidy it up after each major session with the computer, while you can still remember what all the files are.

So called wild cards can be used to save typing when performing these 'housekeeping operations'. The wild card '*' can be used in MSDOS commands to indicate that parts of a file name can be filled in by the system. For example:

del ch2*.lis

will delete all files in your area beginning with 'ch2' and ending '.lis'. If any of the following files were to be found in your area they would be deleted:

ch2.lis ch2ass1.lis ch2a.lis

Deleting files should of course be done with care. It is good practice to try the file specification you are going to type with del with dir first, e.g.

dir t*.r*

before you type del t*.r*

Testing

Use dir to list only those files that begin with 'd'. Use dir to list only those files which have the extension 'mtw'. Now delete all the files you no longer need. Leave any with an extension you do not recognise (see Chapter 3 for a discussion of file extensions that indicate files that should not be deleted).

ASSIGNMENT

1. Retrieve the data from the assignment for Chapter 3, Question 3.

(a) What is the regression equation for predicting minutes-spent-talking from extraversion?

(b) What is r?

(c) What proportion of the variance in minutes-spent-talking can be explained by the variance in extraversion scores?

2. Appendix B, Table B.1, contains some real data collected by a student at York. Children were asked to repeat back 40 non-words such as 'bomat'. A score out of 40 was recorded, depending on how many non-words they repeated back accurately. Previous research predicts that their ability to do this should correlate with their ability to learn new words and so the size of their vocabulary. This is because both abilities depend on being able to perceive and remember briefly new combinations of sound.

The childrens' vocabulary is measured with the British Picture Vocabulary Scale (BPVS). This requires the child to name objects depicted with pictures. In addition there are two measures of general intellectual ability: The British Ability Scale (BAS) and a raw score from Raven's Matrices non-verbal intelligence test (ignore the column 'Age Group').

These data may have already been saved in a file. Ask your system administrator for the full name of this file and write it down in the space below and in the appendix

Name of file containing data in Appendix B, Table B.1 ....

Draw up a table with the mean and standard deviation for each of these four scores (i.e., ignoring the column 'Age Group'). Report the correlations between the scores as a correlation matrix. Describe these correlations (e.g. are they positive or negative, how do they compare in size, is the prediction supported?)

3. Appendix B, Table B.3, contains the scores for a 20-item test of arithmetical ability. Each item is an arithmetic problem scored out of five. These data may have been saved on a file also. Ask your system administrator for the name of the file and write it down in the space below and in the appendix

Name of file containing data in Appendix B, Table B.3 ....

Use the let command to compute a new column containing the total score on the test obtained by each of the 48 subjects.

(a) What are the mean and the standard deviations of these scores?

(b) Compute a new column with the total for the even items only and another for the odd items only. What is the correlation between these two scores.

(c) What is the split-half reliability of this test? (Use the Spearman–Brown formula.)

4. Consider the data from the work sheet relating the time in minutes taken to perform some skilled task with years experience.

(a) Draw a scattergram of these data (by hand). Draw the regression line (obtained from Minitab) for predicting minutes from years onto this graph.

(b) Use the let and regression commands in Minitab to complete the following table.

Subject	Minutes (observed)	Predicted minutes (linear prediction from years)	Deviation
1	4.1	4.567	−.467
2	2.2	...	...
3	...	...	...
4	...	...	...
5	...	...	...
6	...	...	...
7	...	...	...
8	...	...	...
9	...	...	...

(c) Which subject shows the biggest negative deviation?

(d) Which subject shows the biggest positive deviation?

5. Retrieve the Scale A and exam scores for the 12 subjects in Table 4.1. You will remember that the regression equation is the linear formula which gives the smallest deviance. In what follows you will show by experimentation that using formulae other than the regression equation gives a larger deviance. In the section 'Computing r^2 the hard way' in the work sheets we used the let and ssq commands to compute the deviance for the regression equation

predicted_exam_score = 55.4 + 1.55 Scale_A_score

The answer was 353.59. Now compute the deviance for the equations:

(a) predicted_exam_score = 50 + 1.55 Scale_A_score

(b) predicted_exam_score = 60 + 1.55 Scale_A_score

(c) predicted_exam_score = 55.4 + 1.00 Scale_A_score

(d) predicted_exam_score = 55.4 + 2.00 Scale_A_score

In all cases the deviance is greater than 353.59 showing that increasing or decreasing the intercept, and increasing or decreasing the slope, results in a worse fit (higher deviance).

Similarly the mean observed score gives the least deviance of all the models which predict exam score as a single constant.

predicted_exam_score = 71.25

has a deviance of 834.25. Now compute the deviance for the equations:

(e) predicted_exam_score = 70

(f) predicted_exam_score = 74

SUMMARY OF DCL COMMANDS LEARNED SO FAR

Logging in

1. Refer to the form 'Arrangements for using the computer', at the end of Chapter 1, in which you have summarised the procedure for switching on and connecting your terminal.

2. Press <↵return>.

3. Enter your user name when prompted for it.

4. Enter your password.

You are successfully logged in when you get the '$' prompt.

DCL commands

logout (lo)	**rename (ren)**
whois	**copy**
help	**type**
directory (dir)	**print**
mail	**delete (del)**

Mail commands

    <↵return> (show next message)

    send

    help

    exit

Wild cards for use in file specifications

* (any, or no letters here) % (any one letter here)

Start Minitab session

    minitab

SUMMARY OF MSDOS COMMANDS LEARNED SO FAR

Switching on and off

Refer to the page headed 'Arrangements for using the computer', at the end of Chapter 1, in which you have summarised the procedure for switching on and booting up your computer and for ending a session at the computer.

MSDOS commands

date

ren   (the first file name given is the 'from' file,
                      the second the 'to' file)

copy   (again 'from' 'to')

dir   **type**

del   **print**

Wild card for use in file specification

* (any, or no letters here)

Start Minitab session

minitab

SUMMARY OF MINITAB COMMANDS LEARNED SO FAR

set   (indicate you have come to the end of the data with end)

read (ditto)   **erase**

name   **save** 'name'

info   **retrieve (retr)** 'name'

print   **outfile** 'name'

let   **nooutfile**

describe (desc)

mean   **regress (regr)**

stdev   (e.g. **regr c1 1 c2**)

sum   **correlation (corr)**

ssq

table

histogram (hist)

stem-and-leaf

boxplots

plot

help commands

stop

CHAPTER 5

INFERENCE WITH STATISTICS

Statistical concepts introduced in this chapter: The null hypothesis, p value, significance level, sign test, significance of a correlation.

INTRODUCTION

The problem

Chapter 1 showed how an initial question is refined into an experiment. This is the business of science. The question considered in Chapter 1 may not be of great scientific importance but it serves to illustrate this process. The general question was 'Do people prefer butter to margarine?' There are various ways that this general question could be translated into an experiment and two are described below. In Chapter 1 and Experiment 1 below, the more specific experimental question asked was 'Do people who taste butter give higher or lower preference ratings compared with people who taste margarine?'

Chapters 2, 3 and 4 described how the results of experiments can be summarised. In this case the summary statistic used would be the mean. The mean preference rating for a group tasting butter is compared with the mean preference rating for a group tasting margarine. The results of other experiments might be summarised using a contingency table or a correlation.

A result from an experiment can be thought of as providing evidence for or against some hypothesis. Say that the butter group gives a higher mean rating than the margarine group. This supports the hypothesis that 'butter gives higher preference ratings'. Let us assume that the experiment was a fair test of this hypothesis. There is still a potential problem when interpreting the result. It may not be reliable, e.g. there might not be any real difference in preference rating, and just by chance the result has come out this way. If this were the case and we were to repeat the experiment with some new subjects at some time in the future we might draw the opposite conclusion.

Scientists need to be sure that if they repeat an experiment they will come to the same conclusion. Three imaginary experiments are described below. In each case two research teams, A and B, both carried out the experiment and came to differing conclusions. Examine these conclusions and the data they are derived from. Which research team do you feel is producing the most trustworthy results, i.e. which research team's results are most likely to be repeatable?

Experiment 1—Preferences for butter and margarine when the taster samples only one fat

Tasters are given one sample of fat and asked to make a preference rating on the scale 'very nasty' to 'very nice' as described in Chapter 1.

Box 5.1   Results for Experiment 1

Team A results

15 subjects were given butter—their ratings were:

34 38 60 44 47 31 58 53 37 37 46 43 54 35 44

Mean 44.07, Standard deviation 8.99.

15 subjects were given margarine—their ratings were:

32 31 19 38 34 41 40 27 28 19 51 27 30 34 29

Mean 32.0, Standard deviation 8.32.

Conclusion: People rate butter more highly.

Team B results

10 subjects were given butter—their ratings were:

36 5 48 46 44 42 59 44 44 29

Mean 39.70, Standard deviation 14.43.

10 subjects were given margarine—their ratings were:

58 62 55 39 63 38 70 43 3 45

Mean 47.6, Standard deviation 19.13.

Conclusion: People rate margarine more highly.

Experiment 2—Preference for margarine or butter in a forced choice discrimination

Tasters are given two samples of fat. They know that one sample is margarine and the other is butter but not in which order they are presented. Half the subjects have the order butter–margarine, the other half margarine–butter. They are required to state which sample they prefer, the first or the second, after tasting both samples.

Box 5.2   Results for Experiment 2

Team A results

16 subjects were tested, 14 chose the sample which was butter.

Conclusion: People prefer butter.

Team B results

10 subjects were tested, 7 chose the sample which was margarine.

Conclusion: People prefer margarine.

Experiment 3—The relationship between extraversion and the use of extreme categories in a rating scale

People vary in their willingness to use the extremities of a rating scale such as 'very nice' or 'very nasty'. Some tend only to use more central ratings. The question is whether this can be predicted from personality tests. Subjects are given a sample of butter and asked to rate its taste on a 100 mm scale 'very nasty' to 'very nice' as in Experiment 1. Their willingness to use the ends of the scale is established by measuring the distance of the mark they make from the centre of the line. Before they do this they fill in a personality questionnaire which gives an extraversion score. Previous work has established that overall preference for butter cannot be predicted from extraversion.

Box 5.3   Results of Experiment 3

Team A results

Figure 5.1(a) is a scattergram plotting extraversion against distance from the centre. There is a positive relationship evidenced by a correlation coefficient of .87

Conclusion: The more extraverted subjects are more likely to use the extremities of the scale.

Team B results

Figure 5.1(b) is a scattergram plotting extraversion against distance from the centre. There is a negative relationship evidenced by a correlation coefficient −.33

Conclusion: The more extraverted subjects are less likely to use the extremities of the scale.

Team A's results versus Team B's

In all three experiments Team A's results seem more trustworthy. Were the experiments to be repeated one would expect to come to the same conclusions.

Team B's results seem to contain much more random fluctuation than Team A's. Perhaps they did not take the trouble to put the subjects at ease, perhaps they did not give clear instructions or sufficient practice. Whatever the cause, their conclusions appear to be unreliable given the data presented.

For example, in Experiment 1 the difference in means obtained by Team B is small

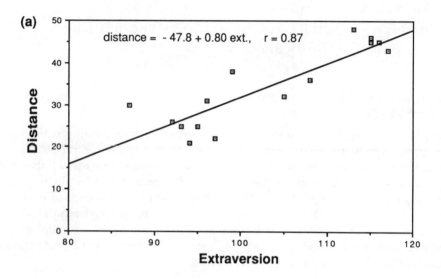

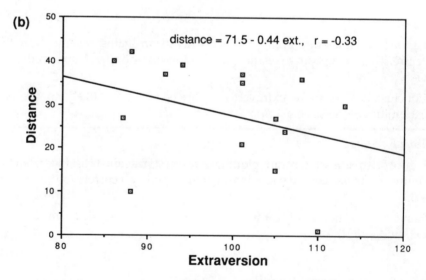

Figure 5.1 Scattergrams depicting the relationships between extraversion score and the distance of the rating made from the centre of the scale: (a) results from Team A, (b) results from Team B

compared with the random variation within groups. It is quite likely that the difference observed in the mean scores could have arisen from these random fluctuations. In contrast, the means obtained by Team A differ more than one would expect from the within-group variation. In Experiment 2, Team B found more subjects prefer the sample which is margarine but only 7 out of 10. If they had been responding at random one might have got 7 out of 10 responses in one direction rather than the other. Team A, on the other hand, found 14 out of 16 preferred butter. This is very unlikely to have happened if they were responding at random. Finally, in Experiment 3 the scatter in Team B's results is considerable and the correlation is only –.33 (11% of the variance). It would not be surprising if the regression line sloped in the opposite direction when the experiment is repeated. Figure 5.1(a) shows very much less scatter. The correlation might not be exactly .87 if the experiment were to be repeated but it would be surprising if it forced a change in conclusion because it sloped in the opposite direction.

It is possible to check whether a result is repeatable by doing the experiment again. Scientists do repeat experiments, indeed important results need to repeated, if possible by different investigators. This is known as replicating an experiment. However, we also need a way of estimating how trustworthy an individual result is without actually having to repeat it. This is the purpose of statistical inference.

Statistical inference

A chance result is inherently unreliable, since on one occasion we may draw one conclusion and on another the opposite. The purpose of tests based on statistical inference is to reject this possibility. This is done by computing the probability of getting a result as extreme as the one obtained, by chance. If that probability is very small the possibility that the result was due to chance is rejected. Technically we say that the result is *significant*.

The logic of statistical inference is as follows:

(a) We have a result to evaluate. We wish to draw some conclusion from this result (e.g., X is greater than Y).

(b) We want to know if we would come to the same conclusion were we to repeat the experiment, i.e. is it a reliable result?

(c) If the result arose by chance then it is by definition unreliable (e.g., it could turn out X greater than Y or Y greater than X).

(d) If we can somehow reject the possibility the result arose by chance then it probably is a reliable result.

As explained above, statistical tests apply this logic by computing a probability. This is the probability that the result arose by chance. If this is small we say the result is 'statistically significant' and reject the possibility that the result occurred by chance. To do this we have to define precisely what is meant by chance and, as with the computation of any *a priori* probability, make certain assumptions. The different statistical tests you will learn in this book all follow this logic. They differ in the way 'chance' is defined and the assumptions made to compute the probability. The definition of chance used by the test is known as the *null hypothesis*.

This process can be illustrated by considering Experiment 2.

1. The experimental hypothesis is that people can discriminate butter from margarine and that the probability of choosing butter is not the same as the probability of choosing margarine.

2. The null hypothesis is that each individual is equally likely to choose each of the fats, i.e. the probability of choosing butter is .5 and the probability of choosing margarine is .5.

3. One further assumption is necessary to compute a probability using this null hypothesis. This is that the choices made are independent of one another, i.e. one subject's choice had no effect on any other subject's choice.

4. The probability of getting a result as extreme as 14 out of 16 subjects choosing butter purely by chance is .0042. This is known as the p value and is usually written 'p = .0042'

5. .0042 is a very small probability. An event with probability .0042 will only occur 42 times in every 10,000, i.e. 4.2 times in every 1000 or 0.42%. We would expect to have to repeat this experiment on average about 240 times before getting a result as extreme as this by chance. This could be that occasion but that is most unlikely. It would seem quite safe to reject the null hypothesis and conclude there is a real effect. People do prefer butter.

Now consider Team B's results. The probability of getting a result as extreme as 7 out of 10 is .3438 (p = .3438). This is not a small probability. An event with probability .3438 will occur 34% of the time. If we performed the experiment 10 times we would expect about three of those experiments to produce results as extreme as this. It would seem unwise to reject the null hypothesis in this case. The result could well have occurred by chance. If so, were the experiment to be repeated, the conclusion drawn might be quite different.

Significance levels

The null hypothesis can be rejected when the probability of getting a result, assuming the null hypothesis is true, is very small. But how small does the probability have to be? The answer is set by convention as something smaller than .05. When the null hypothesis can be rejected the result is said to be significant and the maximum probability which is acceptable is said to be the significance level. Experience has shown that .05 (1 in 20) is small enough to prevent us from building theories on chance results but not so strict that experiments become extremely expensive to run because very large quantities of data have to be collected in order to rule out the possibility of a chance result.

Some authors refer to the .05 level of significance as the '5% level of significance'.

This is simply a matter of style. It is more common to refer to a significance level as a probability than a percentage and this is the convention which will be followed in this book.

Box 5.4 summarises the last two sections.

Box 5.4   The steps taken when a statistical test is applied to some data

There is a result to be evaluated (in our example, 14 out of 16 choose butter). We wish to distinguish between a chance result and a real result. A chance result is by definition unreliable.

(a) Precisely what is meant by 'chance' must be formulated. This is the null hypothesis. (In our example this is that the probability of one individual choosing butter is .5.)

(b) A p value, the probability of getting the result being evaluated, or something even more extreme, is computed under the assumption that the null hypothesis is true. This involves making certain further assumptions about the data. (In our example this is that choices are independent.)

(c) If p is very small, i.e. less than the significance level of .05, the null hypothesis is rejected and the result is said to be significant. It is very unlikely that this result, or something better, could have arisen by chance so it probably is a real result. (In our example p = .0042 so the result is significant at the .05 level).

The binomial test (sign test)

The computation used to illustrate statistical inference above is known as a binomial test, or sometimes the sign test. This statistical test was considered first because the null hypothesis used is easy to understand. This is that each individual had an equal probability of preferring butter and margarine. The computation uses something called the binomial expansion and the probabilities generated are said to form a binomial distribution. There is no need to understand the precise nature of the computation. Minitab does most of the work of computing a p value for you. Box 5.8 in the Minitab work sheet for this chapter details the procedure to be followed.

This statistical test is also known as the sign test because it can be used in situations where one counts the number of subjects whose results show differences in some predicted direction. For example, in Experiment 2 one might have had subjects rate each of the fats by making a mark on the preference scale used in Experiment 1. The prediction is that butter will receive a higher rating. For each subject, it is possible to subtract the rating made for margarine from the rating made for butter. This gives a difference score the sign of which indicates whether the prediction is supported. A positive difference supports the prediction, a negative difference goes against it. Counting the number of positive signs indicates how many subjects prefer butter to margarine.

In Experiment 2, as originally described, there was no difference score to compute and so no signs to count, but the principle is the same in that the subjects supporting a hypothesis are counted. There are better tests for use with difference scores (see Chapter 7) and so the binomial test is rarely used by counting positive or negative signs. It is nearly always used with data like those in Experiment 2 where the subject makes some response which is classified as being for or against the hypothesis.

Technical note—What 'a result as extreme as' means in this context

The probability to be computed is the probability of getting 'a result as extreme as 14 out of 16 choosing butter', not the probability of precisely '14 out of 16 choosing butter'. The probability of precisely 14 out of 16 subjects choosing butter, under the null hypothesis, is .0018 (this is computed using something called the binomial expansion). The p value computed in a binomial test is .0042. This discrepancy arises because when we say that a result of 14 out of 16 is significant we are really setting a criterion. Clearly if 14 out of 16 is acceptable then so is 15 or 16 out of 16. So if the criterion for significance is 14 out of 16 the probability of getting 14, 15 or 16 out of 16 must be less than .05. The probability of getting 14, 15 or 16 out of 16 is .0021.

Now imagine that the result was actually 2 out of 16 choosing butter (14 out of 16 choosing margarine). Even though the experimental hypothesis was that butter is most likely to be chosen we would not discard such a result. This means that 0, 1 or 2 out of 16 choosing butter must also be included in our class of 'interesting' results. Thus the probability we want is the probability of getting 0, 1, 2, 14, 15, or 16 out of 16. This probability, the p value, is .0042.

The t-test and other tests for comparing means

Statistical tests for evaluating the significance of differences between means are discussed more fully in Chapters 6 and 7 but the results of Experiment 1 will be considered briefly here for completeness. The mean preference rating for butter could be compared with the mean preference rating for margarine by using one of these tests. Here a real result is a true difference in the mean rating response. The null hypothesis is that there is really no difference but that the apparent difference arose from the random fluctuations observable in the variance within the two groups. The t-test, to be introduced in Chapter 6, is one way of computing probabilities under this null hypothesis. Having done so the procedure is the same as for the sign test. If the p value is less than or equal to .05 the result is said to be significant. If it is not we cannot reject the null hypothesis.

A t-test performed on the results of Experiment 1, for Team A, shows that the probability of getting a difference as big or bigger than 12.07 (44.07 – 32.0), given the fluctuations apparent within the two groups, is .0007 (p = .0007). This is smaller than .05, the result is significant at the .05 level. We can be confident that if Team A were to repeat the experiment they would come to the same conclusion.

The same cannot be said of Team B's results. A t-test shows that a difference of 7.9 (47.6 – 39.7) or more, given the larger variation within groups for Team B, has a probability of .31 of occurring (p = .31). This is not significant at the .05 level. The difference between these two means may well be a chance difference. If Team B were to do the experiment again they might well come to the opposite conclusion.

The significance of r

With a correlation the conclusion to be drawn concerns the direction of the relationship. Is X positively related to Y so that X increases when Y increases, or are they negatively related so that as one increases the other decreases?

A real result in Experiment 3 is a true trend, either a positive trend such that the higher a subject's extraversion score is the more extreme the ratings they make, or a negative trend such that the lower a subject's extraversion score the more extreme the ratings. The null hypothesis is that the true regression line has no slope and so the 'real' correlation is zero but, because of random scatter (i.e., chance fluctuations), the observed regression has some slope. The Minitab regress command computes the probability under this null hypothesis.

Team A obtained a correlation, r = .87. The conclusion to be drawn is that there is a positive trend. The probability that a correlation as strong as this or stronger could occur by chance is .0001 (p = .0001). This is less than .05 so the correlation is significant. If Team A were to repeat Experiment 3 they might not get a correlation of exactly .87 but they are likely to come to the same conclusion.

Team B's correlation is much weaker, r = −.33. The probability that a trend as strong as this or stronger could occur by chance is .227 (p = .227). This is not significant at the .05 level and may well be a chance result. If Team B were to repeat the result they might well come to the opposite conclusion.

Critical values of r—Table A.1

Minitab computes a p value for a correlation as part of the regress command (see Box 5.7 in the work sheets for a step by step procedure to follow). An alternative way of assessing the significance of a correlation is to use Table A.1. This has been constructed by working out the minimum correlation that would be significant for a sample of a particular size. The larger the number of subjects in the sample (N) the smaller the correlation coefficient can be and still be significant. These values are known as critical values of r. If the r you have just computed is greater than the critical value (ignoring the sign of the correlation) then it is significant at the .05 level.

Both teams tested 15 subjects (N = 15). The critical value from Table A.1 is thus .514. .87 is larger than .514 so the correlation obtained by Team A is significant at the .05 level. We ignore the sign of the correlation when using Table A.1 and .33 is smaller than .514 so the correlation obtained by Team B is not significant at the .05 level.

Table A.1 may be particularly useful when determining which correlations are significant in a correlation matrix generated by the corr command in Minitab. N will be the same for all the correlations and so it is only necessary to look up the critical value of r for that N and then see which correlations are larger than or equal to that value. A step by step procedure to compute a correlation matrix and then evaluate it using Table A.1 is specified in Box 5.6 in the work sheets.

Note that quite small correlations can be significant if there are large numbers of subjects. For example, Table A.1 shows that a correlation of .2 is significant for a sample of 102 subjects. Such a correlation only accounts for 4% of the variance (r^2 = .04). Significance indicates that the sign of the slope of the regression is likely to be the same if the experiment is repeated. It does not necessarily say anything about the amount of variance that regression accounts for. So to indicate the strength of a correlation quote r^2. In general, the significance of any effect should not be taken as an indication of its strength.

Advanced note—How Minitab computes the p value for a particular r^2

Chapter 4 introduced the correlation coefficient through the concept of the deviance of a regression equation. r^2 was defined as

$$\frac{\text{deviance of the mean} - \text{deviance of the regression equation}}{\text{deviance of the mean}}$$

The deviance of the mean was viewed as a baseline against which the regression equation was evaluated. The example used was the correlation between exam scores and a measure of arithmetical ability, Scale A. The deviance of the regression equation for predicting exam scores from Scale A was 353.59 and the

Box 5.5 Regression of exam score on Scale A score from Chapter 4—emphasis (bold face) added

```
MTB > regr 'exam' 1 'ScaleA'

The regression equation is

exam = 55.4 + 1.55 ScaleA

Predictor        Coef        Stdev       t-ratio          p
Constant       55.370        4.636         11.94      0.000
scalea         1.5493        0.4202          3.69      0.004

s = 5.946        R-sq = 57.6%       R-sq(adj) = 53.4%

Analysis of Variance

SOURCE            DF          SS          MS          F          p
Regression         1      480.67      480.67      13.59      0.004
Error             10      353.58       35.36
Total             11      834.25

MTB >
```

deviance of the mean was 834.25, so adding Scale A to the equation reduces the deviance by 480.66.

When Minitab computes the p value for a correlation coefficient as part of the regress command it does so by computing an F ratio from these deviances. The deviances computed 'by hand' in Chapter 4 can be found in the display generated by the regress command. Box 5.5 contains the display generated by Minitab for these data. The deviances can be found in the table headed 'Analysis of variance'. They are printed in bold in Box 5.5. This table also included the F ratio and the p value computed from the F ratio. The F ratio evaluates the significance of the reduction in deviance. The null hypothesis is that there really is no correlation and the reduction in deviance is due to chance. p = .004 and so the F ratio is significant at the .05 level.

Precisely how the F ratio is constructed, and some more about the rationale behind its construction, will be considered in Chapter 8 in the sections headed 'Degrees of freedom' and 'The F ratio'.

One- and two-tailed tests

Some statistics books give procedures for performing one- and two-tailed tests. In this book we consider only two-tailed tests. The distinction has to do with the form the experimental hypothesis takes. A one-tailed hypothesis is strongly 'directional'. In Experiment 2 for example, we might have predicted that butter would be preferred to margarine. If the prediction was so strong that a result in the opposing direction would simply not be considered then we have a one-tailed hypothesis. Thus, under a one-tailed hypothesis, finding that more people prefer margarine is equivalent to finding that exactly half prefer margarine. There is no point in further analysing either result.

In Psychology hypotheses are very rarely so strongly directional. We might *expect* butter to be preferred, but if it turns out the other way around we are unlikely to discard the result. A one-tailed binomial test for Team A, Experiment 2, would be to compute the probability of getting 14, 15 or 16 out of 16. The two-tailed test, used here, computed the probability of getting 0, 1, 2, 14, 15 or 16 out of 16. For binomial and t-tests the p value for a one-tailed hypothesis is half that for the two-tailed test.

How to report a correlation

When writing up the results of statistical tests in a paper or some other form of report it is important to give the right amount of detail. The reader of the report will not want to be swamped with unnecessary information such as part calculations or the explanation of statistical concepts such as significance. On the other hand sufficient detail is required to show that the appropriate test has been performed. A statistical test is used to evaluate a result so the first step should be to report that result. Here the result to be evaluated is a correlation and the first thing to be reported is that correlation and the conclusion it suggests. Having done this the significance of the correlation is reported.

When interpreting a correlation it is often useful to know the mean and standard deviation of each of the scores. This allows one to judge whether the range of scores obtained is typical of the population concerned. One might also plot a scattergram to illustrate the relationship graphically. The correlation coefficient r indicates the strength of the linear relationship between the variables. A strong non-linear relationship would show up in a scattergram but not as a high r.

Team A's results for Experiment 3 might be written up as follows.

Results:-

There is a positive correlation (r = .87) between extraversion score and the extremity of the rating made (distance from the central point of the rating scale). This strong positive relationship is in line with the predictions made. The correlation is significant at the .05 level.

Table 5.1 gives the mean and standard deviation for each of the scores. Figure 5.1(a) is a scattergram using these data. There is no evidence of any additional non-linear relationship.

Table 5.1   Means and standard deviations, Experiment 3, Team A

	Mean	Std.Dev.
Extraversion score	102.8	10.4
Extremity of rating	34.2	9.5

How to report a binomial test

Similar principles apply to the reporting of the results of a binomial test. Here it is sufficient to report the number of individuals who support the hypothesis and the total number of individuals considered. Since binomial tests are often (incorrectly) reported as one-tailed probabilities it is worth saying that you have used a two-tailed test.

Team A's results for Experiment 2 might be written up as follows.

Results:-

Sixteen subjects were tested of whom 14 chose the sample which was butter. A two-tailed binomial test shows this to be significant at the .05 level (p = .0042).

Summary

1. Inferential statistics is the name given to a set of procedures for assessing whether a result is likely to be repeatable, i.e. whether one will come to the same conclusion if the experiment is performed again.

2. All these procedures work as follows:

(a) A chance result is inherently unreliable. If we can reject the possibility that a result is due to chance then it is probably a repeatable result.

(b) 'Chance' is defined as a null hypothesis, a 'no effect' hypothesis which can be stated with sufficient precision to make possible the calculation of probabilities.

(c) The probability of getting our particular result, or one which is more extreme, under the null hypothesis is computed. This is the p value.

(d) If that probability is less than or equal to the significance level the null hypothesis is rejected and the result is said to be significant.

(e) The most common significance level, and the one used consistently through this book, is .05. If the probability of getting the result, under the null hypothesis, is less than or equal to .05 it is probably repeatable.

(f) If it is greater than the significance level it is not possible to reject the null hypothesis.

3. The binomial test works as follows (See Box 5.8 for the detailed procedure to use):

(a) Each subject is classified as supporting the hypothesis (+) or not supporting it (−). The number of + subjects is counted, let us say that it is M out of N.

(b) The null hypothesis is that the probability of an individual subject being + is equal to the probability they are − (.5).

(c) Minitab uses the binomial expansion to compute a p value. The underlying assumption is that each subject's result (+ or −) is independent of the result of every other subject.

(d) If that probability is less than .05 the result is said to be significant at the .05 level.

(e) If it is greater than .05 we cannot reject the null hypothesis.

4. The Minitab command regress computes the p value of r by first computing an F ratio (see Box 5.7 in the work sheets for the procedure to follow).

5. As an alternative, a critical value of r can be looked up in Table A.1 in the appendix. If the correlation to be evaluated is larger than this critical value then it is significant at the .05 level (see Box 5.6 for detailed procedure).

Tests for comparing means are discussed in more detail in Chapters 6 and 7.

WORK SHEETS

MINITAB

Minitab commands introduced in this chapter: cdf (cumulative distribution function for computing p values).

Using Table A.1 with the corr command

The corr command was described in the Minitab work sheet for Chapter 4 where it is was used to generate a correlation matrix. Box 5.6 describes a general procedure to produce a correlation matrix and assess the significance of each correlation using Table A.1. Work through the Minitab commands in the example given in the box to illustrate the procedure. Save the data when you have finished.

Note Box 5.6 is the first of the ten step by step procedures listed on Page xv immediately after the Preface. Each procedure is delimited by a *square cornered box without a border*. Even when you are very familiar with the Minitab procedure for applying some statistical technique, it is a good idea to follow the procedure as outlined in one of these boxes. Use your knowledge of the technique as an additional check that you have not made any mistakes.

Box 5.6   Step by step procedure to compute a correlation matrix and assess the significance of these correlations using Table A.1

Step 1—Tabulate the data with one row for each subject and one column for each score obtained (you will probably have already done this).

e.g. Fifteen subjects are assessed using three tests

	Test 1	Test 2	Test 3
S1	118	194	122
S2	70	152	116
S3	91	185	121
S4	113	243	129
S5	124	369	196
S6	137	321	138
S7	104	285	163
S8	132	314	156
S9	147	167	37
S10	141	311	178
S11	66	250	179
S12	130	249	147
S13	134	258	131
S14	144	311	152
S15	23	168	87

Step 2—Enter the data into Minitab using the read command
   e.g.

```
name c1 'Test 1' c2 'Test 2' c3 'Test 3'
read 'Test 1' 'Test 2' 'Test 3'
118  194  122
70  152  116
  .
  .
  .
23  168  87
end
```

Step 3—Check the data with the print command and correct any mistakes using let (see Chapter 2)
e.g.

print 'Test 1' 'Test 2' 'Test 3'

Step 4—Use the corr command to compute a correlation matrix
e.g.

corr 'Test 1' 'Test 2' 'Test 3'

This gives a correlation matrix of the form

```
            Test 1        Test 2
Test 2  .534
Test 3  .142          .784
```

Step 5—Look up the critical value of r in Table A.1. To do this you will need to know N, the number of subjects
e.g.
N = 15 so the relevant part of Table A.1 is
N   Critical value of r
. .
14 .532
15 .514
16 .497
. .

The critical value of r is .514.

Step 6— The significant correlations are those greater than the critical value of r
e.g.
Significant correlations in bold below

```
            Test 1        Test 2
Test 2      .534
Test 3      .142          .784
```

Testing

Table 5.2 contains the exam and Scale A scores used in Chapter 4 along with the IQ and reading age in months of each child. Enter these data and save them. Use the corr command to create a correlation matrix. The correlation between exam score and IQ should be .766. Use Table A.1 in the appendix to see if this is significant. (There are 12 subjects so the smallest r which would be significant is .576. .766 is larger than this critical value so it is significant at the .05 level).

Table 5.2

Scale A	Reading age	Exam	IQ
11	102.8	76	104
8	102.0	60	99
11	102.2	65	98
9	97.6	61	93
7	98.8	74	113
17	105.8	79	100
7	101.8	67	98
18	111.0	89	119
12	103.8	74	100
5	99.4	62	93
13	102.6	78	107
5	106.2	70	90

Finding the significance of a correlation using the regress command

The regress command was also introduced in Chapter 4. Box 5.7 describes a general procedure for computing a correlation and its p value using the regress command. Again work through the Minitab commands in the example. Steps 1 to 3 can be omitted if you saved the data the first time.

Box 5.7 Step by step procedure for determining a correlation and whether it is significant using the regress command

Step 1—Tabulate the data with one row for each subject and one column for each score obtained (you will probably have already done this).

e.g. as for Box 5.6. Fifteen subjects are assessed using three tests

	Test 1	Test 2	Test 3
S1	118	194	122
.	.	.	.
.	.	.	.
.	.	.	.
S15	23	168	87

Step 2—Enter the data into Minitab using the read command
   e.g.

   name c1 'Test 1' c2 'Test 2' c3 'Test 3'
   read 'Test 1' 'Test 2' 'Test 3'
   118 194 122
   70 152 116
   .
   .
   .
   23 168 87
   end

Step 3—Check the data with the print command and correct any mistakes using let (see Chapter 2)
   e.g.

   print 'Test 1' 'Test 2' 'Test 3'

Step 4—Use the corr command to compute r for the two scores you are interested in comparing
   e.g.

   corr 'Test 1' 'Test 2'

   Correlation of Test 1 and Test 2 = 0.534

Step 5—Use the regress (regr) command to compute r2 between the same two sets of scores
   e.g.

   regr 'Test 1' 1 'Test 2'

   The results will be as follows. To help you find them here, r2 and the p value are printed in bold

```
The regression equation is
Test 1 = 40.7 + 0.281 Test 2
```

Predictor	Coef	Stdev	t-ratio	p
Constant	40.72	32.15	1.27	0.227
Test 2	0.2815	0.1237	2.28	0.040

s = 30.94   R-sq = **28.5%**   R-sq(adj) = 23.0%

```
Analysis of Variance

SOURCE              DF          SS        MS         F        p
Regression           1      4961.0    4961.0      5.18    0.040
Error               13     12446.6     957.4
Total               14     17407.6

Unusual Observations
Obs.    Test 2       Test 1           Fit Stdev.Fit   Residual
St.Resid
   9       167       147.00         87.73      13.18      59.27
2.12R
  15       168        23.00         88.01      13.09     -65.01       -
2.32R

R denotes an obs. with a large st. resid.
```

Step 6—Extract r^2 and the p value from the resulting display. The correlation is significant at the .05 level if p is less than .05.

e.g.

$r^2 = .285$, $p = .040$, the correlation is significant at the .05 level

Testing

Retrieve the data from Table 5.2. Use the regress command to compute a p value for the correlation between exam scores and IQ. It should be .004 which indicates that the correlation is significant.

Binomial test

A p value for a binomial test can be computed with the cdf command in Minitab. cdf stands for cumulative distribution function. The cdf command can be used to compute p values under a variety of statistical assumptions, or as a statistician would say 'using a number of statistical distributions'. Because it can be used to compute p values for other theoretical distributions as well as the binomial expansion it is necessary to specify the distribution required as well as the value to work from. Let us say we wish to compute a p value for getting 14 out of 16 as a binomial test result. We type

    cdf 2;
    binomial 16 .5 .

Several things may be puzzling about the above command.

(a) It is the first Minitab we have encountered with a sub-command. The command 'cdf 2' finishes with a ';' indicating that there is more to follow. Minitab signals that the next line belongs to the last by changing the prompt from 'MTB>' to 'SUBC>' rather as it changes to 'DATA>' when using the set or read command.

The sub-command finishes with a '.' If this is omitted Minitab assumes there are more sub-commands to follow.

(b) We don't just specify the name of the distribution in the sub-command but also the number of subjects (N) and the probability of an individual result (the null hypothesis). Although the sign test always assumes this is .5 it is possible to use the binomial expansion to compute probabilities with other null hypotheses.

(c) The result we had was 14 out of 16 choosing butter yet the value entered in the command is 2. This is because the probability we wished to compute is that of getting 0, 1, 2, 14, 15 or 16 out of 16. cdf gives the probability of getting a value less than or equal to the stated value, in this case 0, 1 or 2 out of 16. The probability we want, the p value, is obtained by doubling that probability. If you have entered the command correctly the result given by Minitab will be

```
K   P( X LESS OR = K)

2.00        0.0021
```

So, the probability of getting 0, 1, 2 out of 16 is .0021. By symmetry the probability of getting 0, 1, 2, 14, 15, or 16 out of 16 is $2 \times .0021 = .0042$.

Box 5.8 gives a generalised procedure for doing a binomial test with Minitab. Work through the Minitab commands in the example. Beware, cdf gives an answer if you omit the ';' and sub-command; however, it is an answer to a different question!

Box 5.8   Step by step procedure for doing a binomial test

Step 1—If they are not already in a suitable form, tabulate the data so that subjects can be classified as falling into one of the two categories, supports (+) or goes against (–) the hypothesis. Subjects who provide no evidence in either direction can be dropped at this stage.

e.g. 15 children are asked to copy 3 figures before and after a training procedure. Each figure is judged to be copied correctly or incorrectly. It is hypothesised that children will tend to get more figures correct after training.

	Number correct Before	After	Category	
S1	1	3	+	
S2	2	3	+	
S3	0	1	+	
S4	2	1	–	
S5	2	2		S5 and S13 provide no
S6	2	3	+	information in either
S7	0	1	+	direction so they are
S8	2	3	+	dropped from further
S9	3	2	–	calculations
S10	1	2	+	
S11	1	2	+	
S12	1	3	+	
S13	0	0		
S14	0	1	+	
S15	1	2	+	

Step 2—Count the number of subjects falling into each of the two categories. Call the smaller of these two numbers M.
e.g.

11 +, 2 –, M = 2

Step 3—Count the total number of subjects that can be classified. Call this N
e.g.

N = 13 (two of the original 15 were dropped as there was no difference in their scores)

Step 4—Enter M and N into the cdf command (binomial). Do not forget the ';' to indicate there is a sub-command to follow and the '.' after the sub-command.
e.g. M = 2 and N = 13 so

cdf 2;
binomial 13 .5 .

This gives the answer

```
    K   P( X LESS OR = K)
    2.00                0.0112
```

Step 5—Double the value obtained, the answer is the p value. If this is less than .05 the result is significant at the .05 level.
e.g.

p = 2 × .0112 = .0224, this is less than .05, significantly more children improve than get worse.

Testing

In Experiment 2 Team B found that seven of the ten subjects tested chose the margarine as the preferred sample. The probability of getting 7 out of 10 is .3438. Make sure you can get this value using Minitab and your calculator before you go on.

DCL

DCL commands introduced in this chapter: Editing the command line using the up arrow and ^A; ^S and ^Q. More mail commands: del, del/all, select.

The up arrow key

DCL allows you to edit a command line before pressing <⏎return> by using the left and right arrow keys. The up arrow key will recall the last command you typed. Leave Minitab and enter the following set of DCL commands

dir a*.*
dir b*.*
dir c*.*
dir d*.*

The last command will list all the files you have beginning with d. Now press the up arrow key. The last DCL command you typed will appear on the screen (dir d*.*). Press it again and it will be replaced by the command before that (dir c*.*). Press <↵return> and the command will be executed (of course nothing will happen if you don't have any files beginning with 'c').

Press the up arrow key until you get the command Minitab. Do NOT press <↵return>.

Having recalled a previous command in this way you can change it using the left and right arrow keys and the <←del> key. Press the <←del> key four times and then 'o'. The command will now read 'mino'. Press <↵return> and you will get some sort of message indicating that DCL cannot understand your command.

Press the up arrow key until the command 'dir c*.*' appears. The marker that indicates where a letter will appear when you type it is called the 'cursor'. It may be a block or an underline character and it may flash on and off. Pressing the left arrow key moves this leftward. Pressing the right arrow key moves it rightward. Try these keys. Press the left arrow key until the cursor is over/under the d of 'dir'. Press the right arrow key until it is at the right-most position.

We are going to 'edit' 'dir c*.*'to 'dir ch*.mtw'. Move the cursor back so that it is over/under the first * (if you overshoot use the right arrow key). Now type 'h*.mtw'. The command will now read 'dir ch*.mtw'. Pressing <↵return> will list any .MTW files you have beginning with ch.

Testing

Press the up arrow key. Change the command to 'dir ch2*.mtw' and press <↵return>.

Control-A (^A)

In the operations we just performed everything we typed replaced the existing letters. In this particular case it would have been much more convenient to insert a character rather than replace the existing characters. Let us say we want to change the command 'dir ch2*.mtw' to 'dir ch2ass*.mtw'. Press the up arrow to recall the command to be edited. Move the cursor until it is under/over the character '2'. This is where we want to insert the characters 'ass'. We can change from 'replace mode' to 'insert mode' by pressing control-A. To do this hold down the <control> key while you press 'A' (it may be spelt <ctrl> or <ctl> on your keyboard, it will be on the left hand side). Now type 'ass'.

<control> is a bit like a second shift key. Pressing <shift> changes the meaning of the keys typed while it is down, 'a' becomes 'A', 'b' becomes 'B' and so on.

<control> has a similar effect except that it makes the key into a character that has a special meaning to the computer. Pressing 'a' while the <control> key is down does not result in anything appearing on the screen, instead DCL interprets it as a message to change from replace to insert mode or vice versa. Control-A is normally written ^A.

Testing

Type the command 'dir ch*.mtw' but do not press <↵return>. Using ^A, edit this to read 'dir ch2*.mtw' without retyping any of the original letters.

Editing the command line in Minitab

In Minitab you may only be able to recall the last command you gave. All the other operations work however.

^S and ^Q

When you are viewing a large file with the DCL type command the information you want will often scroll off the screen before you have time to see it properly. In order to demonstrate this we will enter Minitab and make a large file by plotting three graphs.

```
minitab
read c1 c2 c3
1 5 20
2 8 18
3 9 15
4 6 7
5 10 10
6 8 6
end
outfile 'threeplots'
plot c1 c2
plot c1 c3
plot c2 c3
stop
type threeplots.lis
```

You will have had very little time to study the first plot. ^S (said control-S) stops the display to prevent this happening. ^S is typed by holding down the <control> key while you press 'S'. To start the display again press ^Q (hold down the <control> key and press 'Q').

Testing

Recall the last command ('type threeplots') with the up arrow. Ready yourself to press ^S and then press <⏎return>. Stop the display with the first plot on the screen. Start it again and stop it with the second plot on the screen. Repeat the operation until you are confident.

Note: Terminals with 'smooth scrolling' may not respond to ^S. If this is a problem consult your system manager.

Tidying up mail

Mail saves you messages in a 'folder' unless you explicitly ask for them to be deleted. It is anti-social to build up enormous mail files and you should delete your old messages every so often. If you enter mail when there are no new messages you will automatically be given access to the folder of old messages.

dir will list them all.

del and then a number will delete that message.

del/all will delete them all.

There are other useful mail commands you can learn about using the help command from within mail. Try

help folders

When you have read this get back to the mail> prompt by pressing <⏎return> and try

help select

To get back to the mail> prompt this time you will have to press <⏎return> twice.

MSDOS

MSDOS commands introduced in this chapter: Editing the command line, <F3> and ^S.

<F3>

MSDOS allows you to edit a command line before pressing <⏎return> by using the left and right arrow keys. The key engraved 'F3' (left of the main keyboard) will recall the last command you typed. Leave Minitab and enter the following MSDOS command:

dir c*.*

If there are any files beginning with c they will be listed on the screen. Now press <F3>. The last command you typed will reappear on the screen. Press <⏎return> and the command will be executed again.

Press <F3> again but do NOT press <⏎return>.

Having recalled a previous command in this way you can change it using the left and right arrow keys and the <←–del> key. Press the <←–del> key twice and then 'm'. The command will now read 'dir c*m'. Press <↵return> and you will get a listing of all the files with names beginning with c and ending with m (if any).

Press <F3> again. The marker that indicates where a letter will appear when you type it is called the 'cursor'. It may be a block or an underline character and it may flash on and off. Pressing the left arrow key moves this leftward. Pressing the right arrow key moves it rightward. Try these keys. Press the left arrow key until the cursor is over/under the d of 'dir'. Press the right arrow key until it is at the right-most position.

We are going to edit 'dir c*m' to 'dir ch*.mtw'. Move the cursor back so that it is over/under the * (if you overshoot use the right arrow key). Now type 'h*.mtw'. The command will now read 'dir ch*.mtw'. Pressing <↵return> will list any .MTW files you have beginning with ch.

Testing

Press <F3>. Change the command to 'dir ch2*.mtw' and press <↵return>.

<insert>

In the operations we just performed everything we typed replaced the existing letters. In this particular case it would have been much more convenient to insert a character rather than replace the existing characters. Let us say we want to change the command 'dir ch2*.mtw' to 'dir ch2ass*.mtw'. Enter the command

    ch2*.mtw

Move the cursor until it is under/over the character '2'. This is where we want to insert the characters 'ass'. We can change from 'replace mode' to 'insert mode' by pressing <insert>. This key will be found on the bottom row of the keyboard on the right hand side, it may be spelt <ins>. Now type 'ass'.

Testing

Type the command 'dir ch*.mtw' but do not press <↵return>. Using <insert>, edit this to read 'dir ch2*.mtw' without retyping any of the original letters.

Editing the command line in Minitab

In Minitab you can similarly recall and edit the last command you gave.

^S

When you are viewing a large file with the MSDOS type command the information you want will often scroll off the screen before you have time to see it properly. In order to demonstrate this we will enter Minitab and make a large file by plotting three graphs.

```
minitab
read c1 c2 c3
1 5 20
2 8 18
3 9 15
4 6 7
5 10 10
6 8 6
end
outfile 'threeplots'
plot c1 c2
plot c1 c3
plot c2 c3
stop
type threeplots.lis
```

You will have had very little time to study the first plot. ^S (said control-S) stops the display to prevent this happening. ^S is typed by holding down <control> (it may be spelt <ctrl> or <ctl> on your keyboard, it will be on the left hand side) while you press 'S'. To start the display press ^S again.

<control> is a bit like a second shift key. Pressing <shift> changes the meaning of the keys typed while it is down, 'a' becomes 'A', 'b' becomes 'B' and so on. <control> has a similar effect except that it makes the key into a character that has a special meaning to the computer. Pressing 'S' while the <control> key is down does not result in anything appearing on the screen, instead MSDOS interprets it as a message to stop or start the display.

In Minitab you can also recall the last command you gave by using <F3> and edit commands in exactly the same way.

Testing

Recall the last command ('type threeplots') with the up arrow. Ready yourself to press ^S and then press <↵return>. Stop the display with the first plot on the screen. Start it again and stop it with the second plot on the screen. Repeat the operation until you are confident.

ASSIGNMENT

1. Fill in the rest of this table of sign tests.

Ss supporting (+)	Ss not sup. (−)	N	p	Significance
7	3	10	.3438	no
8	2	10	...	...
9	1	...	...	...
10	0	...	...	...
12	4	...	...	...
14	6	...	...	...

2. Retrieve the data on exam scores, Scale A and so on from Table 5.2.

(a) What is the critical correlation coefficient for these data?

(b) Copy out the correlation matrix for these four variables and circle those correlation coefficients which are significant at the .05 level.

(c) Use the regr command to compute the p value for the correlation between IQ and Scale A.

(d) Use the regr command to compute the p value for the correlation between IQ and reading age.

(e) Use the regr command to compute the p value for the correlation between Scale A and reading age.

3. Retrieve the data on pronunciation accuracy and so on used in Chapter 4, Assignment 2 (Appendix B, Table B.1). Compute a correlation matrix. Circle the correlations which are significant at the .05 level. What do you conclude from this pattern of results?

SUMMARY OF DCL COMMANDS

Logging in

1. Refer to the form 'Arrangements for using the computer', at the end of Chapter 1, in which you have summarised the procedure for switching on and connecting your terminal.

2. Press <⏎return>.

3. Enter your user name when prompted for it.

4. Enter your password.

You are successfully logged in when you get the '$' prompt.

DCL commands

logout (lo)	**rename (ren)**
whois	**copy**
help	**type**
directory (dir)	**print**
purge	**delete (del)**
mail	

Up arrow recalls the last command. ^A toggles between overtype and insert modes. ^S stops the display from scrolling. ^Q restarts it.

Wild cards for use in file specifications

* (any, or no letters here) % (any one letter here)

Mail commands

<⏎return> (show next message)

send	**select newmail**	(folder of unread messages)
help	**select mail**	(folder of read messages)
exit	**select wastebasket**	(folder of deleted messages
del		retained until you exit)
del/all		

Start Minitab session

minitab

SUMMARY OF MSDOS COMMANDS

Switching on and off

Refer to the page headed 'Arrangements for using the computer', at the end of

Chapter 1, in which you have summarised the procedure for switching on and booting up your computer and for ending a session at the computer.

MSDOS commands

 date

 ren   (the first file name given is the 'from' file,
       the second the 'to' file)

 copy   (again 'from' 'to')

 dir type

 del print

<F3> recalls the last command. <insert> toggles between overtype and insert modes. ^S stops the display from scrolling. Pressing ^S again restarts it.

Wild card for use in file specification

* (any, or no letters here)

Start Minitab session

 minitab

SUMMARY OF MINITAB COMMANDS LEARNED SO FAR

set (indicate you have come to the end of the data with end)	
read (ditto)	**erase**
name	**save** 'name'
info	**retrieve** **(retr)** 'name'
print	**outfile** 'name'
let	**nooutfile**
describe **(desc)**	**regress** **(regr)**
mean	(e.g. **regr c1 1 c2**)
stdev	**correlation** **(corr)**
sum	
ssq	
table	
histogram **(hist)**	
stem-and-leaf	
boxplots	
plot	

cdf value ;   (value is the number of subjects in the smaller category,
  binomial N **.5** .   N is the total number of subjects. The p value is obtained
                                     by doubling the probability obtained.)

help commands

stop

CHAPTER 6
COMPARING MEANS

Statistical concepts introduced in this chapter: The t-test, the Mann–Whitney U test.

INTRODUCTION

This chapter is concerned with the problem of evaluating a difference between means. The example developed in Chapter 5 was the comparison of two mean preference ratings, one from a group tasting butter and the other from a group tasting margarine. Team A obtained a mean rating of 44.1 from the butter group and 32.0 from the margarine group. The conclusion is that butter gives higher ratings. Team B got a mean rating of 39.7 for their butter group and 47.6 for their margarine group which would lead one to the opposite conclusion. In Chapter 5, Team B's results were dismissed because the difference between the two means was small compared with the large variation of scores within groups. Given this large 'error' variation the difference between the means could easily have arisen by chance. The purpose of this chapter is to show how this intuition is quantified in statistical tests.

Table 6.1 A population of scores

71	61	48	40	50	53	35	62	19	39	42	59	40	63	61	36	39	69	37
40	27	63	52	61	20	76	40	42	38	46	54	41	54	38	38	23	47	28
54	44	62	53	39	48	68	49	37	51	55	52	46	60	71	36	69	41	34
56	43	22	44	59	55	27	7	49	35	49	71	27	34	26	89	61	71	23
51	58	76	57	39	51	67	49	43	24	45	61	38	52	49	71	58	61	48
57	42	53	51	70	28	32	57	62	60	71	47	52	39	42	23	67	65	45
91	46	14	67	48	46	37	41	23	58	56	64	54	60	52	88	50	50	64
66	58	57	37	43	47	71	37	64	35	46	62	69	28	50	41	60	60	76
49	41	57	51	61	58	53	40	67	50	47	41	46	21	49	72	26	58	64
43	67	92	40	53	45	60	36	37	31	54	46	52	72	60	54	26	50	42
69	52	74	42	61	43	51	36	45	64									

The null hypothesis

Table 6.1 contains 200 randomly generated numbers. Imagine they were obtained by getting a rating from all the students on a particular statistics course. Each student is given a sample of butter and asked to make a rating, from 'very nasty' to 'very nice' as in Chapter 1. Ten values are randomly sampled from this population of scores:

71, 27, 34, 26, 89, 61, 71, 23, 51, 58 (Mean = 51.1)

Sampling another ten scores at random

46, 52, 72, 60, 54, 26, 50, 42, 69, 52 (Mean= 52.3)

gives a slightly different mean. You may want to repeat this process. Choose ten numbers from the table using a pin. It is very unlikely that your sample will have the same mean as either of the other two samples. This is because each sample mean is only an estimate of the population mean (49.92). The above exercise illustrates the null hypothesis when comparing means. This is that the two samples to be compared in fact come from the same population and the means differ only through chance.

So, the statement that Team B's results 'could have arisen by chance' is reformulated more precisely as the null hypothesis that 'the two sets of scores come from the same population of scores'. Giving one group one fat and the other another has had no effect. If we could reject this null hypothesis because the probability of getting a difference of this magnitude or greater is very small (less than .05) then we could say that the result was significant, i.e. the result is likely to be replicable. As we saw in Chapter 5, we cannot reject the null hypothesis when evaluating Team B's results and so there is the possibility that the means do differ only by chance. If the experiment were to be repeated we might come to the opposite conclusion that butter is preferred to margarine.

The problem then is to compute the probability that the two sets of scores to be compared have been drawn from the same population of scores. As with the computation of any *a priori* probability it is necessary to make assumptions. There are two ways of doing this, and they are described in the sections that follow.

The normal distribution

Statisticians have shown that many distributions observed in 'nature' have a characteristic shape which can be described by a mathematical function known as the normal or Gaussian distribution function. A normally distributed variable arises when that variable is determined by a large number of independent factors. Height is the classic example. The height of an individual is determined by many different genes in the individual's genotype and by many different environmental factors. Figure 6.1 is a histogram drawn from the 200 points in Table 6.1. It conforms to this general shape, being approximately symmetrical about the mean, with the most common values being central. As values deviate further

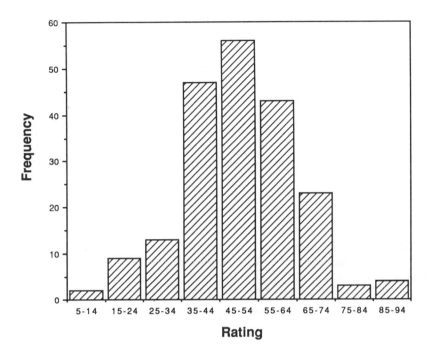

Figure 6.1 Frequency distribution based on the data in Table 6.1. Even though it is slightly asymetric, this approximates to a normal distribution

from the mean they become less frequent, giving the distribution a characteristic symmetrical bell shape.

The normal distribution is convenient for statistical calculations as it can be described completely by two 'parameters', its mean and its standard deviation. Thus it is known, for example, that 68.26% of all the scores in a normal distribution will fall within one standard deviation either side of the mean and 95.44% within two standard deviations either side of the mean. This is of considerable practical importance. Imagine you are screening infants for abnormalities in a clinic. One thing of interest is the circumference of the infant's head. An abnormally large or abnormally small head may be indicative of a clinical problem. The nurse taking the measurements has to be given criteria, a lower and an upper limit. If the infant's head is outside of these limits they should be referred for more specialist tests. National statistics are collected to determine the mean and standard deviation of head circumference for a range of ages. Let us say that at a particular age the mean head circumference is 50 cm and the standard deviation is 5 cm. Setting a lower limit of 45 cm and an upper limit of 55 cm would result in 31.7% (100 − 68.26) of the infants measured being referred for further tests. Setting a lower limit of 40 cm and an upper limit of 60 cm would result in 4.56% (100 − 95.44) being referred. In this way the normal distribution function can be used to set criteria which will result in the desired proportion of the population being referred for further testing.

Parametric tests

To recap, the objective is to evaluate the difference between two means with respect to the inherent 'error' variation in the scores. The null hypothesis is that the two sets of scores that the means were computed from both came from the same population of scores, i.e. the manipulation had no effect. We need to compute the probability that the two means could differ as much as they do, or more, assuming that the null hypothesis is true. We hope to be able to reject the null hypothesis because that probability is very small. To compute a probability or 'p value' further assumptions have to be made. Statistical tests that assume the scores all come from the same normal distribution are known, for somewhat obscure reasons, as parametric tests. The F ratio computed to evaluate the significance of a regression equation in Chapter 5 was a parametric test. The parametric test for comparing means used in this chapter is the t-test.

The t-test makes the assumption that all the scores come from the same normal distribution. Another theoretical distribution, known as Student's t distribution, is then used to compute a p value. Student's t distribution is derived from the normal distribution. Applying this test to Team A's results, Minitab gives a p value of .0007 This is less than .05 so the difference is significant, the mean rating for the butter group is significantly higher than that for the margarine group. Were the experiment to be repeated, they might not get precisely the same means, but they are likely to come to the same conclusion. The same is not true of Team B's results. The p value computed by Minitab for these data is .31 which is greater than .05. We cannot reject the null hypothesis. On the basis of Team B's data we cannot tell whether tasting butter or margarine gives the highest ratings. It is very likely that were the experiment to be repeated we could come to the opposite conclusion to that suggested by the present data.

When the assumptions are violated

With some kinds of data the assumption that the scores come from a normal distribution may be hard to justify. If this is the case then the validity of the p value computed using a parametric test may not be trustworthy. Reaction time is a classic example. With small measurements of time the underlying distribution is not normal. This is because it is generally easier to take a relatively long time to make a response than to take a relatively short time. In the limit it is impossible to respond in anything much less than about 200 ms.

Figure 6.2 plots some real data from a reaction time task. The two graphs are for two experimental conditions, the first results in generally longer reaction times. In both cases there is a clearly defined modal value but the distributions are not symmetrical about this value. The distribution extends further to the right of the modal value than to the left. As is often the case the decrease in modal reaction time is accompanied by a corresponding decrease in variance, that is the spread of scores in Figure 6.2(a) is much less than in Figure 6.2(b). This is another sign that the underlying distribution is not normal because it is generally easier to increase than to decrease reaction time.

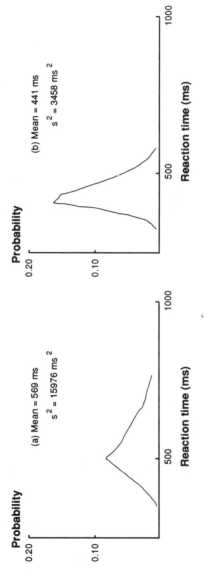

Figure 6.2 Distributions of reaction time under two conditions giving different means (real data—each graph is based on about 600 observations)

Were smaller samples to be drawn from these two distributions and their means compared in a t-test one might be sceptical about the validity of the p value computed. The null hypothesis for a t-test is that the two samples were drawn from the same normal distribution. The asymmetrical shapes of these distributions and the change in variance which accompanies the change in mean suggest this is not the case. The solution to this problem is to 'transform' the data, i.e. to translate each score into some other more suitable scale. With small reaction times it is common to take the logarithm of the time as the dependent variable rather than the time itself. Log reaction time has been found to be reasonably normally distributed. The approach adopted in this book is to transform the scores to ranks. The ranks of ten scores will always be the numbers one to ten (assuming there are no tied ranks) and so fewer assumptions have to be made when computing a p value.

Statistics using ranks

Consider the data in Table 6.2 from an experiment in which the dependent variable is the number of typing errors made in creating a document. The subjects are instructed to avoid errors at all costs and so the number of errors made is in general small. The experiment is to determine whether music, played through headphones, can improve performance by cutting out the normal auditory distractions present in an open plan office.

Table 6.2 Error scores on a typing task

Experimental group (music) (Median = 10.5, N = 8)	5,	2,	23,	35,	7,	15,	10,	11
Control group (no music) (Median = 21, N = 9)	8,	65,	83,	21,	18,	20,	43,	27,	12

Like small times, small frequencies will also generally violate the assumptions of parametric tests and so the scores are transformed to ranks (Table 6.3).

Table 6.3 Ranking the scores—E indicates a score from the experimental group, C a score from the control group

Score	2	5	7	8	10	11	12	15	18	20	21	23	27	35	43	65	83
Rank	1	2	3	4	5	6	7	8	9	10	11	12	13	14	15	16	17
Group	E	E	E	C	E	E	C	E	C	C	C	E	C	E	C	C	C

The smallest score in the whole data set comes from the experimental group so that is assigned a rank of 1. The next smallest is 5 and so that is assigned a rank of 2, 7 gets a rank of 3 and 8, from the control group, a rank of 4. This continues up to the score 83 which is the largest in the data set and so that has a rank of 17, there being 17 subjects altogether. The transformed scores can be gathered together again as in Table 6.4.

Table 6.4   Ranks and mean ranks for each group

Experimental group (music) (Mean rank = 6.375)	2,	1,	12,	14,	3,	8,	5,	6
Control group (no music) (Mean rank = 11.333)	4,	16,	17,	11,	9,	10,	15,	13, 7

A difference between mean ranks can be evaluated with the Mann–Whitney U test which tests the degree to which the two samples overlap. In these data the higher ranks tend to be from the control group and the lower ones from the experimental group but there is some overlap. Minitab computes a statistic U which reflects the degree of overlap and then computes the probability that an overlap as small as that could have occurred by chance, i.e. if the subjects had been randomly assigned ranks. This requires making assumptions about the data but they are generally less demanding assumptions than those required for parametric tests. For the above data p is .0485 and so we can reject the null hypothesis. The difference in mean rank is significant at the .05 level.

When to use the t-test and when the Mann–Whitney U test

You have just collected some data from two groups of subjects. There is an apparent difference in the mean scores for these two sets of scores and you need a statistical test to determine whether it is significant. How do you decide whether to use the t-test or the Mann–Whitney U test?

The 'power efficiency' of a statistical test refers to the number of subjects which have to be tested in order to gather sufficient evidence to reject the null hypothesis. The statistical theory is that your two sets of scores are samples from two populations of scores. There will be a minimum sample size which is capable of demonstrating some given difference in the means of these two populations of scores. Intuitively one can see that a sample of three individuals from each population is unlikely to provide sufficient evidence to reject the null hypothesis that the scores came from the same distribution. At the other extreme, a sample of 100 individuals from each population ought to be sufficient to demonstrate any difference of practical importance. The minimum needed for a particular statistical test to demonstrate a real effect of some particular size can be estimated and will lie between these two extremes. In general, parametric tests have a greater power efficiency than statistics based on ranks, that is they require less data to reject the null hypothesis if there really is an effect. The reason for this is that in transforming the scores to ranks some information is lost. In Table 6.3 the lowest three scores all come from the experimental group. The lowest control group score is 8 so the mean ranks would not be changed if the number of errors made by these subjects were 0, 1 and 2 or 5, 6 and 7 instead of 2, 5 and 7. The ranks do not distinguish between these different scores, the information they provide is lost.

The disadvantage of the t-test is that it makes more stringent assumptions. If the assumptions used to compute a p value are violated then we can no longer believe that p value. For the t-test the basic assumption is that all the scores come from the same normal distribution. It has already been noted that small measurements of time and small frequencies, such as error counts, may violate this assumption. Proportions suffer the same problems. It is likely to be harder to improve one's score from say 95% to 99% than from say 45% to 49%. As with small times this distorts the distribution. Proportions of one kind and another are the most common form of data collected by behavioural scientists. Any test or performance measure, where each subject gets some score between zero and a known maximum, can be expressed as a proportion.

So, statistical theory recommends the use of the t-test because it has a greater power efficiency than the Mann–Whitney U but cautions against it because much of the data one is likely to collect will not be normally distributed. In practice both tests almost always give the same answer. That is, if one test shows that a difference is significant so will the other and if one test does not give a p value sufficiently small to reject the null hypothesis, neither will the other. There are two reasons for this. Firstly, it turns out that the power efficiency of the Mann–Whitney U is only slightly less than that of the t-test. Secondly, the t-test has been shown to be 'robust to violations of its assumptions'. If there are equal numbers of subjects in each of the two groups and the distribution is not seriously skewed then the p value obtained can be trusted even if the data are to some extent non-normal.

The reader who is looking for practical advice about when to use the t-test and when to use the Mann–Whitney U test may be getting impatient with this section by now. The data collected in a single small scale experiment are unlikely to be sufficient to distinguish between a normal and a non-normal distribution. Anyway, 'small' deviations from normality are known not to be a problem. Deciding which test to use on the basis of the statistical theory is thus not easy to do. It is possible to suggest guidelines or rules of thumb which will be acceptable to most statistical authorities. In general parametric tests, such as the t-test, should NOT be used.

1. If there is evidence for serious skew in the distribution (see Chapter 2). The signs of this are

(a) there are extreme outliers, perhaps scores greater than three standard deviations from the group mean;

(b) the range of score in one group is very much larger than (say more than twice) that in the other;

(c) there are ceiling or floor effects;

2. If there is not the same number of subjects in one group as the other.

A floor effect will occur when a test is too hard. If many (say more than 20%) of the subjects score close to zero then there is probably a floor effect. This will make the range of scores in whatever condition raises scores larger than that in the other. For this reason 1(a) and 1(c) usually go together. A ceiling effect is the same problem at the other end of the scale. A ceiling effect will occur when the test is too easy. Ceiling and floor effects may also make it harder to demonstrate any effect of the manipulation. There should be an equal number of subjects in each group if you are using a t-test because the robustness of the test against violations of its assumptions depends crucially on this and very few variables used in the behavioural sciences can be trusted to be truly normal.

Given the high power efficiency of the Mann–Whitney U test a practical and very reasonable strategy is to always use it in place of the t-test. However, the t-test has a venerable history, it would seem churlish to abandon it except in the above circumstances!

How to report the results of the t-test and the Mann–Whitney U test

As stated in Chapter 5, when writing up the results of statistical tests it is important to give the right amount of detail. Part calculations should not be presented nor should basic concepts such as significance be explained. On the other hand sufficient detail is required to show that the appropriate test has been performed. A statistical test is used to evaluate a result so the first step should be to report that result. In this chapter the results to be evaluated are differences between means so the first thing to be reported should always be the means and the conclusion they suggest. Having done this the results of the test used to assess the significance of the effect is reported.

Some statistics books discuss the use of one- or two-tailed t-tests. In the behavioural sciences the use of one-tailed tests can rarely be justified (see Chapter 5). For this reason Minitab computes two-tailed probabilities. The t-test we have considered here is a 'two-tailed between-subjects t-test'. The meaning of 'between-subjects' will be explained in the next chapter.

Team A's results might be written up as follows:

Results:-

The marks made by the subjects on the rating scale were turned into scores between 0 and 100 by measuring the distance from the 'very nasty' end. Table 6.5 gives the mean rating and standard deviation for each group. The mean rating for the butter group is higher than that for the margarine group indicating that butter tends to result in higher ratings. This difference can be shown to be significant at the .05 level using a two-tailed between subjects t-test (t = 3.82, p = .0007).

Table 6.5   Results of tasting experiment, rating

	Mean	Std.Dev.
Butter group	44.07	8.99
Margarine group	32.00	8.32

Note that summary statistics are presented in the report and not the raw scores. Large tables of numbers are hard for a reader to digest and best separated from the text, perhaps in an appendix.

A Mann–Whitney U test compares ranks not raw scores. The dependent variable being examined is now the rank and not the raw score so it is important that the mean rank for each group is reported along with the results of the test. Also, if the guidelines suggested above are followed then data which require a Mann–Whitney U test, rather than a t-test, are likely to come from skewed distributions. This being the case the median will be a more representative measure of central tendency than the mean (see Chapter 2). In the example which follows the mean, median and mean rank are all reported but the median is foregrounded as the 'prize result'.

Results:-

The number of errors made in typing the test document was determined for each subject. Table 6.6 gives the median, mean and standard deviation for the experimental group (with music) and the control group (no music). The median error score is higher for the control group suggesting that music may have had a beneficial effect. Raw error scores were transformed to ranks in order to perform a Mann–Whitney U test. The mean ranks differ in the same direction as the medians (see Table 6.6) and the effect was found to be significant at the .05 level (p = .0485).

Table 6.6   Results of the typing test, number of errors in document

	Median	Mean	Std.Dev.	Mean rank
Experimental group (music)	10.5	13.50	10.82	6.375
Control group	21	33.00	25.65	11.333

Both the above examples were significant effects. When reporting a non-significant result a similar format can be used. Note that not being able to reject the null hypothesis is not the same thing as concluding that there is no effect. The independent variable really may not have any effect but it is also possible that the experiment was not sufficiently sensitive. Team B's results might be reported as follows:

Results:-

The marks made by the subjects on the rating scale were turned into scores between 0 and 100 by measuring the distance from the 'very nasty' end. Table 6.7 gives the mean rating and standard deviation for each group. Although there is an apparent difference in favour of the margarine group this was not found to be significant at the .05 level when evaluated with a two-tailed between subjects t-test (t = 1.04, p = .31).

Table 6.7   Results of the tasting experiment, ratings (Team B)

	Mean	Std.Dev.
Butter group	39.7	14.4
Margarine group	47.6	19.1

Summary

1. This chapter is concerned with evaluating experiments where there are two groups of subjects. Each subject gives us one score and the conclusions drawn depend on the difference in mean score for each group (other types of experiment will be discussed in the next chapter).

2. The scores vary within each group owing to random error of measurement. There is thus the possibility that the difference in mean score, between the groups, is due to chance. If the difference between the means is due to chance then the result is probably not repeatable, i.e. if the experiment were to be repeated we might draw the opposite conclusion.

3. The null hypothesis (what we mean by 'chance') is that all the scores were drawn from the same population. Their division into groups is essentially random.

4. By making assumptions about this population of scores we can compute the probability of getting two groups which differ in their measure of central tendency as much as was observed in the experiment. If this probability, or 'p value', is small (less than or equal to .05) then the null hypothesis is rejected and the result is said to be significant.

5. Two statistical tests are considered, each using different assumptions in order to compute a p value.

(a) The t-test assumes that the scores come from a normal distribution (parametric test).

(b) The Mann–Whitney U test makes less demanding assumptions (non-parametric test). The scores are ranked and the computation is based on the degree to which the ranks of subjects in the two groups overlap.

6. The parametric test (t-test) will generally require less data in order to demonstrate the significance of an effect of some given size. However, calculations show that this difference in 'statistical power efficiency' is small. The t-test is robust to violations of its assumptions so long as there is an equal number of subjects in each group and the underlying distribution is not seriously skewed. As a rule of thumb the Mann–Whitney U test should be used if:

(a) there are more subjects in one group than the other

(b) there are extreme outliers (scores greater than three standard deviations from the group mean)

(c) the range of scores in one group is very much larger than, say more than twice, that in the other

(d) there are large ceiling or floor effects.

7. When reporting the results of one of these tests, first describe the result being assessed, e.g. the means to be compared. A t-test is reported as a t value and a p value. Mean ranks should be reported with the p value for the Mann–Whitney U test. If the Mann–Whitney U test is being used because it is suspected that the data distribution is skewed then medians may be more representative measures of central tendency than the group means.

WORK SHEETS

MINITAB

Minitab commands introduced in this chapter: twot, twos (independent samples t-tests), mann (Mann–Whitney U test).

Comparing two groups

Consider the following data from an experiment on the effect of temperature on typing performance. One randomly selected group type as accurately as possible for two days in a warm environment (24°C) and an other in a normal environment (19°C). The scores are the number of errors made in completing all the work set.

> Warm: 28 24 47 30 45 37 30 28 25 11 26 13
>
> Normal: 34 31 40 25 52 31 39 48 42 40 30 36

Login, start Minitab and then put this data into a single column, c1. The first 12 values in the column will be the warm group and the last twelve the normal group. Now create a second column containing 12 '1's and then 12 '2's (i.e., a '1' for each subject in the warm group and a '2' for each subject in the normal group.

```
name c1 'Errors' c2 'Temp_grp'
print c1 c2
boxplots c1;
by c2.
```

You should get two box-plots, one above the other. If you don't you have probably forgotten the ';' or '.', 'by c2' is a sub-command.

Note the difference in central tendency (the plus sign is the median) and the degree of overlap between these two groups. What would you conclude from these results without doing any further statistical tests? Guess whether that conclusion will be shown to be significant by a t-test, i.e. guess whether one may safely assume one would come to the same conclusion were the experiment to be repeated.

t-test with the twot command

We can now do a t-test on these data using the twot command (there is a command 'ttest' but that does something different!).

```
twot 'Errors' 'Temp_grp';
pooled.
```

twot has a sub-command 'pooled'. This makes Minitab do a standard t-test as found in most introductory statistics books. If this sub-command is not appended it does a less common variant which 'corrects' for the fact that the two samples have different variances. This usually has little effect on the final result, i.e. whether the difference is significant or not.

twot 'Errors' 'Temp_grp'

Compare the results of this command with the last.

t-test with the twos command

Sometimes it is convenient to put the data from each group into a separate column. twos is a version of the twot commands for dealing with this data format.

Create two new columns, one containing only the data from the warm group and one containing only the data from the normal group. Let us say these are columns 3 and 4 respectively.

name c3 'Warm' c4 'Normal'

print c3 c4

desc c3 c4

twos c3 c4;

pooled.

twos c3 c4

Save all these data.

Testing

Use the twot command on columns 1 and 2 again and check you get the same answers.

The Mann–Whitney U test

Two groups of subjects from Brighton are asked to rate a set of 10 photographs of buildings as to how modern they are. Half of the subjects are told that all the buildings are in London, half are told that they are in Berlin. The theory developed by the authors predicts that the latter group will tend to see the buildings as being more modern. The rating scale runs from 1 to 7, with 7 being labelled 'very modern'. The mean rating for each subject is given below.

London group: 3.4 3.6 2.2 3.6 5.9 2.5 2.7 4.6

Berlin group: 2.0 6.1 5.1 6.5 4.9 6.1 5.6 6.3

Put these scores into columns c5 and c6 and name them appropriately. The command mann does a Mann–Whitney U test on data where each group occupies a separate column (there is no equivalent of the twot commands).

mann c5 c6

Most of the results displayed can be ignored. The medians may be useful if you have not already computed them with desc. The p value is given as 'The test is significant at'. Write down the median for each group and the p value. When quoting the results of a Mann–Whitney U test it is conventional to quote the mean rank of each group. Minitab gives a statistic 'W' which is the total ranks for the first group specified, in this case c5. The mean rank for c5, the London group, is thus W/8. The sum of the ranks of N scores will always be N(N+1)/2 so we can easily work out the sum of the ranks of the other group (c6) as N(N+1)/2 − W, where N is the total number of subjects. The mean rank is obtained by dividing by the number of subjects in the group. In terms of our example:

$$W = 47 \qquad N = 16 \qquad \text{so } N(N+1)/2 = 136 \qquad \text{and } 136 - 47 = 89$$

Or alternatively the mann command can be used a second time:

    mann c6 c5

giving W= 89. So:

	Sum of ranks	Number of subjects	Mean rank
London group	47	8	5.88
Berlin group	89	8	11.13

Testing

Do a Mann–Whitney U test on the data for Warm and Normal typists we used to try out the twos command. You should get a p value of .0243. The mean rank for the Warm group is 9.21. For the Normal group it is 15.79. Check you can get the same results.

Comparing the t-test and the Mann–Whitney U test

Compare the results obtained with twos and mann on the rating data example (London and Berlin groups).

    twos c5 c6
    mann c5 c6

The data were generated from a normal distribution and so the conclusions are similar. Add an outlier to the Berlin group by making the score for subject 4 100 (O.K. I know it's supposed to be out of 7!).

    let c6(4)=100
    print c5 c6
    twos c5 c6
    mann c5 c6

Notice that this has a large effect on the mean but no effect on the median. Notice that it also makes the t-test non-significant, as the error variance is much increased, but leaves the non-parametric test significant.

Box 6.1 summarises the above as a general purpose procedure for evaluating a difference between the mean scores obtained from two groups of subjects. Work through the example used to illustrate the procedure.

Box 6.1   Step by step procedure for comparing means (two groups)

Step 1—Tabulate the data so that there is one set of figures for each group.
e.g.

Score out of 100 for Experimental and Control Groups

Experimental		Control	
S1	75	S2	21
S3	42	S4	48
S5	75	S6	26
S7	97	S8	28
S9	56	S10	40
S11	89	S12	69
S13	64	S14	55
S15	76	S16	30

Step 2—Enter the data as two columns in Minitab and name the columns appropriately
e.g.

name c1 'Exptl' c2 'Control'
set 'Exptl'
75 42 75 97 56 89 64 76
end
set 'Control'
21 48 26 28 40 69 55 30
end

Step 3—Check the data with the print command and correct any mistakes using let (see Chapter 2).
e.g.

print 'Exptl' 'Control'

Step 4—Decide whether you are going to do a t-test or a Mann–Whitney U. Use the latter test (Step 5b) if (a) there are unequal numbers of subjects in each group, (b) there are extreme outliers, (c) the range of scores in one group is very much larger than that in the other or (d) there are obvious ceiling or floor effects.

e.g.
None of the above apply. A t-test would be appropriate.

Step 5a—Do a t-test using the twos command and copy down the t and p values obtained.

e.g.

twos 'Exptl' 'Control';
pooled.

This gives the following output:

```
TWOSAMPLE T FOR Exptl VS Control
            N       MEAN      STDEV    SE MEAN
Exptl       8       71.8      17.6      6.22
Control  8       39.6      16.6      5.87

95 PCT CI FOR MU Exptl - MU Control: (13.77, 50.48)

TTEST MU Exptl = MU Control (VS NE): T= 3.76   P=0.0021
DF=  14
```

So t = 3.76 and p = .0021.

Step 5b—If you decide not to do a t-test do a Mann–Whitney U test using the mann command and copy down the p value obtained. Compute the mean rank for each group from W.

e.g. (If you had not done Step 5a)

mann 'Exptl' 'Control'

This gives the following output

```
Mann-Whitney Confidence Interval and Test

 C1            N =   8     MEDIAN =          75.00
 C2            N =   8     MEDIAN =          35.00
 POINT ESTIMATE FOR ETA1-ETA2 IS          34.50
 95.9  PCT C.I. FOR ETA1-ETA2 IS (    12.00,     50.00)
 W =     95.0
  TEST  OF  ETA1  =  ETA2   VS.    ETA1  N.E.  ETA2  IS
SIGNIFICANT AT   0.0054
```

p = .0054

Mean rank for Experimental group = 95.0/8 = 11.875

mann 'Control' 'Exptl'

This output is used to compute the mean rank for the Control group

```
Mann-Whitney Confidence Interval and Test

Control    N =   8      MEDIAN =          35.00
Exptl      N =   8      MEDIAN =          75.00
POINT ESTIMATE FOR ETA1-ETA2 IS        -34.50
95.9  PCT C.I. FOR ETA1-ETA2 IS (   -50.00,    -12.00)
W =       41.0
   TEST  OF  ETA1  =  ETA2    VS.    ETA1  N.E.  ETA2  IS
SIGNIFICANT AT  0.0054
```

Mean rank for Control Group = 41.0/8 = 5.125

Step 6—If the p value obtained is less then .05 then the result is significant.
e.g. (having followed Step 5a)

$p = .0024$, the mean score for the Experimental group is significantly larger than the mean score for the Control group (.05 level).

e.g. (having followed Step 5b)

$p = .0054$, the mean score for the Experimental group is significantly larger than the mean score for the Control group (.05 level).

ASSIGNMENT

1. A group of 12 male students and 12 female students are compared on two tests of spatial ability. Their scores are given below.

Male:		Female:	
Test 1	Test 2	Test 1	Test 2
28	46	29	75
28	75	6	84
36	70	24	41
35	49	20	24
29	8	19	71
32	67	27	86
29	24	13	31
22	76	36	60
25	75	33	38
27	57	19	87
41	67	22	60
23	66	19	74

(a) Printout box-plots comparing males and females for each of these tests. Cut them out of the printout and stick them into your report. Describe the differences in central tendency.

(b) Compute the following statistics for each of these two tests and put them into a table: mean for males, mean for females, t, p of t-test, significance (yes or no), median for males, median for females, mean rank for males, mean rank for females, p of U, significance.

2. Retrieve the data on pronunciation accuracy used first in the assignment for Chapter 4, Question 2 (Appendix B, Table B.1). The second variable is age group. Group 1 were 4 and 5 year olds, Group 2 were 6 and 7 year olds. Compare these two groups on the four variables recorded in the data set. What conclusions can you draw?

3. Design and run your own experiment to look at verbal reasoning and spatial manipulation. The two tasks you are to use are described below and include instructions you can copy out and give to your subjects. Feel free to change these tasks, or the instructions, as you see fit but record exactly what you did in the report. Before you test the subjects on these tasks record what sex they are, what subject they are studying and any other variable you think may be interesting. Your analysis will compare male and female scores (and means for any other dichotomies you think may be interesting). You will also compute a correlation between the results on the two tests across all the subjects tested. The correlation is interesting because these are very different tests and so a correlation would be evidence for the concept of general intelligence (Spearman's g). It has also been found that males tend to do better on spatial tasks and females on verbal tasks.

Testing will only take a few minutes so you can do it in a corridor or in a student's room. You should work in groups. Aim to test about 15 to 20 students each so that you end up tabulating the results from around 50 students.

Verbal reasoning test

This task was devised by Baddeley at the Applied Psychology Unit in Cambridge, and involves judging whether sentences are true or false.

Instructions

Your job is to read each sentence and decide whether it is a true or false description of the letter pair which follows it. If you think the sentence describes the letter pair correctly circle 'T' (true). If you think the sentence does not give a true description of the letter order circle 'F' (false). This is illustrated in examples 1 and 2 below. When you have read 1 and 2, try examples 3, 4, 5 and 6.

Examples

1. A follows B - BA	T	F
2. B precedes A - AB	T	F
3. A is followed by B - BA	T	F
4. B is not followed by A - BA	T	F
5. B is preceded by A - BA	T	F
6. A does not precede B - BA	T	F

When you start the main test, work as quickly as you can without making mistakes. Start with sentence 1 and work systematically through the test leaving no blank spaces.

[The main test will consist of 20 sentences on a separate sheet which you will have to make up yourselves by combining 'follows', 'proceeds', 'is followed by', 'is preceded by' with a particular order of A and B in the sentence and '-AB' or '-BA' at the end. Some sentences should have 'not' in them.]

[Stop the subjects after 1 minute and count how many they got right.]

Spatial manipulation task

This task was invented by Brookes. It requires a subject to manipulate a mental image.

Instructions

Imagine you are looking at a block letter F like so:

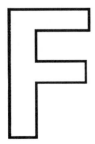

Starting at the top left corner go around the block letter in a clockwise direction saying what sort of corner it is, 'inside' or 'outside'. The first three corners of F are 'outside', the fourth is 'inside'. Now try it without looking at this sheet.

I shall give you a series of letters, work as quickly as you can without making mistakes.

[Letters to use: E, T, H, L. Work out what the correct sequences are before you start.]

[Have them do these four letters twice and time them. Caution them immediately they make a mistake. Subjects making errors on more than two letters will have to be discarded.]

Writing the report

The report you write should have the following headings:

Title — something appropriate to the subject of your enquiries

Method — about a page on what you did when collecting the data, it should be sufficiently detailed that someone else could repeat your procedure. Divide this section into subsections as in the assignment for Chapter 1.

Results — divide this into two subsections: the first describing the complete set of results (means, standard deviations etc. and the correlation between verbal and spatial ability scores) and the second the comparison of different subgroups in your sample. Restrict yourselves to independent variables with two levels, e.g. male/female, science/arts.

SUMMARY OF DCL COMMANDS
See end of Chapter 5

SUMMARY OF MSDOS COMMANDS
See end of Chapter 5

SUMMARY OF MINITAB COMMANDS LEARNED SO FAR

set   (indicate you have come to the end of the data with end)

read (ditto)	**erase**
name	**save** 'name'
info	**retrieve** (**retr**) 'name'
print	**outfile** 'name'
let	**nooutfile**
describe (**desc**)	**regress** (**regr**)
mean	(e.g. **regr c1 1 c2**)
stdev	**correlation** (**corr**)
sum	
ssq	
table	
histogram (**hist**)	
stem-and-leaf	
boxplots	
plot	

cdf value ;
   binomial N .5 .   (value is the number of subjects in the smaller category, N is the total number of subjects. The p value is obtained by doubling the probability obtained.)

twot c1 c2   (between subjects t-test, first column gives data, second specifies the group)

twos c1 c2   (ditto, first column gives data for group 1, second data for group 2)

mann c1 c2   (Mann–Whitney U test, data as for twos. p value specified as 'is significant at'. The mean rank for c1 is W/n_1, the mean rank for c2 is $(N(N+1)/2 - W)/n_2$; where n_1 is the number of subjects in c1, n_2 the number in c2 and $N=n_1+n_2$. Alternatively use the command **mann** c2 c1, the mean rank for c2 is then W/n_2)

help commands
stop

CHAPTER 7
TWO EXPERIMENTAL DESIGNS

Statistical concepts introduced in this chapter: Within-subjects designs (alias: repeated measures, correlated or matched samples), between-subjects designs (alias: independent samples, completely random), within-subjects t-test, Wilcoxon matched-pairs signed-ranks test, chi squared, choosing the appropriate test.

INTRODUCTION

Within- and between-subjects designs

The previous chapter described two statistical tests for evaluating a difference in central tendency between two groups. Each subject experiences only one of the levels of the independent variable and so contributes just one score to the analysis. This way of arranging an experiment will be described in this book as a *between-subjects design*. It is so called because the experimental manipulation distinguishes between subjects—either they are in the butter group or they are in the margarine group. The alternative to a between-subjects design is a *within-subjects design*. Here each subject experiences both levels of the independent variable and so contributes two scores to the analysis. It is called a within-subjects design because the manipulation is made within the experience of each subject. Some examples of these two experimental designs will make this distinction clear. The first (Box 7.1) was used in the last two chapters. Compare that with the within-subjects design described in Box 7.2.

Box 7.1   A between-subjects design

Hypothesis: Subjects tasting butter will rate it more highly on a scale from 'very nasty' to 'very nice' than subjects tasting margarine.

Experimental design: Between subjects, 15 subjects taste a sample of butter and another 15 a sample of margarine. Each subject rates the taste of the one sample. The independent variable is 'fat tasted' and the dependent variable the rating.

Data:

Table 7.1   Rating data

Butter group		Margarine group	
S1	34	S2	32
S3	38	S4	31
S5	60	S6	19
S7	44	S8	38
S9	47	S10	34
S11	31	S12	41
S13	58	S14	40
S15	53	S16	27
S17	37	S18	28
S19	37	S20	19
S21	46	S22	51
S23	43	S24	27
S25	54	S26	30
S27	35	S28	34
S29	44	S30	29
Mean	44.07	Mean	32.0

Conclusion: The mean rating for the butter group is higher than the mean rating for the margarine group as predicted.

Null hypothesis for significance testing: The two groups are random samples from the same population (the independent variable 'type of fat' had no effect on the scores).

Box 7.2   A within-subjects design

Hypothesis: Subjects will respond faster to a red light than to a green light in a simple reaction time experiment.

Experimental design: Within subjects, 10 subjects press a response button whenever a light comes on. There are 200 trials. On half of these trials the light is red and on half it is green. The sequence of red and green lights is odd trials red and even green for half the subjects and even trials red and odd green for the other half. The mean reaction time to the red light and the mean reaction time to the green light is computed for each subject. The independent variable is 'colour of stimulus' and the dependent variable is mean reaction time.

Data:

Table 7.2   Reaction time data

	Red	Green	Difference
S1	632	644	12
S2	571	631	60
S3	472	514	42
S4	848	926	78
S5	567	681	114
S6	505	511	6
S7	572	638	66
S8	729	713	−16
S9	577	597	20
S10	770	752	−18
Mean	624.3	660.7	36.4

Conclusion: The red light is responded to faster than the green light as predicted.

Null hypothesis: The differences are sampled from a distribution with a mean of zero (the independent variable 'colour' has no effect on reaction time).

Note that in the within-subjects design the scores are paired up and a difference can be computed. While the scores in the between-subjects design are tabulated with the score for subject 1 next to the score for subject 2 and so on, this arrangement is completely arbitrary. There is no reason why the score for subject 1 should not have been tabulated next to the score for subject 16, say. It would make no sense to compare individual scores in these data.

Because it is possible to pair up the scores in a within-subjects design and then compute a difference score, a different null hypothesis is called for and hence different statistical tests. For a within-subjects design the null hypothesis is that the 'real' difference between the pairs of scores is zero, but, because of the random error present in all behavioural data, this is not what is observed. More precisely the null hypothesis is that the differences are sampled from a hypothetical distribution which has a mean of zero. The test computes the probability that the mean difference for the sample could deviate this much from zero by chance. If this p value is less than .05 the null hypothesis is rejected and the difference is said to be significant.

Again there are parametric and non-parametric tests for computing p. The parametric test is a *within-subjects t-test*. The non-parametric test, the equivalent of the Mann–Whitney U test, is the Wilcoxon matched-pairs signed-ranks test. These are described below. First the other names by which these two experimental designs are known will be discussed.

Other names

Unfortunately the authors of statistical textbooks and computer programs cannot agree on labels for these two experimental designs. In Minitab they are distinguished as *one-sample* or *two-sample* tests. The command ttest takes a single set of numbers (one sample) and tests whether their mean is significantly different from zero (the null hypothesis). If you start off with pairs of scores these have to be converted to differences before the test can be applied. In contrast the twosample command (twos for short), introduced in the last chapter, is used with between-subjects designs. As it is not possible to compute a difference score in this case, this command takes two columns of data (two samples). In this case the null hypothesis is that both samples are drawn from the same population. As these two t-tests use different null hypotheses they will give very different answers. The test used must be appropriate for the experimental design.

Between-subjects designs are sometimes referred to as *independent-samples designs*, within-subjects designs as *correlated-* or *matched-samples* designs. The labels within and between subjects are used here because they are useful for thinking about more complex experimental designs in behavioural science which you will encounter if you go on to consider other experimental designs outside of the scope of this book.

Matched samples designs

This term is used to describe within-subjects designs where the sampling unit or 'subject' is a pair of matched individuals. For example, you might be interested in some rather rare disease of the nervous system. You can scrape together a group of 12 such individuals but they are a very heterogeneous group as they vary widely in age, IQ, and so on. The hypothesis is that they have a deficit in verbal reasoning. Simply comparing them with a sample of normal individuals is unsatisfactory as matching the mean age, IQ and so on may be difficult and the wide variation in reasoning ability due to age and IQ within the group will mean that the experiment will only be sensitive to very large differences between groups. One solution is to match each patient to a normal control of the same age and IQ. This will guarantee that the mean age and mean IQ for the normal subjects are well matched to those for the patients. In addition, the data can be taken in pairs and difference scores computed. This could be thought of as a 'within pairs' design and could be evaluated with a within-subjects t-test. The new sampling unit (normally subjects) is the pair.

t-test for within-subjects designs

This t-test uses the null hypothesis that the differences come from a normal distribution with mean zero. This is a parametric test like the between-subjects t-test considered in the previous chapter. If this assumption of normality is seriously compromised because the distribution of differences is very skewed then the alternative Wilcoxon matched-pairs signed-ranks test described in the next section should be used. In a small sample outliers are the main evidence for skew. If one or two of the differences of one sign are very large (say more than three standard deviations from the mean difference) then the t-test should not be used.

The Wilcoxon matched-pairs signed-ranks test

To perform this test the differences are ranked, irrespective of sign. For example take the differences from the reaction time experiment above. Table 7.3 tabulates the absolute size of the differences from Table 7.2. The smallest difference is 6, this is given a rank of 1. The next smallest is 12 and the next 18 and so on. The largest absolute difference is 114. That is given a rank of 10.

Table 7.3   Ranked absolute differences for the reaction time data

Subject	1	2	3	4	5	6	7	8	9	10
Difference (ignoring size)	12	60	42	78	114	6	66	16	20	18
Rank	2	7	6	9	10	1	8	3	5	4
Sign	+	+	+	+	+	+	+	−	+	−

If there was no difference between the red and green conditions one would expect the sum of the ranks for the differences with a positive sign to be the same as the sum of the ranks of the differences with negative ranks. In these data, when sign is taken into account, there is a net positive difference (mean difference 36.4) and this can be seen in the rankings. There are more positive differences than negative and the negative differences tend to be smaller than the positive ones. The Wilcoxon test uses the null hypothesis that the ranks of the negative and positive differences are assigned at random to compute a p value. In this case it is .041 so the difference is significant at the .05 level.

The same arguments, developed in Chapter 6, that apply when choosing between the between-subjects t-test and the Mann–Whitney U test also apply in choosing between a within-subjects t-test and the Wilcoxon test. Any test based on ranks will require more evidence to reject the null hypothesis than an equivalent test using untransformed scores but the Wilcoxon matched-pairs signed-ranks test has a high power efficiency. It should always be used when there are signs of serious skew in the distribution of difference scores such as is signalled by the presence of extreme outliers.

Designing your own experiments

There are advantages and disadvantages for both of these experimental designs which you should be aware of when designing your own experiments or reading about those of others.

The advantage of a within-subjects design is that a difference score may be a more sensitive dependent variable than either of the raw scores that are used to compute it. Reaction time for example is a variable with large individual differences. Subjects differ from one another a great deal, although within a given subject's performance reaction time may be relatively stable. Looking at the reaction time data in Table 7.2 it is clear that S2 is considerably better at this kind of task than S4. Nevertheless the difference between red and green reaction times is similar for the two subjects. By computing a difference score we remove the error variance due to individual differences. In a between-subjects design it is not possible to do this and so very many more subjects may need to be tested in order to provide sufficient evidence to reject the null hypothesis.

The disadvantage of a within-subjects design is that experiencing one experimental condition (one level of the independent variable) may affect the subject in some way so that the second experimental condition has a different effect than it would have had this not been the case. Take the following example. It has been found that instructions to form mental images linking the words in a list makes that list easier to learn. An experiment might be performed to demonstrate this. In one of the experimental conditions instructions are given to form visual images, in the other no such instructions are given. Consider a subject who has imagery instructions for the first list learnt and no instructions with the second. If imagery really makes the task easier then he is likely to use it with both lists. Even if he is instructed not to use imagery with the second list the experience of learning the first list is likely to affect the way he approaches the task of learning the second. This carry over effect will decrease the size of the difference score. Alternatively he may perform the control condition (no instructions) first and then the experimental condition (instructions). This does not suffer from the above problem but if only subjects who experience the conditions in this order are tested then any advantage observed could be due to practice effects. Practice would be expected to increase the recall of the second list learned anyway. However, it is conceivable that giving the instruction to image words changes the nature of the task so radically that any practice effect is cancelled. All in all it would be very difficult to interpret the results of either of these experiments.

Randomising the order in which different subjects get the different conditions will control unwanted effects like practice but only if the effects are unchanged by the experimental manipulation. The reaction time example was chosen because it is practical to have a long sequence of red and green stimuli and to interleave red and green trials. A less satisfactory design would have been to perform the experiment as two blocks of trials, half the subjects responding to 100 red trials and then 100 green and half doing it the other way round. By doing it this way it is hoped that averaging across the two groups of subjects any practice effects will be cancelled. This depends on the assumption that the practice effect is the same for red and green stimuli. In this case there is no reason to believe this is not true but there might be some subtle effect of this kind. If the conditions are interleaved then there will be red and green trials at the beginning, middle and end of the experiment so differential order effects which could change the result would have to be extremely subtle.

The possibility of order effects of one kind and another has been used to argue that within-subjects designs should not be used under any circumstances. A more pragmatic approach is to use them with dependent variables which make between-subjects designs impractical because of the large number of subjects required. Reaction time is nearly always used in within-subjects designs. Every so often someone has to replicate an important result obtained in a within-subjects design using a between-subjects design. That way the investigators in a particular area of research can check that the assumptions they are all making in order to interpret the results of their within-subjects experiments are justified.

Sampling bias and self selection

The major source of potential bias in a between-subjects design comes in choosing the groups for the experiment. Groups must be randomly sampled from the same population. This requirement is generally upheld if subjects are assigned arbitrarily to groups before they appear at the experiment. A good procedure is to use a rule of the form 'The first subject who turns up will be put into Group A the second into Group B and so on'. Since neither you nor they know in advance whether they will turn out to be odd or even numbered subjects this is an effective way of randomly assigning people to groups.

If subjects choose the condition they perform in there may well be bias. Had the subjects in the tasting experiment chosen whether they would like to be in the butter or margarine groups the result might have been to select rather different types of people for the two groups. For example, the people who particularly dislike margarine might insist on being in the butter group.

A more subtle form of self selection may occur when subjects have to be rejected after or while they are performing the experiment. Consider the following rather extreme example. It is proposed that punishment is a more effective motivation than reward. In a prior experiment the monetary reward required to get people to suffer a large electrical shock of a given size has been accurately determined so that the reward and the punishment for the present experiment are matched in subjective strength. All the subjects have to learn a set of nonsense syllables. The reward group of ten subjects are given an appropriate sum of money every time they get more than half the list correct. The punishment group, originally ten subjects, are given the shock every time they get less than half the list correct. Five of the ten subjects in the punishment group refuse to go on after they have received a few shocks, however, averaging the results from the remaining five subjects gives a mean which is significantly better than that for the ten reward group subjects.

The problem when interpreting this result is that subjects have effectively selected themselves. Only the best subjects will avoid the shocks and carry on to the conclusion of the experiment. It is not surprising that the mean for the five best subjects in one sample is better than the mean of all of another sample. This is an extreme example but the same potential problem arises whenever subjects are lost during or after an experiment and the loss could be attributed to the experimental condition experienced. Losses due to equipment failure, where this is not the case, can be replaced by running more subjects without compromising the interpretation of the results.

A test for use with nominal data—chi squared (χ^2)

Most of this book is concerned with data in the form of scores. Each subject is assigned a number or numbers which quantify some aspect of behaviour. However, readers will remember that in Chapter 2 we considered summarising data in the form of a contingency table. Here subjects do not provide scores to the analysis, rather the subjects are put into categories. As an example consider a survey where the sample is classified according to whether they drive or not and whether they suffer from lower back pain. Table 7.4 shows how many people fell into the four categories: drivers with L.B.P, drivers without L.B.P., non-drivers with L.B.P. and non-drivers without L.B.P. In addition the table gives the total number of drivers and non-drivers (the column totals) and the total number of L.B.P. sufferers and non-sufferers (row totals).

Table 7.4   The association between lower back pain (L.B.P.) and driving (fictional data)

	Drivers	Non-drivers	
Lower back pain	172	58	230
Not having L.B.P.	248	489	737
	420	547	967

This is known as a two by two contingency table (see Chapter 2). The variables are both dichotomies, lower back pain or not and driving or not. There is clearly an association between these variables—41% of the drivers have lower back pain whereas only 11% of the non-drivers do (these are fictional data!). If the incidence of lower back pain was independent of whether you drive or not then these proportions should be the same.

To illustrate this possibility Table 7.5 gives some data where there is no association between the variables. There are fewer males than females and there are fewer people with lower back pain than with it but the proportion of males suffering lower back pain is very similar to the proportion of females (29% and 30% respectively).

Table 7.5   The association between lower back pain (L.B.P.) and sex (fictional data)

	Male	Female	
Lower back pain	35	64	99
Not having L.B.P.	86	148	234
	121	212	333

The chi squared (χ^2) test evaluates the null hypothesis that the two dichotomies are independent by comparing the observed frequencies with what would be expected if this null hypothesis were true. If the null hypothesis were true then one would expect the frequencies in the cells of Table 7.4 (172, 58, 248, 489) to be determined by the row and column totals (230, 737, 420, 547). Thus as the proportion of drivers in the sample is 420/967 and the proportion of people having lower back pain 230/967 then the proportion expected to drive *and* have lower back pain is

$$\frac{420}{967} \times \frac{230}{967}$$

As there were 967 people in the sample then the expected frequency of such people is

$$967 \times \frac{420}{967} \times \frac{230}{967} = 99.90$$

The observed frequency, 172, is much higher than this expected frequency. More people who drive have lower back pain than would be expected (by chance). Table 7.6 gives the expected frequencies for all four cells of Table 7.4. As one would expect given the above finding for drivers with lower back pain, the observed frequency for lower back pain in non-drivers is lower than expected, for drivers not having lower back pain it is lower than expected and for non-drivers not having lower back pain it is more than expected.

Table 7.6   Expected frequencies for Table 7.4

	Drivers	Non-drivers
Lower back pain	99.9	130.1
Not having L.B.P.	320.1	416.9

Table 7.7   Expected frequencies for Table 7.5

	Male	Female
Lower back pain	36.0	63.0
Not having L.B.P.	85.0	149.0

Table 7.7 gives the expected frequencies for the observed frequencies in Table 7.5. For these data the observed and expected frequencies are very similar. There is no sign of an association between the sex of the subjects and whether they suffer from lower back pain or not. The data conform closely to the null hypothesis for the chi squared test which is that the two dichotomies are independent.

Minitab computes a chi squared statistic by comparing expected and observed frequencies. For the data in Table 7.4 Minitab gives a chi squared of 120.714. For any 2 by 2 contingency table chi squared has to be greater than 3.84 to reject the null hypothesis at the .05 level. This association between driving and lower back pain is thus significant at the .05 level. On the other hand the chi squared statistic computed by Minitab for the data in Table 7.5 is 0.059. This is less than the critical value of 3.84 so there is no evidence for a significant association in this case.

Chi squared can be computed for nominal variables where people are put into more than two categories (e.g., experienced drivers, novice drivers and non-drivers). It is much more common for the variables concerned to be dichotomies as in the examples above. There are also problems interpreting a significant chi squared when the variables are not dichotomies. This book only considers 'two by two' (or '2 × 2') chi squared tests i.e., chi square when applied to a contingency table based on two dichotomies.

N.B. for technical reasons a two by two chi squared test can only be applied when all of the expected frequencies are five or more. This means there must be *at least* twenty subjects.

Reporting the results of a within-subjects t-test and the Wilcoxon test

The within-subjects t-test is used to evaluate a mean difference and so the means for the two experimental conditions being compared should be reported first. The difference between the means is equal to the mean difference and so it is not necessary to report the latter statistic. Having described the means you can then quote the t statistic and the p value. You should always make it clear what kind of t-test (i.e., within or between subjects) has been performed and that you have used a two-tailed test (see Chapter 5). The reaction time experiment might be presented as follows.

Results:-

The mean reaction time to the red lights and the mean reaction time to the green lights was computed for each subject. The means and standard deviations of these scores are given in Table 7.8. Averaging across subjects, the mean reaction time to the red light is less than that to the green light. This difference can be shown to be significant at the .05 level using a two-tailed within subjects t-test (t= 2.67, p= .026). (While reaction time can produce skewed distributions there is no evidence of outliers in the difference scores and so a parametric test can be justified for these data.)

Table 7.8   Reaction times to red and green lights

	Mean	Std. Dev.
Red	624.3	120.6
Green	660.7	120.9

The Wilcoxon test is similarly reported. If the guidelines suggested above are followed then the data that require the use of a Wilcoxon test, as opposed to a within-subjects t-test, are likely to come from a skewed distribution. In such cases the median may be a more representative measure of central tendency than the mean. It is good practice to quote the means and standard deviations as well as the medians for the two sets of scores. The Wilcoxon statistic is written as 'T' (note that this is a capital, 'T', whereas the t-test uses a lower case 't'). This is the sum of the ranks for the differences with the less frequent sign. It is conventional to quote this statistic along with the p value. The full name 'Wilcoxon matched-pair signed-rank test' should be used. Wilcoxon had to do with developing the Mann–Whitney U test and so some people refer to that test as a Wilcoxon test also.

If the reaction time experiment had been evaluated with a Wilcoxon matched-pair signed-rank test the results might be reported so:

Results:-

The mean reaction time to the red lights and the mean reaction time to the green lights was computed for each subject. The means, medians and standard deviations of these scores are given in Table 7.9. Averaging across subjects, the median reaction time to the red light is less than that to the green light. This difference can be shown to be significant at the .05 level using a Wilcoxon matched-pairs signed-ranks test (T = 48, p = .041).

Table 7.9 Reaction times to red and green lights

	Mean	Median	Std. Dev.
Red	624.3	575	120.6
Green	660.7	641	120.9

Reporting the results of a chi squared test

The chi squared test is used to evaluate an association in a contingency table. The contingency table should be reported first. It is often useful to turn the frequencies into percentages. For example, in Table 7.4 there are more non-drivers than drivers and many more people without lower back pain than with it. This makes it difficult to judge the extent of the association. In many cases one can think of one of the two dichotomies as being a dependent variable and the other an independent variable. In this example having or not having lower back pain can be thought of as a dependent variable (the result) and driving or not driving as the independent variable as it forms the contrast of interest. In such cases it makes sense to report proportions within each of the categories corresponding to the independent variable. Thus here the proportion of drivers suffering lower back pain and the proportion of non-drivers suffering lower back pain are reported. Having described the contingency table, chi squared and significance can be quoted. An example is given below.

Results:-

The total number of subjects falling into the four categories, drivers with lower back pain, drivers without lower back pain, non-drivers with lower back pain and non-drivers without lower back pain are given in Table 7.4 (see above). The proportion of the drivers having lower back pain and the proportion of the non-drivers having back pain are 41 and 11% respectively. This association between lower back pain and driving can be shown to be significant at the .05 level by a chi squared test, chi square being 120.714.

Choosing a test—Figure 7.1

This far in this book we have considered eight statistical tests. Figure 7.1 should allow you to determine which one is applicable to a particular set of data. To use it first determine what sort of data you are dealing with. Data of the type labelled A in Figure 7.1 have an independent variable with two levels (conditions or groups), and a dependent variable which is a score of some kind. The alternatives are Type B, where a correlation is to be computed (no levels), and Type C, where a chi squared or binomial test is to be applied. In the latter case the subjects are classified rather than given a score as such. A common mistake is to try to apply a chi squared test to other data where counts are obtained (e.g., the number of errors made by a subject). These are scores, so the data are of type A or B.

One then follows lines in the figure to determine the precise test to be used. In the case of Type A this involves deciding whether the design is within- or between-subjects and then whether a t-test is appropriate. The box containing a general step by step procedure to be used when applying the test is referenced in the figure.

It should be noted that the tests described in this book, and thus covered in Figure 7.1, do not exhaust the potential experimental designs and experimental hypotheses which can be statistically evaluated. In particular we have not considered experimental designs where there is more than one independent

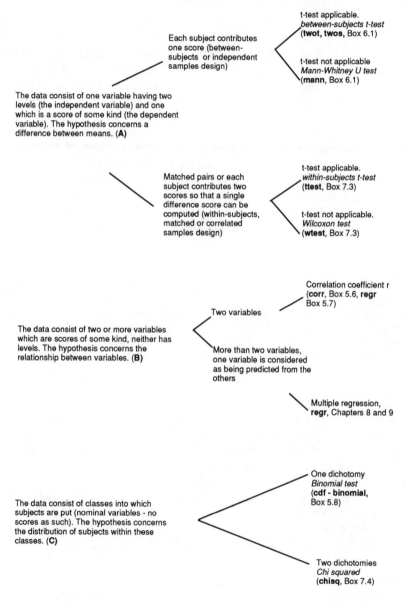

Each subject contributes one score (between-subjects or independent samples design)

t-test applicable.
between-subjects t-test
(**twot, twos,** Box 6.1)

t-test not applicable
Mann-Whitney U test
(**mann,** Box 6.1)

The data consist of one variable having two levels (the independent variable) and one which is a score of some kind (the dependent variable). The hypothesis concerns a difference between means. **(A)**

Matched pairs or each subject contributes two scores so that a single difference score can be computed (within-subjects, matched or correlated samples design)

t-test applicable.
within-subjects t-test
(**ttest,** Box 7.3)

t-test not applicable.
Wilcoxon test
(**wtest,** Box 7.3)

Two variables

Correlation coefficient r
(**corr,** Box 5.6, **regr** Box 5.7)

The data consist of two or more variables which are scores of some kind, neither has levels. The hypothesis concerns the relationship between variables. **(B)**

More than two variables, one variable is considered as being predicted from the others

Multiple regression, **regr,** Chapters 8 and 9

One dichotomy
Binomial test
(**cdf - binomial,** Box 5.8)

The data consist of classes into which subjects are put (nominal variables - no scores as such). The hypothesis concerns the distribution of subjects within these classes. **(C)**

Two dichotomies
Chi squared
(**chisq,** Box 7.4)

Figure 7.1 How to choose the appropriate test (see Chapter 6 for a discussion of when a t-test is applicable

variable (factorial designs), independent variables with more than two levels or nominal variables which are not dichotomies. These tests will however be sufficient for the majority of experiments. The experimental designs to which they are applicable have the considerable advantage of being straightforward to interpret. When designing your own experiments there is a lot to be said for restricting yourself to these designs, even if you do know how to analyse the alternatives.

Summary

1. In the previous chapter we considered a design for experiments where each subject contributes one score to the data. Two groups are compared on their mean scores. An alternative design for an experiment is to have each subject provide two scores, one for each experimental condition. The former arrangement is called a between-subjects design, the latter a within-subjects design.

2. Between-subjects designs are also sometimes called independent or unrelated samples designs. Within-subjects designs are sometimes known as repeated measures, correlated samples or matched samples designs.

3. Different experimental designs require different statistical tests. For testing the significance of the difference between means in a between-subjects design the null hypothesis is that all the scores come from the same distribution. In the case of a within-subjects design it is that the difference between the scores has a true mean value of zero.

4. The independent samples t-test and the Mann–Whitney U test considered in the last chapter are used for between-subjects designs, the former when the assumptions underlying parametric tests are met, the latter when they are not. The within-subjects t-test and the Wilcoxon matched-pairs signed-ranks test is used with within-subjects designs, again the former when the assumptions underlying parametric tests are met, the latter when they are not.

5. The third test to be introduced in this chapter was the chi squared test for association in a two by two contingency table. The null hypothesis for this test is that the marginal totals, i.e. the distribution of values in each dichotomy, independently determine the cell totals.

6. Figure 7.1 summarises how to recognise data for which one of the eight statistical tests considered in this book is applicable. The first step is to determine whether one is: (A) comparing means, i.e. there is an independent variable with two levels and a dependent variable which is a score; (B) testing a relationship between continuous variables; or (C) looking at nominal data, i.e. subjects who have been categorised in some way but not assigned scores. Further distinctions are made in order to arrive at the particular test required.

WORK SHEETS

MINITAB

Minitab commands introduced in this chapter: ttest, wtest, chisq.

Statistics for comparing means from within-subjects (correlated samples) designs—ttest and wtest

The experiment using photographs of buildings from Chapter 6 is repeated as a within-subjects design. In this case twenty photographs are used. For each subject taking part, they are randomly divided into two sets of ten, one supposedly from London and another from Berlin. The order in which they are presented is also randomly determined independently for each subject. Mean ratings are determined as before.

Subject	London set	Berlin set
1	3.1	3.5
2	4.0	6.6
3	3.9	4.7
4	3.6	4.8
5	3.9	6.2
6	3.8	4.3

Minitab describes within-subjects or correlated samples tests as one-sample tests. To use ttest or wtest the scores have first to be transformed into differences.

> **name c1 'London' c2 'Berlin' c3 'Diff L-B'**
> **read c1 c2**
> **3.1 3.5**
> **4.0 6.6**
> **3.9 4.7**
> **3.6 4.8**
> **3.9 6.2**
> **3.8 4.3**
> **end**
> **let c3=c1-c2**
> **print c1-c3**
> **desc c1-c3**

ttest uses a correlated samples t-test to test the hypothesis that the mean of these differences is zero, i.e. that the means of the two original sets of scores are equal.

> **ttest c3**

t is 3.39 which has a p value of .019 so these means are significantly different at the .05 level. wtest similarly evaluates this column of differences:

> **wtest c3**

This gives a T (Wilcoxon statistic) of 0 and a p value of .036. The difference is significant when evaluated this way as well.

Box 7.3 provides a general procedure for comparing means from a within-subjects design. Work through the example given.

Box 7.3 Step by step procedure for comparing means (within- subjects design)

Step 1—Tabulate the data so that there is one row for each subject and one column for each experimental condition.

e.g.
An experiment on reaction time before and after taking a strong analgesic.

	Before	After
S1	560	624
S2	502	594
S3	473	471
S4	415	418
S5	512	506
S6	611	685
S7	523	605
S8	441	543
S9	505	549

Step 2—Enter the data as two columns in Minitab and name the columns appropriately.

e.g.

```
name c1 'Before' c2 'After'
read 'Before' 'After'
560 624
502 594
473 471
415 418
512 506
611 685
523 605
441 543
505 549
end
```

Step 3—Check the data with the print command and correct any mistakes using let (see Chapter 2).

e.g.

```
print 'Before' 'After'
```

Step 4—Compute the difference score using let.
e.g.

name c3 'Diff B-A'
let 'Diff B-A' = 'Before' - 'After'
print 'Before' 'After' 'Diff B-A'

gives

```
ROW  Before  After  Diff B-A
  1     560    624       -64
  2     502    594       -92
  3     473    471         2
  4     415    418        -3
  5     512    506         6
  6     611    685       -74
  7     523    605       -82
  8     441    543      -102
  9     505    549       -44
```

Step 5—Decide whether you are going to do a within-subjects t-test or a Wilcoxon matched-pairs signed-ranks test. In general the t-test will be applicable unless there are extreme outliers in the difference scores (more than three standard deviations from the mean difference say).
e.g. There are no extreme outliers so a t-test is applicable

Step 6—Do a t-test by using the ttest command on the difference scores, or a Wilcoxon matched-pair signed-rank test using the wtest command on the difference scores. Write down the t or T statistic and p value obtained.
e.g. If the t-test is to be used

ttest 'Diff B-A'

gives

```
TEST OF MU =  0.0 VS MU N.E.  0.0

                N    MEAN   STDEV  SEMEAN     T        P
VALUE
Diff B-A    9   -50.3    42.3    14.1   -3.57   0.0074
```

t = 3.57, p = .0074.

e.g. If the Wilcoxon test is to be used

wtest 'Diff B-A'

gives

```
TEST OF MEDIAN = 0.000000000 VERSUS MEDIAN N.E.
0.000000000

                    N FOR    WILCOXON              ESTIMATED
              N     TEST    STATISTIC  P-VALUE      MEDIAN
Diff B-A      9       9         4.0      0.033      -48.00
```

T = 4, p = .033.

Step 7—If the p value obtained is less than .05 then the result is significant
e.g. If the t-test was used

p = .0074, the mean reaction time before was significantly faster than the mean reaction time after (.05 level).

e.g. If the Wilcoxon test was used

p = .033, the mean reaction time before was significantly faster than the mean reaction time after (.05 level).

Testing

As when we compared the independent samples t-test (twos) with the Mann–Whitney U test in Chapter 7, it is instructive to look at the effect of adding an outlier to the scores on the conclusions drawn from parametric and non-parametric tests. Make the Berlin score for subject 5 100 and repeat the two tests (don't forget to recompute 'Diff,L-B').

Chi squared

The chisq command takes a table of frequencies as specified in some number of columns and computes the chi squared statistic. For example, consider the data in Table 7.4. Minitab is used to get chi squared as follows:

```
read c4 c5
172 58
248 489
end
chisq c4 c5
```

This command gives marginal totals and expected frequencies. Check all the expected frequencies are 5 or more. For a 2 by 2 table chi squared must be greater than 3.84 to be significant at the .05 level. The value of chi squared computed by Minitab is 120.714. This is considerably higher than the critical value. The association between driving and back pain is significant (remember all the data in this book are fictional!).

Box 7.4 is a general procedure for evaluating a two by two contingency table. Work through the example used.

Box 7.4   Step by step procedure for evaluating a two by two contingency table

Step 1—Tabulate the data in a two by two contingency table, if you have not already done so.
  e.g.

Students are classified as to whether they are ever late for lectures and whether they are male or female

	Male	Female
Late	25	8
Never Late	15	16

Step 2—Enter the two by two contingency table as two columns in Minitab.
  e.g.

```
name c1 'Male' c2 'Female'
read 'Male' 'Female'
25 8
15 16
end
```

Step 3—Use the chisq command to compute expected frequencies and chi squared.
  e.g.

```
chisq 'Male' 'Female'
```

gives

```
Expected counts are printed below observed counts

            Male    Female    Total
    1        25         8        33
           20.63     12.38

    2        15        16        31
           19.37     11.62

 Total       40        24        64


 ChiSq =  0.928 +  1.547 +
          0.988 +  1.647 = 5.109
 df = 1
```

Step 4—Check all the expected frequencies are 5 or more. If any are less than 5 the test cannot be used.

   e.g.

   The lowest expected frequency is 11.62 so the test can be used.

Step 5—Write down chi squared. If it is greater than 3.84 the test is significant at the .05 level.

   e.g.

   Chi squared = 5.109, the association between lateness and gender is significant at the .05 level.

ASSIGNMENT

Seven experiments are described below. For each answer the following questions:

(a) What variables are measured and manipulated in the experiment?

(b) With reference to Figure 7.1, what kind of data has been collected: A, B, or C?

(c) For type A:

(i) Specify the independent variable.

(ii) Specify its levels.

(iii) Specify the dependent variable.

(iv) Give a summary of the results, numerically and in words. Do the results support the hypothesis suggested in the question?

(v) Perform the relevant statistical test to assess the significance of the conclusion stated in (iv). If applicable, both parametric and non-parametric tests should be used. The relevant statistics, the p value and the significance level should be quoted.

For Types B and C:

(i) Summarise the results, numerically and in words. Do the results support the hypothesis suggested in the question?

(ii) Perform the relevant statistical test to assess the significance of the conclusion stated in (i). The relevant statistics, the p value and the significance level should be quoted.

1. An experiment is performed to determine whether subjects can discriminate false suicide notes from real ones. Ten of each kind of note are presented in a randomised sequence and the subjects rate them for the probability they are real. A rating of 7 indicates highly probable, a rating of 0 indicates highly improbable. Mean ratings are obtained for each kind of note for each subject. These are given below.

Subject	Real notes	False notes
1	5.1	4.2
2	3.1	3.9
3	4.3	2.5
4	6.5	6.7
5	2.5	2.0
6	4.9	3.3
7	5.1	5.3
8	3.9	2.5
9	4.3	3.3
10	5.2	4.2

2. In an experiment on social judgement subjects judge a short video film for 'gratuitous violence'. The film is divided into 12 'scenes' and subjects indicate which scenes they feel are gratuitously violent. It is predicted that females will judge more scenes as violent than males.

Number of scenes judged violent out of 12:

Males: 5, 6, 4, 3, 7, 4, 4, 3, 1, 3

Females: 7, 9, 8, 2, 5, 10, 7, 7, 6, 8

3. It has been proposed that dog and cat owners recover better from heart attacks than people who do not own dogs or cats. All the admissions suffering from heart attacks at a certain hospital are classified as to whether they survive the first heart attack or not. Two groups of 30 patients are selected to be matched for sex, age and socio-economic status. Group 1 have cats or dogs, group 2 do not. The number of patients surviving the first attack is computed (see below).

	Surviving	Not surviving
With pets	21	9
Without pets	15	15

4. A new pain killer is thought to cause lapses of attention. A vigilance task is devised, in which subjects watch a video screen for small changes in a pattern of dots. 200 changes are made in a five hour period. The subject has to pull a lever as soon as a change is detected. The number of responses within one second of the change occurring is counted for each subject. The experimental group are given the drug and the control group a placebo, two hours before testing commences.

Experimental   78, 64, 75, 45, 82, 31, 41

Control   110, 70, 53, 51, 90, 83, 79, 97

5. A positive relationship between sensation seeking and testosterone level is predicted.

Sensation seeking was measured using a questionnaire including statements such as 'I enjoy wild uninhibited parties'. Students rate each statement for how much they agree with it. Testosterone levels were assessed from a blood sample. The following scores were obtained for a group of 12 students.

	Sensation seeking	Testosterone level
S1	82	42
S2	98	46
S3	87	39
S4	40	37
S5	116	65
S6	113	88
S7	111	86
S8	83	56
S9	85	62
S10	126	92
S11	106	54
S12	117	81

6. The effect of nursery school education on social perceptiveness is to be assessed. It is hoped that schooling will increase socialisation in general.

Eight pairs of twins were found. One twin from each pair was randomly assigned to attend nursery school for one term. At the end of the term all 16 children were given a test of social perceptiveness using a standardised procedure in which questions are asked about pictures depicting various social situations. A 'double blind' situation is used so that the person testing the children does not know whether they went to nursery school or not. The scores obtained were as follows:

Pair	Twins going to nursery school	Twins staying at home
1	82	63
2	69	42
3	73	74
4	43	37
5	58	51
6	56	43
7	76	80
8	82	65

7. It is planned to introduce a new computer terminal which is considerably less expensive than those in current use. One is installed and 30 computer users are asked to do their normal work on it for a total of 5 hours. They then fill in a questionnaire. One of the questions in it is 'Is this terminal easier to use than the one you normally work with?'. 21 responded 'yes' to this question and 9 'no'.

SUMMARY OF DCL COMMANDS
See end of Chapter 5

SUMMARY OF MSDOS COMMANDS
See end of Chapter 5

SUMMARY OF MINITAB COMMANDS LEARNED SO FAR

set   (indicate you have come to the end of the data with end)

read (ditto)	**erase**
print	**save** 'name'
let	**retrieve (retr)** 'name'
describe (desc)	**outfile** 'name'
mean	**nooutfile**
stdev	
sum	**regress (regr)**
table	(e.g. **regr c1 1 c2**)
histogram (hist)	**correlation (corr)**
stem-and-leaf	
boxplots	
plot	
name	
info	

cdf value ;   (value is the number of subjects in the smaller category,
   binomial N .5 .   N is the total number of subjects. The p value is
                          obtained by doubling the probability obtained.)

twot c1 c2   (between subjects t-test, c1 gives data, c2 specifies
                          the group)

twos c1 c2   (ditto, c1 gives data for group 1, c2 data for group 2)

mann c1 c2   (Mann–Whitney U test, data as for twos. p value
                          specified as 'is significant at'. The mean rank for c1 is
                          W/n_1, the mean rank for c2 is $(N(N+1)/2 - W)/n_2$; where
                          n_1 is the number of subjects in c1, n_2 the number in c2 and
                          $N=n_1+n_2$. Alternatively use the command **mann** c2 c1, the
                          mean rank for c2 is then W/n_2)

ttest c1   (within subjects t-test on difference scores)

wtest c1   (Wilcoxon matched-pairs signed-ranks test on difference
                          scores)

chisq c1 c2   (chi squared test for 2 by 2 contingency table. Critical
                          value 3.84, no expected frequency can be less than 5)

help commands

stop

CHAPTER 8
MULTIPLE AND STEPWISE REGRESSION

Statistical concepts introduced in this chapter: Multiple regression, R, stepwise regression, partial correlation.

INTRODUCTION

Multiple regression—the problem

Chapter 4 introduced simple regression and the correlation coefficient, r, to describe the relationship between two variables. Very often there are more than two variables to correlate with one another. In previous chapters we have dealt with this by computing a correlation matrix. Every variable is correlated with every other variable. Table 8.1 for example, shows high correlations between exam score and three other variables. There are also moderate correlations between Scale A and IQ and Scale A and reading age.

Table 8.1   A correlation matrix

	Exam	Scale A	IQ
Scale A	.76		
IQ	.77	.59	
Reading age (RA)	.74	.64	.39

Correlation matrices are not always easy to interpret and various statistical techniques for characterising them have evolved. This chapter describes one such technique. Multiple regression is used to ask questions about the relationship between some single variable and some combination of variables. For example, one might use multiple regression to ask whether combining Scale A, IQ and reading age gives a better prediction of exam scores than Scale A alone, or, if one were to choose just two of those three in combination which would be the best two to choose.

We shall describe the single variable (exam scores) as the predicted variable and the variables used in combination (Scale A, IQ and reading age) as the predictor variables. As with simple regression, it is very unusual for anyone to want to predict individual scores using a regression equation. We ask what the best prediction might be in order to determine the strength of the relationship. In that sense the predicted variable is like the dependent variable in an experiment where two groups or conditions are compared. The dependent variable is only predicted in that it reflects the result of the experiment. In the same way the predictor variables are equivalent to the independent variable in such an experiment. An independent variable is a predictor in that it is expected to affect the dependent variable.

Simple regression

Before describing multiple regression, simple regression will be quickly reviewed. Simple regression is based on the linear equation

$$y = c + mx$$

In Chapter 4 the example used was

predicted_exam_score = 55.4 + 1.55 Scale_A_Score

This is the best fitting linear equation of this form, where best fitting is defined as the equation with the smallest deviance. The deviance of an equation is computed by finding the squared difference between the predicted and observed exam score for each subject and then summing these squared differences. Deviance was also used to define the correlation coefficient r:

$$r^2 = \frac{\text{deviance of the mean} - \text{deviance of the regression equation}}{\text{deviance of the mean}}$$

One can think of the deviance of the mean as a baseline against which the deviance of the regression equation is measured. In moving from the equation

predicted_exam_score = 71.25

to the equation

predicted_exam_score = 55.4 + 1.55 Scale_A_score

we reduce the deviance of the prediction from 834.25 to 353.59. r^2 is that improvement, expressed as a ratio of the baseline deviance.

$$r^2 = \frac{834.25 - 353.59}{834.25} = .58$$

Extending the linear equation

In multiple regression the equation is extended to include more than one predictor variable. For example, the best linear combination of IQ and Scale A for predicting exam scores might be determined. This is given by the formula

predicted_exam_score = 10.3 + 0.963 Scale_A_score + 0.505 IQ

'Best' is again defined with regard to the deviance of the prediction. The first student's Scale A score is 11 and his IQ 104 so his predicted exam score is

$$10.3 + 0.963 \times 11 + 0.505 \times 104 = 73.413$$

His observed exam score is 76 so the deviation between observed and predicted is 2.587. As before, squaring the deviations for all the subjects and summing gives the deviance. Table 8.2 contains: Scale A and IQ scores; predicted and observed exam scores; deviations and squared deviations. The deviance is 222.21 which is better than the deviance when predicting with Scale A alone (353.58).

Table 8.2 Computing the deviance of a multiple regression

Subj.	Scale A	IQ	Pred. exam score	Observed ex. sc.	Deviation	Sq.Dev
1	11	104	73.413	76	2.587	6.6926
2	8	99	67.999	60	−7.999	63.9840
3	11	98	70.383	65	−5.383	28.9767
4	9	93	65.932	61	−4.932	24.3246
5	7	113	74.106	74	−0.106	0.0112
6	17	100	77.171	79	1.828	3.3452
7	7	98	66.531	67	0.469	0.2200
8	18	119	87.729	89	1.271	1.6154
9	12	100	72.356	74	1.644	2.7027
10	5	93	62.080	62	−0.080	0.0064
11	13	107	76.854	78	1.146	1.3133
12	5	90	60.565	70	9.435	89.0192
			Sum of squared deviations or Deviance			222.21

Again, as with simple regression, we can compute a correlation coefficient:

$$R^2 = \frac{\text{deviance of the mean} - \text{deviance of the regression equation}}{\text{deviance of the mean}}$$

R is the multiple correlation coefficient and it is computed in exactly the same way as r.

$$R^2 = \frac{834.25 - 222.21}{834.25} = .734$$

Simple regression with Scale A alone gave an r^2 of .576 so the correlation is considerably improved by adding IQ to the regression equation.

The regr command in Minitab will compute multiple as well as single regressions giving the best fitting equation, R^2 and the deviance of the regression. You will never have to do the computations shown in Table 8.2 except in artificial exercises of the kind found in this statistics book.

Stepwise regression—linear equations as models

The three linear equations considered for predicting exam scores can be considered as different models that are fitted to the data. The deviance of the equation is the 'error' left after the model is fitted. The simplest, let us call it Model 0, is that exam score can be predicted from a single constant. The mean exam score turned out to be the constant which gives the least deviance so Model 0 is

predicted_exam_score = 71.25

this has a deviance of 834.25. The next model to be fitted, Model 1, was that exam score can be predicted from Scale A. The best linear equation for doing this was

predicted_exam_score = 55.4 + 1.55 Scale_A_score

and this has a deviance of 353.58. Finally Model 2 predicts exam score from Scale A and IQ

predicted_exam_score = 10.3 + 0.963 Scale_A_score + 0.505 IQ

and this model has a deviance of 222.21. This is summarised in Table 8.3.

Table 8.3   Three linear models

	Deviance
Model 2 (Regression of exam score on Scale A score and IQ)	222.21
Model 1 (Regression of exam score on Scale A alone)	353.58
Model 0 (Deviance of the mean exam score)	834.25

Moving from Model 0 to Model 1 can be thought of as a 'step' in which Scale A is added to the equation. Similarly, moving from Model 1 to Model 2 can be thought of as a step in which IQ is added to the equation. R^2 evaluates Model 2 against Model, 0 i.e.,it says how good the prediction using Scale A and IQ together is compared with no predictors at all. It is also possible to evaluate Model 2 against Model 1. This says how much one has gained by adding IQ to an equation already containing Scale A. This is known as stepwise regression.

There are two basic ways of doing this stepwise regression. One is used when there is a hypothesis to test and the other as a way of describing the relative strengths of predictors when used in combination. We shall consider these two uses of stepwise regression after a discussion of how the significance of a correlation is assessed. This will involve introducing the concept of degrees of freedom.

Degrees of freedom

Given that we are always looking for the best possible prediction it is not surprising that predicting with two things is better than predicting with one. Indeed it can be shown that a regression equation with N terms (N – 1 predictors and a constant) can always be found to predict the scores of N subjects with zero deviance.

Each time a new term is added to the model the opportunity for prediction to fail is reduced. This notion is expressed in a parameter known as the 'degrees of freedom' (d.f.). The deviances computed for this example and their associated degrees of freedom are retabulated in Table 8.4.

Table 8.4 Deviances and degrees of freedom (d.f.) for three models

	Deviance	d.f.
Model 2 (Regression of exam score on Scale A score and IQ)	222.21	9
Model 1 (Regression of exam score on Scale A alone)	353.58	10
Model 0 (Deviance of the mean exam score)	834.25	11

Model 0, deviance of the mean, has 11 degrees of freedom, there being 12 subjects. Model 1 (Scale A only) has 10 degrees of freedom and Model 2 (Scale A and IQ) has 9. To make the deviances comparable one can express them as deviance per degree of freedom. This statistic is known as the mean square and can be thought of as a kind of variance (in the case of Model 0 it *is* the variance of the exam scores).

The Minitab regress command computes these deviances, degrees of freedom and mean squares and displays them as an 'Analysis of Variance' table. The tables produced by Minitab for the simple and multiple regressions respectively are given in Tables 8.5 and 8.6.

Table 8.5 Analysis of variance, predictor Scale A (Model 1)

SOURCE	DF	SS	MS	F	p
Regression	1	480.67	480.67	13.59	0.004
Error	10	353.58	35.36		
Total	11	834.25			

Table 8.6 Analysis of variance, predictors Scale A and IQ (Model 2)

SOURCE	DF	SS	MS	F	p
Regression	2	612.04	306.02	12.39	0.003
Error	9	222.21	24.69		
Total	11	834.25			

The column DF gives the degrees of freedom. Deviance (sum of the squared deviations) is abbreviated as SS for sum of squares and mean square is abbreviated as MS. The 'Error' SS is the deviance of the regression equation. This is because the deviance of the regression equation is the 'error' left when one has fitted the model. The 'Total' SS is the deviance of the mean. The SS labelled 'Regression' is the difference between the other two, that is the reduction in deviance. This may be slightly confusing. The authors of Minitab have labelled this row in the table 'Regression' as it may be thought of as the SS explained by the regression equation. It may be better to think of it as the 'reduction in deviance'.

Comparing the error MS we see that the deviance of Model 2 is smaller that that of Model 1, even when the smaller degrees of freedom of the former is accounted for (24.69 versus 35.36). However, comparing the Regression mean squares (306.02 versus 480.67) we see that the reduction in deviance gained by fitting a model which uses up two degrees of freedom is not twice as much as that gained by fitting a model which uses up one degree of freedom.

The F ratio

Tables 8.5 and 8.6 contain p values obtained from the F ratios given to their left. The F ratio is a statistic like t or chi squared with a known distribution from which a p value can be computed. F is in turn computed from two mean squares.

Where there is a p value there must be a null hypothesis! For the simple regression evaluated in Table 8.5 this is that Scale A score does not in fact predict exam scores. The scores are randomly scattered on the scattergram and the variability represented by the regression line is the same as the general variability in the scores.

For convenience the 'Error' MS will be written MS_{Error} the 'Regression' MS, $MS_{Regression}$. The two mean squares which go into the F ratio are viewed as independent estimates of the true variance due to the regression line ($MS_{Regression}$) and the true variance about the regression line (MS_{Error}). So the null hypothesis is that they are both independent estimates of the same random fluctuation. Now if the true $MS_{Regression}$ equals the true MS_{Error} then

$$\frac{\text{true } MS_{Regression}}{\text{true } MS_{Error}} = 1$$

so F should be 1. However, they are only estimates of the true state of affairs. MS_{Error} may be a chance under-estimate and $MS_{Regression}$ may be a chance over-estimate. These possibilities are important because if Scale A did predict exam scores then $MS_{Regression}$ would be larger than MS_{Error}, i.e. the alternative to the null hypothesis is that F is greater than 1.

By making assumptions about how the data arose statisticians, notably Fisher who gives his name to this statistic, have worked out how to compute the probability that an F greater than some value could occur by chance from two independent estimates of the same true variance. If that probability is small (less than .05) then we can reject the null hypothesis and accept that r is significant. The logic of using F to compute the significance of a regression equation is the same logic as was introduced in Chapter 5 for all statistical tests. It is summarised in Box 8.1.

Box 8.1 Statistical inference with the F ratio

(a) A chance result is inherently unreliable. If we can reject the possibility that a result is due to chance then it is probably a repeatable result.

(b) 'Chance' is defined as a null hypothesis, in this case that MS_{Error} and $MS_{Regression}$ are independent estimates of the same random variation.

(c) The probability of getting our particular result, or better, under the null hypothesis is computed. In this case the probability of getting an F ratio greater than or equal to 13.59 when the larger MS has d.f. 1 and the smaller d.f. 10.

(d) If that probability is less than or equal to the significance level the null hypothesis is rejected and the result is said to be significant. .004 is less than .05 so the correlation is significant.

In Chapter 5 the significance of r was interpreted in terms of the reliability of the slope of the regression. In the case of R this is not possible. The significance of R can only be interpreted by reference to deviance (SS). A significant R indicates that the deviance explained by the regression equation is unlikely to be due to chance.

Stepwise regression—statistical control

Having considered degrees of freedom and F ratios we can return to the practical analysis problems mentioned earlier. The first is the problem of assessing the effect of a 'nuisance variable' on a correlation. What this means is best explained by an example.

Table 8.7 is a correlation matrix derived from an experiment which measured the ability of children to recall lists of words (see Appendix B, Table B.4). These data were collected to see how recall changes with age.

Table 8.7 Correlation matrix for recall experiment (ignoring IQ)

	Recall	Age
Age	.87	
Time	.05	.50

The experimental procedure used to collect these data was not entirely satisfactory and subjects vary in the amount of time they spent learning the list.

There is a moderate correlation (.50) between age and time spent learning the list which indicates that the latter variable does not vary randomly with respect to age. Time spent learning the list can be described as a nuisance variable which covaries with the predictor variable we are interested in (age). As older subjects tend to spend more time learning the list this alone could account for any apparent effect of age on recall. It would have been best to control this variable experimentally but failing this the effect of time spent learning can be 'statistically controlled'. The problem then is to assess the effect of age on recall after partialling out the effect of time spent learning. In stepwise regression this is done as follows.

1. Compute the regression equation and deviance for the nuisance variable to be partialled out, in this case the regression equation for predicting recall from time spent learning the list (Model 1). This can be thought of as the new baseline deviance.

2. Add the predictor variable we are interested in to the equation, i.e. compute the deviance for the regression equation for the nuisance variable plus the predictor variable. In this case this is the regression equation for predicting recall from time spent learning and age (Model 2).

3. The decrease in deviance in making the step between Models 1 and 2 indicates the strength of the relationship between the predictor and predicted variables when the nuisance variable is statistically controlled. When converted to a mean square, this reduction in deviance is the variance in the recall scores left for the predictor to account for when the variance attributable to the nuisance variable has been removed.

Table 8.8 Stepwise regression (statistical control)

Predictor(s)	Deviance	d.f.	Dev. reduced
None (Model 0)	102.4	9	
Time (New baseline, Model 1)	102.18	8	0.22
Time and age (Model 2)	3.505	7	98.675

Table 8.8 records these computations including, for completeness, the step from no predictors (Model 0) to Model 1. Adding age to the equation considerably reduces the deviance. It is apparent that age still has plenty of predictive power even when the variance due to time taken to learn the list has been statistically controlled.

Partial correlation

Stepwise regression, when used in this way, is equivalent to partial correlation. A partial correlation can be computed from the correlation matrix as follows. The correlation between recall and age will be written r_{ra} and that between time to learn the list and recall r_{tr} and so on. The partial correlation $r_{ra.t}$ is the correlation between recall and age after partialling out the effect of time spent learning the list. This can be computed from the other correlations using the formula

$$r_{ra.t} = \frac{r_{ra} - r_{tr}\, r_{ta}}{\sqrt{(1 - r_{tr}^2)(1 - r_{ta}^2)}}$$

$$= \frac{.873 - .046 \times .501}{\sqrt{(1 - .046^2)(1 - .501^2)}}$$

$$= .983$$

$$r_{ra.t}^2 = .9657$$

$r_{ra.t}$ is in fact stronger than r_{ra} (.87). Controlling for time spent learning the list has improved not worsened the correlation between recall and age.

It is not immediately obvious how this formula works. However, the same figure can be computed from the stepwise regression depicted in Table 8.8 where the motivation behind the computation may be clearer. It will be recalled that to compute a correlation (r^2) the reduction in deviance in moving from Model 0 (no predictors) to Model 1 (one predictor) is expressed as a proportion of the deviance for Model 0. In terms of our example

$$r_{ra}^2 = \frac{102.4 - 24.381}{102.4} = .762$$

The partial correlation is computed similarly but using the new baseline deviance (Model 1) in place of Model 0. In terms of our example

$$r_{ra.t}^2 = \frac{\text{dev. of reg. on time} - \text{dev. of reg. on time and age}}{\text{dev. of regression on time}}$$

$$= \frac{102.18 - 3.501}{102.18}$$

$$= .9657$$

Significance testing in stepwise regression—statistical control

The significance of a partial correlation can be looked up in the Table A.1 if the N is reduced by one. It is preferable to test the significance of a partial correlation in an analysis of variance table. Table 8.9 does this for our example. Notice first that the partial correlation has a very high F ratio and so a very low p value. The correlation between recall and age is significant at the .05 level when time to learn the list is statistically controlled.

Table 8.9 is constructed in the same way as the analysis of variance table for the step from Model 0 to Model 1 except that the new baseline deviance is used instead of the deviance of Model 0. For comparison Table 8.10 gives the analysis of variance table for the correlation between recall and age.

Table 8.9 An analysis of variance table, stepwise regression for statistical control

	DF	SS	MS	F	p
Reduction in deviance	1	98.675	98.675	197.07	<.0001
Time and age	7	3.505	.5007		
Time	8	102.18			

Table 8.10 An analysis of variance table, correlation

	DF	SS	MS	F	p
Reduction in deviance	1	78.019	78.019	25.60	<.0001
Age	8	24.381	3.048		
Model 0 (no predictors)	9	102.4			

In both tables the reduction in deviance SS and d.f. are computed by subtraction. Mean squares (MS) are computed by dividing SS by d.f. and F is the reduction in deviance MS divided by the other MS as in Table 8.5 above. Box 8.3 in the work sheets gives a step by step procedure for computing a partial correlation and constructing an analysis of variance table.

More complex hypotheses

In the above calculations stepwise regression was used to test a reasonably sophisticated psychological model of how recall scores relate to other variables. It is straightforward to generalise these calculations to more complex models with more than one nuisance variable and more than one predictor. For example, had there also been a correlation between IQ and age indicating a bias in the sampling for say older children to be more intelligent, then IQ might have been used as a second nuisance variable. The significance of the model is tested by evaluating the change in deviance from a baseline deviance as above. The only difference is that the baseline model contains more than one nuisance variable, in this case time and IQ.

Stepwise regression for statistical control is sometimes described as stepwise regression when one or more variables are 'forced' into the equation. This follows from the way the nuisance variables are entered into the equation first (forced in) before the real predictors are considered. This is in contrast to the procedure to be described below where variables enter the equation in an order which is statistically rather than psychologically determined.

Stepwise regression—descriptive use

Let us return to the example of predicting exam scores and expand it by considering a further potential predictor, reading age (RA). Examination of the correlation matrix in Table 8.1 shows that all three predictors, Scale A, IQ and reading age correlate with exam score but they also correlate with one another. Stepwise regression gives us a way of describing these correlations as they relate to the predicted variable exam score. In the above sections, variables have been entered into the equation in an arbitrary order. Here the order they are entered depends on the amount of deviance reduced. Thus the order in which they enter is a way of describing their importance in predicting exam scores. The procedure is as follows.

1. Choose the predictor which correlates best with the predicted variable; this is said to be 'the first variable to enter the equation'. In this case it is IQ.

2. Compute the regression equation and deviance for the first variable to enter the equation in combination with each of the other predictors in turn. IQ and Scale A gives a deviance of 222.21, IQ and reading age 155.82.

3. Choose the combination giving the least deviance. The variable added is the second variable to enter the equation, in this case reading age.

This procedure is repeated until all the predictors are used up. In this case there is only Scale A left. It is said to enter the equation last. The order in which the variables enter reflects their importance as predictors when taken in combination with one another.

Table 8.11 Stepwise regression

Predictor(s)	Deviance	d.f.	
None (Model 0)	834.25	11	Deviance from the mean
Scale A	353.58	10	
Reading age	381.14	10	
IQ	**344.19**	**10**	**IQ enters first**
IQ and Scale A	222.21	9	
IQ and RA	**155.82**	**9**	**RA enters second**
IQ and RA and ScaleA	**138.30**	**8**	**Scale A enters last**

The procedure, as applied to the example, is summarised in Table 8.11. The lines in bold are the 'steps' in the procedure. The initial baseline is no predictors (Model 0). Then three single predictor models are fitted. IQ gives the lowest deviance so the first step is to enter IQ into the equation (in the procedure described above this was done by selecting the highest correlation with exam scores from the correlation matrix, the two procedures are equivalent). Next, the two models with two predictors are considered. One of the predictors must be IQ as it has already 'entered' the equation. IQ with reading age gives the lowest deviance so reading age is entered next. There is only one model with three predictors so Scale A enters as step 3. We conclude that, when used in combination, the importance of the predictors can be ordered: IQ, reading age then Scale A.

It is interesting to note that, although Scale A correlates with exam score better than reading age does (see Table 8.1), it enters the equation last. This is because of the strong correlation between Scale A and IQ. IQ enters first and 'uses up' all the variance which Scale A could explain.

As each variable enters into the equation the improvement in prediction (decrease in deviance) diminishes. The step None to IQ reduces the deviance by 490, the step from IQ to IQ and reading age 188 and the step from IQ and reading age to using all three predictors only 17.5. The next section discusses the use of significance testing as a 'stopping rule' to allow us to determine the point where adding more terms to the equation no longer results in a real gain in predictive power.

The significance of a step in stepwise regression—descriptive use

As well as the deviance of each model from Table 8.11, Table 8.12 gives the reduction in deviance achieved by taking each step and the p value for it. Thus moving from no predictors to IQ only (step 1) reduces the deviance from 834.25 to 344.19. This has a probability of .004 of occurring under the null hypothesis. This step is significant at the .05 level.

Table 8.12   Stepwise regression

Predictor(s)	Deviance	d.f.	Dev. reduced	p
None (Model 0)	834.25	11		
IQ	344.19	10	490.06	.004
IQ and reading age	155.82	9	188.37	.009
IQ and reading age and Scale A	138.30	8	17.52	.344

The reduction in moving from IQ to IQ and reading age (step 2) is 344.19 – 155.82 = 188.37 which has a p value of .009. So this step is significant at the .05 level too. Moving from IQ and reading age to predicting with all three variables (step 3) only reduces the deviance by 17.52. The p value for this step is considerably greater than .05. This step is not significant at the .05 level. It can be concluded that adding Scale A to the equation does not buy you significantly better predictive power and the 'best' prediction is obtained with IQ and reading age.

The analysis tables in which these p values are computed are constructed in the same way as the significance of any step in stepwise regression. Table 8.13 is the analysis of variance table for the first step from no predictors to the best single predictor, IQ. The F ratio computed evaluates the reduction in deviance, 490.06 against the deviance left after adding IQ to the model, 344.19.

Table 8.13   Step 1 in predicting exam score, IQ enters first

	DF	SS	MS	F	p
Reduction in deviance	1	490.06	490.06	14.24	.004
IQ (Model 1)	10	344.19	34.42		
None (Model 0)	11	834.25			

The table we construct to evaluate step 2 has the same form. The bottom line of Table 8.14 is the baseline deviance, this time the deviance of the one predictor model, IQ. The next line up in Table 8.14 gives the deviance of the current model, this time the deviance of the two predictor model, IQ with reading age. The reduction in deviance and its d.f. are computed by subtraction and the MS and F ratio in the normal way.

Table 8.14 Step 2 in predicting exam score, reading age enters secon

	DF	SS	MS	F	p
Reduction in deviance	1	188.37	188.37	10.88	.009
IQ and RA (Model 2)	9	155.82	17.313		
IQ (Model 1)	10	344.19			

Table 8.15 is the analysis of variance table for step 3. Scale A enters last. Its baseline deviance is the deviance of Model 2, the deviance of the current model is the deviance of Model 3.

Table 8.15 Step 3 in predicting exam scores, Scale A enters last

	DF	SS	MS	F	p
Reduction in deviance	1	17.52	17.52	1.01	.344
IQ and RA & Scale A	8	138.30	17.288		
IQ and RA	9	155.82			

For steps 1 and 2 the F ratios are large and the p value shows them to be significant at the .05 level. For step 3, F is very close to one. As the null hypothesis is that the two MS are estimates of the same variance, i.e. they are equal and so F = 1, it is not surprising that the p value is high and not significant.

Box 8.2 summarises the procedure followed. A general step by step procedure for descriptive stepwise regression is provided in the work sheets as Box 8.5.

Box 8.2 The procedure for stepwise regression (descriptive use)

1. The first predictor to be considered is the one that correlates best with the variable to be predicted, here exam score. This variable is said to enter the equation first. The significance of this simple correlation is assessed in the normal way. If it is significant then step 1 is said to be significant. In this case IQ enters first and this first step is significant at the .05 level.

2. Each of the other predictors is tried in combination with the first variable to enter the equation in turn. IQ with reading age gives the lowest deviance so reading age is the next variable to enter the equation. An analysis of variance table is specially constructed to test the significance of this step. Step 2 is shown to be significant at the .05 level.

3. In the general case this procedure is repeated, adding each predictor left to the current model to find the next variable to enter the equation and then testing the significance of the step. In the example here there were only three predictors so Scale A must enter next. The analysis of variance table constructed for this step showed it not to be significant. We conclude that a model with IQ and reading age accounts for all the important variance in exam scores.

Other procedures for stepwise regression as a descriptive technique

The procedure described in Box 8.2 is to start with the simplest model and add variables. At each step the variable which gives the biggest reduction in deviance is added to those already entered into the equation. This is probably the most commonly used procedure. A similar, but not always exactly equivalent, procedure is to start with the full model (all predictors) and progressively remove variables. The variable removed at each step is the one which has least effect on the deviance of the regression equation. There are other variations on this theme. All can be interpreted in the same way as the more common procedure described here.

Reporting the results of multiple and stepwise regression

The multiple correlation coefficient R can be reported along with the regression equation. Its significance can then be reported along with the analysis of variance summary table. Multiple regression is often a way of summarising a correlation matrix and it is good practice with all the techniques described in this chapter to provide a correlation matrix for all the variables being considered. Similarly, a reader will want to verify that the variables are within the expected range for the population tested so a table of means and standard deviations for the variables should also be included. The multiple regression of exam score on Scale A and IQ might be reported as follows.

Results:-

The regression of recall on Scale A and IQ was computed ($R^2 = .734$) and the regression equation is

exam_score = 10.3 + 0.963 Scale_A + 0.505 IQ

R is significant at the .05 level (see Table 8.6 above for the analysis of variance summary table). The correlation matrix describing the correlations between exam score, Scale A, IQ and reading age are given as Table 8.1 (above) and Table 8.16 includes the means and standard deviations for each of these three variables.

Table 8.16   Descriptive data for exam scores, Scale A and IQ

Variable	Mean	Standard deviation
Exam score	71.25	8.71
Scale A	10.25	4.27
IQ	101.17	8.45
Reading age (months)	102.83	3.64

In the case of stepwise regression for statistical control the result is the partial correlation. That should be reported and described along with the correlation between predicted and predictor variables for comparison. It is probably most straightforward to quote the squared partial correlation as this can be determined directly from the stepwise regression. If the sign of the partial correlation is critical then the formula given in the summary for computing a partial correlation from the correlation matrix should be used.

To demonstrate the significance (or otherwise) of the partial correlations give the analysis of variance summary table for the stepwise regression. The experiment looking at the effect of age on recall could be reported as follows.

Results:-

The correlation matrix including the correlations between the three variables is given as Table 8.7 (above). There is a high correlation between recall and age but also a moderate positive correlation between age and time taken to learn the list. To statistically control for this possible confounding variable the squared partial correlation between recall and age, controlling for time spent learning the list, was computed. It is .97. This very high correlation is higher than the correlation between recall and age when time spent learning the list is not statistically controlled ($r^2 = .76$). The significance of the partial correlation was assessed by stepwise regression. The analysis of variance table for this is given as Table 8.9 (above). This shows that the partial correlation is significant at the .05 level. Table 8.17 gives the mean and standard deviation of each of these three variables.

Table 8.17 Descriptive data for the recall experiment

Variable	Mean	Standard deviation
Recall	24.6	3.37
Age (months)	67.5	7.25
Time to learn list (mins.)	16.0	5.70

When reporting a descriptive stepwise regression a correlation matrix and table of means should also be reported. The 'result' in this case is the order in which the variables enter the equation and whether the step in which they entered is significant. One could provide a complete analysis of variance table for each step or just the F ratio, degrees of freedom and significance. The latter option is illustrated below for the exam scores example.

Results:-

The correlation matrix describing the correlations between exam score, Scale A, IQ and reading age are given as Table 8.1. All four variables are intercorrelated and exam score correlates highly with the other three variables. A descriptive stepwise regression was performed to determine the relative predictive power of these variables to predict exam score when used in combination. The first variable to enter was IQ ($F(1,10) = 14.24$, $p < .05$). The next variable to enter was reading age ($F(1,9) = 10.88$, $p < .05$). Scale A entered last. This step was not significant ($F(1,8) = 1.01$, n.s.). Table 8.16 gives the mean and standard deviation of each of these variables.

Notice the convention used to report an F ratio. For example, '($F(1,8) = 1.01$, n.s.)' summarises Table 8.15. The degrees of freedom for the two mean squares are given in brackets, '$F(1,8) =$'. The significance of F is either 'p <.05', meaning significant at the .05 level, or as here 'n.s.', meaning non significant.

Summary

1. Multiple regression is an extension of simple regression. One variable is predicted from more than one predictor. The regression equation is the linear combination of predictors giving the least deviance ('linear combination' means multiplying by constants and then adding as in a linear equation).

2. Different combinations of predictor variables in multiple regression can be thought of as different models to be fitted to the data and the deviance of the equation as the 'error' of the model. Stepwise regression involves the progressive addition of terms to a model.

3. Stepwise regression can be used to statistically control one or more nuisance variables. Here the procedure is to use the regression equation containing the nuisance variable(s) as the baseline deviance rather than the deviance from the mean. The reduction in deviance when the other predictors are added to this baseline model shows how much variance is left to explain when the variance attributable to the nuisance variable(s) has been removed. With one predictor and one nuisance variable this is known as partial correlation.

4. A partial correlation can also be computed from a correlation matrix using the following formula

$$r_{xy.z} = \frac{r_{xy} - r_{zx} r_{zy}}{\sqrt{(1 - r_{zx}^2)(1 - r_{zy}^2)}}$$

where $r_{xy.z}$ is the partial correlation. This gives the correlation between x and y after partialling out the effect of the nuisance variable z. r_{xy} is the correlation between x and y, r_{zx} is the correlation between z and x, and r_{zy} is the correlation between z and y.

5. Stepwise regression can be used to describe how a set of intercorrelated predictor variables relate to one another in the prediction of some other variable. This descriptive technique is most usually structured as follows.

(a) The predictor with the best correlation with the predicted variable enters the equation first.

(b) The predictor which, in combination with the first predictor, gives the least deviance is the second predictor to enter the equation.

(c) The predictor which, in combination with the first and second predictors, gives the least deviance is the third predictor to enter the equation.

(d) and so on.

This is repeated until all the predictor variables are in the equation. The order in which the predictors enter the equation gives an indication of their importance, when used in combination to predict the predicted variable.

6. An analysis of variance table can be constructed to test the significance of r, R or a step in stepwise regression.

(a) In each case there is a current model to be evaluated with respect to a baseline model. For r and R the current model is the regression equation and the baseline the deviance of the mean (Model 0). For stepwise regression the current model is the regression equation after the step has been taken and the baseline model is the regression equation before the step was taken.

(b) The change in deviance in moving from the baseline model to the current model is computed and compared with the deviance of the current model in an F ratio. To do this MS (Mean Squares) are computed by dividing the deviances by their degrees of freedom.

(c) The null hypothesis is that the MS for the change in deviance and the MS for the deviance of the current model are independent estimates of the same random variation and F is only greater than 1 because these estimates are approximate.

(d) By making certain assumptions, statisticians have computed a theoretical distribution for F. Minitab computes the probability of getting an F of the observed size or greater using the F distribution.

(e) If that probability is less than or equal to .05 the change in deviance is said to be significant at the .05 level.

(f) If it is not we are not able to reject the null hypothesis.

The procedures for computing a multiple regression and the two kinds of stepwise regression using Minitab are given in Boxes 8.3, 8.4 and 8.5 in the work sheets.

WORK SHEETS

MINITAB

Minitab commands introduced in this chapter: cdf to compute p for an F ratio.

Some data

The data on recall and age described above are presented in Appendix B, Table B.4, and will probably have been saved in a file. Retrieve this file and examine the data using the info, print, desc and corr commands

```
info
print c1 - c4
desc c1 - c4
corr c1 - c4
```

Looking at the correlation matrix we see that these four variables are all inter-correlated. Age is by far the best predictor of recall. Start off by computing the regression equation for predicting recall from age

```
regress 'recall' 1 'age'
```

The equation is

$$\text{recall} = -.2.83 + .406 \, \text{age} \qquad \text{and} \quad r^2 = .762$$

Testing

Remind yourself how to use the regress command by computing the regression equation and r^2 for predicting recall from time and then for predicting recall from IQ.

Regression with more than one predictor

Each of the three predictors has now been used in turn. The command below predicts recall from age and time

```
regress 'recall' 2 'age' 'time'
```

The equation is

$$\text{recall} = -6.09 + .528 \, \text{age} - .309 \, \text{time} \qquad R^2 = .966$$

Notice R is used rather than r for multiple regression, though Minitab always gives it as R. By using two predictors instead of one we can account for 97% of the variance instead of 76% with age only.

Box 8.3 describes a general procedure for computing a multiple correlation using the regress command. Work through the example given. The data should have been saved when you used them in Chapter 5 (Box 5.6).

Box 8.3 Step by step procedure for determining a multiple correlation and whether it is significant using the regress command

Step 1—Tabulate the data with one row for each subject and one column for each score obtained (you will probably have already done this). Decide which variable is to be predicted from which others, i.e. which is the 'dependent' variable.

> e.g. as for Box 5.6. Fifteen subjects are assessed using three tests. Test 1 scores are to be predicted from Test 2 and Test 3 (the regression of Test 1 on Test 2 and Test 3).

	Test 1	Test 2	Test 3
S1	118	194	122
.	.	.	.
.	.	.	.
.	.	.	.
S15	23	168	87

Step 2—Enter the data into Minitab using the read command.

> e.g.

name c1 'Test 1' c2 'Test 2' c3 'Test 3'
read 'Test 1' 'Test 2' 'Test 3'
118 194 122
70 152 116
.
.
.
23 168 87
end

Step 3—Check the data with the print command and correct any mistakes using let (see Chapter 2).

> e.g.

print 'Test 1' 'Test 2' 'Test 3'

Step 4—Use the regress (regr) command to compute R^2. The single predicted or 'dependent' variable is given first. Then the number of predictor variables and then a list of those variables.

e.g.

Test 1 scores are to be predicted from Test 2 and Test 3. So, Test 1 is specified first
then '2' and then the predictors Test 2 and Test 3.

regr 'Test 1' 2 'Test 2' 'Test 3'

The results will be as follows. To help you find them here, R^2 and the p value are
printed in bold

```
The regression equation is
Test 1 = 53.7 + 0.579 Test 2 - 0.643 Test 3

Predictor          Coef         Stdev      t-ratio          p
Constant          53.74         29.05         1.85      0.089
Test 2           0.5789        0.1761         3.29      0.007
Test 3          -0.6425        0.2984        -2.15      0.052
```

s = 27.35   R-sq = **48.4%**   R-sq(adj) = 39.8%

```
Analysis of Variance

SOURCE            DF           SS          MS         F          P
Regression         2       8429.1      4214.5      5.63      0.019
Error             12       8978.5       748.2
Total             14      17407.6

SOURCE            DF       SEQ SS
Test 2             1       4961.0
Test 3             1       3468.1

Unusual Observations
Obs. Test 2 Test 1      Fit Stdev.Fit  Residual St.Resid
  9     167 147.00   126.64      21.50     20.36     1.20 X
 15     168  23.00    95.09      12.03    -72.09    -2.93R
```

R denotes an obs. with a large st. resid.

X denotes an obs. whose X value gives it large
influence.

Step 5—Extract R^2 and the p value from the resulting display. The correlation is significant at the .05 level if p is less than .05.
    e.g.

$R^2 = .484$, p = .019, the correlation is significant at the .05 level

Testing

Retrieve the data on recall and age again. Obtain the regression equation and R^2 for predicting recall from age and IQ that is the regression of recall on age and IQ (R^2 should be .762). Obtain the regression equation and R^2 for predicting recall from age, time and IQ (the regression of recall on age time and IQ). R^2 should be .979.

Significance of F from the cdf command

When doing stepwise regression we shall have to compute our own analysis of variance tables and F ratios. The significance of these F ratios is determined using the cdf command. To illustrate this we will use cdf to recompute the p value given in Table 8.5.

The cdf command was used to compute p values for the binomial test in Chapter 5. The same command is used to compute the p value for an F ratio except that we have to specify that the F distribution is to be used rather than the binomial distribution. The F value to be assessed and the degrees of freedom of the two mean squares which are divided into one another to make the F ratio also have to be specified. In Table 8.5 these figures are 13.59, 1 and 10 respectively. Find these numbers in Table 8.5 before going any further. The Minitab command required is

> **cdf 13.59 ;**
>
> **f 1 10 .**

f is the type of distribution, 1 and 10 are the degrees of freedom of the greater and lesser MS in the F ratio. Minitab gives a result of the form

> 13.5900   0.9958

meaning the probability of getting an F of 13.5900 or less is .9958. This probability has to be subtracted from 1.000 to get the p value. This is because the p value is the probability of getting an F greater than 13.5900. 1.000 − .9958 = .0042 which is a more precise form of the value given in Table 8.5 (.004).

Stepwise regression—statistical control

Box 8.4 describes a general procedure for stepwise regression for statistical control. The example is that used in the Introduction of evaluating the correlation between age and recall while partialling out the nuisance variable time to learn the list. These data are presented as Appendix B, Table B.4. Work through the example following all the instructions. Refer back to the Introduction if you are unclear about any of the steps taken.

Box 8.4   Step by step procedure for stepwise regression (statistical control)

Step 1—Tabulate the data with one row for each subject and one column for each score obtained. Enter the data, check it and correct any mistakes (see Box 8.3 for details).

Step 2—Decide which are the predicted, predictor and nuisance variables. The predicted (dependent) variable is the one that could alternatively be predicted by the predictor or the nuisance variable. The analysis is to determine whether the predictor still has predictive power when the nuisance variable is statistically controlled.

e.g.

Recall could be predicted by age or by time to learn the list. We wish to see whether recall can be predicted from age when time to learn the list is statistically controlled. Recall is the predicted (dependent) variable, age is the predictor and time the nuisance variable.

Step 3—Draw up a blank analysis of variance table to be filled in as the computation proceeds. Write the headings d.f., SS, MS, F and p. The rows should be headed as follows. The first as 'Reduction in deviance', the second as nuisance & predictor and the last as nuisance alone.

e.g.

	DF	SS	MS	F	p
Reduction in deviance	...	...	...	...	...
Time & Age	...	...	...		
Time	...	...			

Step 4—Use the regress command to compute the baseline deviance that is the regression of the predicted variable on the nuisance variable. The predicted variable is specified first, then '1' then the nuisance variable.

e.g.

regr 'Recall' 1 'Time'

The results will be as follows

```
The regression equation is
Recall = 24.2 + 0.027 Time

Predictor          Coef          Stdev       t-ratio           p
Constant         24.162          3.532          6.84       0.000
Time             0.0274         0.2091          0.13       0.899

s = 3.574          R-sq = 0.2%          R-sq(adj) = 0.0%

Analysis of Variance

SOURCE             DF            SS            MS          F           p
Regression          1          0.22          0.22        0.02       0.899
Error               8        102.18         12.77
Total               9        102.40
```

Step 5—Write the 'Error SS' from this computation and its d.f. into the bottom row of the blank analysis of variance table.

e.g.

	DF	SS	MS	F	p
Reduction in deviance	...	...	...	...	...
Time & Age	...	...	...		
Time	8	102.18			

Step 6—Use the regress command to compute the deviance for the full model, that is the regression of the predicted variable on the nuisance and predictor variables. The predicted variable is specified first, then '2' then the nuisance and predictor variables.

e.g.

regr 'Recall' 2 'Time' 'Age'

The display will be as follows

```
The regression equation is

Recall = - 6.09 - 0.309 Time + 0.528 Age

Predictor        Coef        Stdev      t-ratio          p

Constant       -6.094        2.266       -2.69      0.031

Time          -0.30890      0.04784      -6.46      0.000

Age            0.52795      0.03761      14.04      0.000

s = 0.7076      R-sq = 96.6%      R-sq(adj) = 95.6%

Analysis of Variance

SOURCE          DF          SS         MS          F          p

Regression       2       98.895     49.447     98.74      0.000

Error            7        3.505      0.501

Total            9      102.400

SOURCE          DF      SEQ SS

Time             1        0.219

Age              1       98.675
```

Step 7—Write the 'Error SS', MS and its d.f. into the middle row of the blank analysis of variance table.

e.g.

	DF	SS	MS	F	p
Reduction in deviance	...	...	...	...	...
Time & Age	7	3.505	.501		
Time	8	102.18			

Step 8—Complete the analysis of variance table. d.f. and SS for the reduction in deviance are obtained by subtraction. MS is obtained by dividing SS by d.f.. F is obtained by dividing the MS for the reduction in deviance by the MS for the full model.

e.g.

$102.18 - 3.505 = 98.675$

$8 - 7 = 1$

$98.675 / .501 = 197.0$

	DF	SS	MS	F	p
Reduction in deviance	1	98.675	98.675	197.0	...
Time & Age	7	3.505	.501		
Time	8	102.18			

Step 9—Use the cdf command to compute a p value for F. The subcommand specifies 'f' and the degrees of freedom for the two mean squares. The degrees of freedom for the reduction in deviance are given first. The probability given by Minitab must be subtracted from 1.000 to get the p value.

e.g.

cdf 197.0;

f 1 7.

gives

```
197.0700      1.0000
```

The p value is written 'p < .0001' not 'p = 0' as the probability is really less than one but rounded to 1.0000 by Minitab.

Step 10—Copy the p value into the analysis of variance table and compute the squared partial correlation. This is the reduction in deviance (SS) divided by the deviance (SS) of the baseline model (nuisance alone).

e.g.

Squared partial correlation (recall with age statistically controlling time to learn the list) = 98.675/102.18 = .97

Step 11—If the p value is less than .05 then the correlation between the predicted and predictor variables is significant at the .05 level even when the nuisance variable is statistically controlled.

e.g.

p < .0001 so this partial correlation is significant at the .05 level.

Stepwise regression—descriptive use

Box 8.5 describes a general procedure for descriptive stepwise regression. The example is that of predicting exam scores used in the Introduction. These data were presented in Chapter 5 as Table 5.2. You will have saved them at that point. Work through the example following all the instructions. Refer back to the Introduction if you are unclear about any of the steps taken.

Box 8.5   Step by step procedure for stepwise regression (descriptive use)

Note: Because it is necessary to refer to 'steps' in the stepwise regression the steps in the step by step procedure will be referred to as stages.

Stage 1—Tabulate the data with one row for each subject and one column for each score obtained. Enter the data, check it and correct any mistakes (see Box 8.3 for details).

Stage 2—Decide which is the predicted or dependent variable. The rest are predictors.

e.g.

Exam score is to be predicted by Scale A, IQ and Reading Age (RA).

Stage 3—Use the corr command to compute a correlations matrix for all the variables. The predictor with the highest correlation with the predicted variable enters the equation first. Write it down.

e.g.

IQ is the first variable to enter the equation.

Stage 4—Use the regress command to compute the simple regression of the predicted variable on the first variable to enter the equation.

e.g.

regr 'exam' 1 'IQ'

Stage 5—On a separate piece of paper construct two blank tables which you will fill in as the analysis progresses. The 'Models Table' has the headings:

Model, d.f., Deviance, and MS. The 'Steps Table' has the headings: Step, Deviance reduced, d.f.1, d.f.2, F, p, sig.

Fill in the first two rows of the Models Table. The first row is for Model 0, no predictors. Its deviance is the Total SS in the analysis of variance table produced in Stage 4 (and all of the regression analyses where exam is the predicted variable). Copy down its d.f.. We shall not need its MS. The second row is for Model 1, the first predictor to enter the equation. Copy down the Error SS, its d.f. and MS from the analysis of variance table produced in Stage 4.

Fill in the first row of the Steps Table. This is for Step 1, Model 0 to Model 1. The reduction in deviance, F and p can be copied from the row headed 'Regression' in the analysis of variance table produced in Stage 4. d.f.1 is 1 and d.f.2 the d.f. for the deviance of Model 1 (Models Table).

e.g.

Models Table

Model	d.f.	Deviance	MS
0 (no predictors)	11	834.25	-
1 (IQ)	10	344.19	34.42
2 ...	...	...	...
3 ...	...	...	...

Steps Table

Step	Dev. Red.	d.f.1	d.f.2	F	p	sig.
1 (0 to 1)	490.06	1	10	14.24	.004	<.05
2 (1 to 2)	...	1	...	...	...	...
3 (2 to 3)	...	1	...	...	...	...

Stage 6— Compute a multiple regression for the first variable to enter the equation in combination with each of the other predictors in turn. Write down the 'Error' SS for each regression analysis.

e.g.

regr 'exam' 2 'IQ' 'Scale A'

regr 'exam' 2 'IQ' 'RA'

For IQ and Scale A the deviance (Error SS) = 222.21

For IQ and RA the deviance (Error SS) = 155.82

Stage 7—The second variable to enter the equation is the predictor which, in combination with the first variable to enter the equation, gives the lowest deviance. Complete the next line in the Models Table by copying in the Error SS, d.f. and MS from the appropriate regression analysis computed in Stage 6.

e.g.

Models Table

Model	d.f.	Deviance	MS
0 (no predictors)	11	834.25	-
1 (IQ)	10	344.19	34.419
2 (IQ & RA)	9	155.82	17.31
3 ...	...	...	...

Stage 8—Draw up an analysis of variance table to compute the significance of this step from Model 1 to Model 2. Write the headings d.f., SS, MS, F and p. The rows should be headed: (i) 'Reduction in deviance', (ii) 'Current model' and (iii) 'Baseline'. The baseline d.f. and SS are the deviance and d.f. of Model 1 (Models Table). The current model, d.f., SS and MS are those for Model 2. The reduction in deviance d.f. and SS are computed by subtraction, the MS is the same as the SS. F is the reduction in deviance MS divided by the current model MS.

e.g.

	d.f	SS	MS	F	p
Reduction in deviance	1	188.37	188.37	10.88	...
Current model (IQ & RA)	9	155.82	17.31		
Baseline (IQ)	10	344.19			

Stage 9—Use the cdf command to compute a p value for F. The sub-command specifies 'f' and the degrees of freedom for the two mean squares. The degrees of freedom for the reduction in deviance (1) are given first. The probability given by Minitab must be subtracted from 1.000 to get the p value.

e.g.

cdf 10.88;

f 1 9.

gives

10.8800   0.9907

p = 1.0000 − 0.9907 = .0093.

Stage 10—Complete the next row in the Steps Table (Step 2, Model 1 to Model 2) by adding the reduction in deviance, d.f.2, F and p computed in Stages 8 and 9.

e.g.

Steps Table

Step	Dev. Red.	d.f.1	d.f.2	F	p	sig.
1 (0 to 1)	490.06	1	10	14.24	.004	<.05
2 (1 to 2)	188.37	1	9	10.88	.009	<.05
3 (2 to 3)	...	1	...	...	...	...

Stage 11—Repeat Stages 6 to 10 until all the predictors are used up. The third variable to enter the equation (Model 3) is the predictor which in combination with all the predictors already entered gives the lowest deviance. The deviance etc. for Model 3 is added to the Models Table and an analysis of variance table constructed for Step 3 (Model 2 to Model 3). The values from this is added to the Steps Table.

The procedure can either be repeated until all the variables are used up or until a step proves to be non-significant.

e.g.

When IQ and RA have entered the equation there is only Scale A left so it enters last.

Models Table

Model	d.f.	Deviance	MS
0 (no predictors)	11	834.25	-
1 (IQ)	10	344.19	34.419
2 (IQ & RA)	9	155.82	17.313
3 (IQ & RA & Scale A)	8	138.30	17.288

Steps Table

Step	Dev. Red.	d.f.1	d.f.2	F	p	sig.
1 (0 to 1)	490.06	1	10	14.24	.004	<.05
2 (1 to 2)	188.37	1	9	10.88	.009	<.05
3 (2 to 3)	17.52	1	8	1.01	.344	n.s.

Stage 12—Summarise your findings.

e.g.

The order in which the predictors enter the equation is IQ Reading Age then Scale A. The last step is not significant at the .05 level.

ASSIGNMENT

1. Retrieve the data on pronunciation accuracy and so on first used in Chapter 4, Assignment 2 (Appendix B, Table B.1). Compute the multiple regression of BAS (British Ability Scale) onto Ravens (score on Raven's Matrices test) and BPVS (British Picture Vocabulary Scale).

(a) What is the regression equation?

(b) What is R^2?

(c) What is the F ratio for computing the significance of this R^2?

(d) What is the p value for this R^2 as computed by cdf (four figures after the decimal point)?

(e) Is R^2 significant at the .05 level?

2. The data below were obtained from an experiment looking at the relationship between rate at which people speak (in words per minute), confidence (this is the self rated confidence they have in their ability to communicate the material they have been asked to talk about) and extraversion as measured by a personality test. The subjects were all children between the age of 11 and 12.

Subject	Speech rate	Confidence	Extraversion
1	90	65	101
2	106	75	114
3	88	68	91
4	98	74	94
5	80	66	76
6	103	76	122
7	103	75	92
8	142	77	147
9	103	76	121
10	113	74	96
11	144	76	122
12	134	76	106
13	131	77	118
14	149	78	112
15	147	80	141
16	128	79	109
17	131	77	81
18	131	74	102
19	144	77	121
20	131	78	106

You are advised to name the Minitab columns containing these data and save it as soon as you have checked for typing errors.

(a) Describe these data in terms of means, medians and some measure of dispersion.

(b) Describe the relationships between these variables (how they correlate one with another).

(c) Speech rate is the dependent variable, that is the variable we are trying to predict. Use stepwise regression to describe how confidence and extraversion affect this dependent variable.

(d) Now assume that extraversion is a nuisance variable in this experiment. What is the partial correlation between speech rate and confidence when we take out the effect of extraversion? Give the complete analysis of variance table for evaluating the significance of this partial correlation.

Notes: This is a realistic (and quite advanced) statistics problem. Only general questions are asked and the precise procedure is not specified. The answer to each of these requests to 'describe...' will be: a table of results, significance tests such as analysis of variance summary tables where appropriate, and one or two lines of explanation and conclusion.

SUMMARY OF DCL COMMANDS

See end of Chapter 5

SUMMARY OF MSDOS COMMANDS

See end of Chapter 5

SUMMARY OF MINITAB COMMANDS

set   (indicate you have come to the end of the data with end)

read (ditto)	**erase**
print	**save** 'name'
let	**retrieve (retr)** 'name'
describe (desc)	**outfile** 'name'
mean	**nooutfile**
stdev	
sum regress (regr)	
table (e.g. **regr c1 1 c2**)	
histogram (hist)	**correlation (corr)**
stem-and-leaf	
boxplots	
plot	
name	
info	

cdf value ; **binomial** N .5 .	(value is the number of subjects in the smaller category, N is the total number of subjects. The p value is obtained by doubling the probability obtained.)
cdf value; **f** df1 df2 .	(value is the F ratio to be assessed. df1 is the d.f. for the reduction in deviance, df2 is the d.f. for the other MS. The p value is obtained by subtracting the probability obtained from 1.000)
twot c1 c2	(between subjects t-test, c1 gives data, c2 specifies the group)
twos c1 c2	(ditto, c1 gives data for group 1, c2 data for group 2)
mann c1 c2	(Mann–Whitney U test, data as for twos. p value specified as 'is significant at'. The mean rank for c1 is W/n_1, the mean rank for c2 is $(N(N+1)/2 - W)/n_2$; where n_1 is the number of subjects in c1, n_2 the number in c2 and $N=n_1+n_2$. Alternatively use the command **mann** c2 c1, the mean rank for c2 is then W/n_2)

ttest c1	(within subjects t-test on difference scores)
wtest c1	(Wilcoxon matched-pairs signed-ranks test on difference scores)
chisq c1 c2	(chi squared test for 2 by 2 contingency table. Critical value 3.84)

help commands

stop

CHAPTER 9

PUTTING IT ALL TOGETHER: ANALYSIS OF COVARIANCE

Statistical concepts introduced in this chapter: Comparing means in a regression analysis, analysis of covariance.

INTRODUCTION

The problem and some data

At first sight, the techniques described in Chapter 6 for comparing means and the techniques described in Chapters 4, 5 and 8 for describing the relationships between variables have little in common. This chapter demonstrates how the comparison of means can be thought of as a problem in regression and how one can use a form of stepwise regression, known as the analysis of covariance, to statistically control nuisance variables when comparing means.

Consider an experiment designed to examine the effect of pre-school playgroups on the behaviour of children. Twelve children are selected. Six are randomly chosen to attend a pre-school playgroup, the other six do not. The independent variable then is group. It takes the levels attending playgroup and not attending playgroup. At around the age of five they all go to the same school where, after a two month interval, their behaviour is studied. The dependent variable is a rating made by a teacher for 'social adjustment'.

Table 9.1 gives these social adjustment scores for each of the twelve children and their ages when the rating was made. The mean social adjustment rating, and mean age when rated, are given in Table 9.2 for the two groups. The group attending playgroup get higher ratings than the group who do not but they also tend to be older. This sampling bias is a problem when interpreting the rating data. The difference between the two groups could be due to this difference in age rather than the effect of the manipulation. Analysis of covariance can be used to control, statistically, the effect of age when testing the significance of the difference in mean rating for the two groups.

Table 9.1 Data from pre-school playgroup experiment, Group P attended playgroup, Group C did not

Subject No.	Group	Social adjustment	Age (months)	Group (for regression)
1	C	21	57	0
3	C	23	58	0
5	C	18	61	0
7	C	17	53	0
9	C	15	50	0
11	C	24	55	0
2	P	25	65	1
4	P	26	67	1
6	P	24	69	1
8	P	29	73	1
10	P	23	62	1
12	P	28	63	1

Table 9.2 Mean social adjustment rating and age in months for the groups attending and not attending playgroup (standard deviation in brackets)

	Soc. Adj.		Age		N
Control	19.67	(3.56)	55.67	(3.88)	6
Play group	25.83	(2.32)	66.50	(4.09)	6

Comparing means in a regression analysis

To look at the relationship between the two continuous variables, social adjustment and age, we would use linear regression. The dependent or predicted variable is social adjustment rating and the model fitted (predictor) is age in months. The regression of social adjustment on age is

predicted_social_adjustment = −7.65 + .498 months

This regression has an r^2 of .62 and is significant at the .05 level (see analysis of variance table in Table 9.3).

Table 9.3 Analysis of variance summary table for regression between social adjustment and age

	DF	SS	MS	F	p
Reduction in deviance	1	126.52	126.52	16.28	.002
Months	10	77.73	7.77		
Model 0 (deviance of mean)	11	204.25			

We can use exactly the same calculation to compare two groups of subjects if the independent variable is viewed as a predictor where one level is coded as 0 and the other as 1. The last column in Table 9.1 gives this model or predictor to be fitted to the social adjustment scores. Each child in the group not attending playgroup has a 0 in this column, each child in the group attending playgroup has a 1. Fitting this model gives the regression equation

predicted_social_adjustment = 19.667 + 6.167 group

What the regression analysis does is to fit the group mean as the predicted score for each subject. This becomes apparent if the value of the variable recall (0 or 1) is substituted into the equation. For each of the children who did not go to playgroup, group = 0, and so

predicted_social_adjustment = 19.667 + 6.167 × 0 = 19.667

For each of the children who did go to playgroup, group = 1, and so

predicted_social_adjustment = 19.667 + 6.167 × 1 = 25.833

Comparison of these predictions with the means in Table 9.2 shows that the best fitting regression equation for this predictor takes the mean value of whatever group the child was in as its prediction of social adjustment.

The 'slope' for the predictor group is 6.167. This is the difference between the two means. The analysis of variance summary table for the regression evaluates the significance of this difference. This is given in Table 9.4. There is a large F ratio and the p value is considerably less than .05.

Table 9.4   Analysis of variance for comparing means, social adjustment for two groups

	DF	SS	MS	F	p
Reduction in deviance	1	114.08	114.08	12.65	.005
Group	10	90.17	9.02		
Model 0 (deviance of mean)	11	204.25			

The rationale behind this calculation is as follows. Model 0 (deviance of the mean) can be thought of as the 'total' variance. This is divided into the variance left when the individual group means are fitted (Groups deviance) and the reduction in deviance. The former is the error variance which our null hypothesis says gave rise to the difference in means. The latter is the difference in the means represented as variance. Thus the reduction in deviance can be evaluated against the groups deviance to give an F ratio that tests the significance of the difference between means.

Any data which can be evaluated with a between-subjects t-test can be similarly analysed as a regression of the dependent variable onto the independent variable coded as 0 for one group and 1 for the other. In fact the two tests are mathematically equivalent. t is the square root of F. There is also a statistical test called the 'Analysis of Variance' which is used to assess the significance of differences between means through the computation of an F ratio. This test is normally reserved for experimental designs, beyond the scope of this book, where the independent variable has more than two levels, e.g. the comparison of three groups of subjects. t-tests cannot be used to analyse such experiments.

So, when the independent variable has two levels as in our example, one could ask Minitab to compute a t-test, an analysis of variance or a regression. In each case one would be doing essentially the same computation and all three would give the same p value. Regression and the analysis of variance would give the same analysis of variance summary table, although the labels used would be different. The F ratio given in these two tables would be the square of the t value computed in the t-test.

Analysis of covariance

The possibility of evaluating a difference between means using regression is of more theoretical than practical interest, unless there is a nuisance variable that needs to be statistically controlled. This is the purpose of the analysis of co-variance. The nuisance variable is described as a covariate. The data in Table 9.1 can be analysed in this way.

To reiterate, the mean age in months of the experimental group is 66.5 while the mean age of the control group is 55.67. This is unfortunate because there is a correlation between age and social adjustment such that older children have higher social adjustment scores. There is thus the possibility that the difference in social adjustment arises, not from the training procedure, but rather from bias in the sampling of the two groups. Age is said to be a nuisance variable, or covariate, confounded with group. When considering statistical control by stepwise regression (or partial correlation) a similar problem was outlined. The solution was to compute a new baseline deviance using the nuisance variable and then add the predictor variable to the equation. The reduction in deviance achieved in this step represents the predictive power of the predictor variable when the nuisance variable is statistically controlled.

In the case of the data from Table 9.1 we can use the same procedure. The new baseline deviance is again the deviance for the nuisance variable, in this case age. The independent variable group (coded as 0 or 1) is then added to that equation. The reduction in deviance achieved represents the effect of group on social adjustment when age is statistically controlled. Table 9.5 shows how this can be tabulated.

The reduction in deviance is computed in the normal way by subtraction. The resulting MS is smaller than the MS for the deviance of the current model (months and group) and so the F ratio is less than 1 and cannot be significant. We conclude that statistically controlling age completely nullifies the significant effect of group demonstrated as evaluated in Table 9.4.

Table 9.5 Analysis of covariance, social adjustment with age statistically controlled

Source	DF	SS	MS	F	p
Reduction in deviance	1	5.81	5.81	< 1	n.s
Months and group	9	71.92	7.99		
Months	10	77.73			

It is instructive to look at the regression equation for this regression. It is

predicted_social_adjustment = 0.8 + 0.339 months + 2.49 group

2.49 can be thought of as the 'corrected' difference between the two groups. The original difference of 6.167 has been reduced to 2.49 by adding months to the equation. This is because the mean age differs for the two groups. Substituting these means into the regression equation it can be seen that we are still predicting the original mean observed social adjustment ratings of 19.67 and 25.83 but the difference now arises mainly from the component due to age.

For the group not attending playgroup, Group = 0, and the mean age is 55.67 so the predicted social adjustment rating is

.8 + 0.339 × 55.67 + 2.49 × 0 = .8 + 18.87 = 19.67

For the group attending playgroup, Group = 1, and the mean age is 66.50 so the predicted social adjustment rating is

.8 + 0.339 × 66.50 + 2.49 × 1 = .8 + 22.54 + 2.49 = 25.83

This procedure can be generalised to situations where there is more than one nuisance variable. In these cases the baseline deviance is the deviance of the regression on all the nuisance variables. The current model is to add group to the baseline model. Of course statistical control must always be viewed as a poor second best to proper experimental control. A sampling bias of the kind found in the example above is the result of poor experimental control. There would have to be strong practical reasons for not repeating the experiment to verify the conclusion drawn by our analysis.

Reporting an analysis of covariance

Previous sections describing how to report the results of statistical tests have suggested that the result of the experiment should be reported before the statistical test used to assess it. The same is true here, though the 'result' has a number of components. First there is the mean scores for the dependent variable, in the example used here the mean social adjustment rating for each of the two groups. These means and the results of a t-test evaluating the difference between them should be reported. However, the reason for doing an analysis of covariance is that one suspects these means because there is a correlation between the dependent and nuisance variables and so this correlation is also a part of the result. The mean scores for the nuisance variable are also relevant to the argument. Finally, the analysis of variance summary table for the analysis of covariance should be reported in full.

Results:-

The mean social adjustment rating and age for each group are included in Table 9.2. Children attending playgroup tend to get higher ratings. This difference is significant at the .05 level ($t = 3.56$, p (two tailed) $< .05$). However, there is a positive correlation between the age of the child and its social adjustment rating ($r = .79$) and children attending playgroup tend to be older. This possible confounding factor was statistically controlled in an analysis of covariance, the analysis of variance summary table for which is given as Table 9.5. The dependent variable is social adjustment rating and the covariate or nuisance variable is age. Group is the independent variable. F is not significant at the .05 level. Controlling for age nullifies the apparent difference between groups.

Comparing means with a correlation coefficient

The above sections show how regression can be used to evaluate a difference between means as well as the correlation between two continuous variables. If regression can be generalised in this way what about the correlation coefficient r? The answer is 'yes', though the statistic, the *point biserial correlation,* is very rarely used.

A point biserial correlation is computed by coding group as 0 or 1 and then correlating those values with some continuous variable. Two point biserial correlations can be computed from Table 9.1. The first is computed by correlating the social adjustment ratings with the last column of 0s and 1s. It is .75. This describes the strength of the difference in social adjustment rating for the two groups when evaluated against the within-groups error variance. The second describes the difference in age for the two groups in the same way and is computed by correlating age with the last column of 0s and 1s. This is .83, an equally strong effect. The significance of a point biserial correlation can be established by using Table A.1 or by compiling an analysis of variance table and F ratio in the normal way.

Note that to compute a point biserial correlation one correlates the dependent variable (e.g., social adjustment) with the independent variable (e.g., group) coded as 0s and 1s. Groups 1 and 2 must NOT be coded as 1 and 2. This would be to fit a quite different model.

Analyses with several continuous and nominal variables

Suppose you have some data where each subject provides scores on a number of variables and, in addition, is classified according to several different dichotomies. As an example, consider the sort of data someone answering Question 3 of the assignment for Chapter 6 might have collected. Each subject has a score on the verbal reasoning and the spatial manipulation tests. They are also classified as to whether they were male or female, over or under 21, and whether they were studying an arts (B.A.) or science (B.Sc.) degree. As an initial way of describing these data it would have been quite reasonable to code the dichotomies as 0s and

1s and to compute a correlation matrix showing the association between these five variables. Table 9.6 illustrates what such a correlation matrix might look like.

Table 9.6 A correlation matrix with continuous and discontinuous variables

	Verbal Res.	Spat. Man.	Sex	Over 21
Spat. Man	.32			
Sex	.21	−.35		
Over 21	.11	.09	.07	
Degree	−.45	.38	−.58	.13

The correlation between verbal reasoning and spatial manipulation is easy to interpret as a normal correlation between continuous variables. People who do well on one test tend also to do well on the other. There are also six point biserial correlations. For example, sex is positively correlated with verbal reasoning but negatively correlated with spatial manipulation. This reflects the fact that males do better than females on spatial tasks but worse on verbal tasks. Finally, there are three correlations between nominal variables. These give an indication of how independent the classifications were. Thus sex and degree are not independent dichotomies. The association is negative reflecting the fact that males tend to do B.Sc. degrees and females B.A. degrees. One should not be tempted to evaluate the significance of such a correlation.

While this is a very reasonable way of initially exploring a set of data it would be very unconventional to include such an analysis in a report of the experimental results. Few people use point biserial correlations and r computed on two dichotomies does not have a proper statistical basis. People unfamiliar with the regression approach taken in this book would find these results difficult to understand.

Associations between dichotomies should be presented as contingency tables and evaluated by chi squared (Chapter 7). An association between a dichotomy and a score should be reported as a difference in means and evaluated by a t-test (Chapter 6). Only associations between continuous variables (scores) are conventionally reported and evaluated as correlation coefficients.

Given this kind of data one might also be tempted to compute some multiple regressions with a mixture of continuous and nominal variables. This is only advisable in the case of analysis of covariance, i.e. with a continuous dependent variable, a continuous nuisance variable (though there may be several of these) and a dichotomy as an independent variable.

Independent variables with more than two levels CANNOT be analysed by coding those levels within a single variable (e.g., it is NOT sensible to code groups 1, 2 and 3 as '1', '2' and '3' or even '−1', '0' and '+1'). To apply the regression approach to the analysis of variance with an independent variable having k levels requires k − 1 predictor variables. Experiments with k greater than 2 are beyond the scope of this book.

Attributing causality

In this chapter we have seen how a difference in means can be viewed as a correlation and that the t-test and linear regression can be computationally equivalent. This equivalence gives the lie to a widely held fallacy, that is, that the nature of the statistical test you use determines whether one can attribute causality to an effect. This is simply not true.

Scientists distinguish between experiments where there is a true experimental manipulation and experiments where no variable is manipulated. In the former case the manipulation can be said to have caused the effect, i.e. causality can be attributed to the manipulation. In the latter case it cannot. An example will make this distinction clearer. Consider two studies of the same drug. It is thought this drug produces drowsiness and reduced alertness. This side effect is to be investigated by measuring reaction time. The first study is an experiment in which two randomly selected groups of volunteers take either the drug or a placebo one hour before they are tested. Table 9.7 summarises the results of this experiment.

Table 9.7   The results of Study 1

	Mean reaction time (seconds)	t	p
Drug group	.57	3.12	.003
Control group	.41		

The drug group are significantly slower. All the subjects were treated in an identical manner, except that half are given the drug, so this effect can reasonably be assumed to be caused by the drug.

The second study (Table 9.8) uses patient groups. All those visiting a particular outpatients clinic have their reaction time tested. Two groups of patients are selected. One group have been receiving the drug for a period of at least 3 years, the other group of patients have never taken it.

Table 9.8   The results of Study 2

	Mean reaction time (seconds)	t	p
Drug group	.84	2.80	.007
Control group	.73		

Again the drug group are significantly slower but this time we cannot conclude that the drug caused the effect. It could be that in selecting the subjects for the two groups we have inadvertently selected them to differ in some other characteristic which is the cause of the difference. Perhaps the patients given this drug tend to be older or more ill.

Behavioural scientists would always prefer to be able to come to a clear conclusion about the cause of some effect. The paradox is that the problems that are easiest to test in rigorous experiments tend not to be of practical importance.

Conversely, the problems of most practical importance are often those that are the least amenable to the experimental method. Returning to the two drug studies, the first is sufficiently well controlled to attribute the cause of the effect to the drug. However, the experiment is probably not very representative of the way the drug will be finally used. The dose is small and administered only once. It would probably not be ethically acceptable to give a powerful drug to volunteers for realistically long periods and at realistic dosages. To turn the second study into a true manipulation it is necessary to select a population who would normally have received the drug and then randomly assign patients either to a group who receive the drug or to another group who are given no treatment. This is probably not ethically acceptable either. There is no easy way round this paradox. All one can do is collect converging evidence from as many different sources as possible. Statistical control (analysis of covariance, and partial correlation) can be aids to interpretation but they depend on identifying and reliably measuring the relevant nuisance variables.

The fallacy referred to above is to assume that whether one can attribute causality depends on the statistical test used. Specifically, it is sometimes falsely assumed that if one is using a test to compare means (a t-test say) then significance indicates that the independent variable causes the effect observed on the dependent variable. If one is evaluating a correlation or a contingency table it is assumed that this is not possible. This is rubbish. The attribution of causality depends on the way the experiment is constructed, i.e. whether there is a true manipulation or not. If the independent variable is formed by selecting amongst a population (e.g., male versus female or introverted versus extraverted) rather than randomly sampling and then treating the subjects in some way, then causality cannot be attributed whatever statistic one computes.

The independence of one's ability to attribute causality from the type of test used can be demonstrated by considering different types of tests and thinking of examples where causality can and cannot be attributed. Thus Tables 9.7 and 9.8 are examples of each of these kinds of conclusion but both rest on comparisons of means. Similarly one could imagine versions of both these experiments where the outcome of the study was assessed by classifying subjects according to some dichotomy (e.g., pass versus fail or survived versus died). So both kinds of conclusion can also be drawn from contingency tables. It is true that correlations rarely allow the attribution of causality. This is because it is rare for an experimenter to manipulate a continuous variable according to some broad distribution of values; however, such an experiment is not inconceivable.

Summary

1. The comparison of the means of two groups can be viewed as an instance of regression where the independent variable group is a predictor taking the values 0 and 1. In this way a difference in means can be represented and evaluated as a point biserial correlation coefficient. (This statistic is not widely used.)

2. The significance of the difference between two means can be tested with an F

ratio in the analysis of variance summary table generated for this regression. F is the square of t. (It is more usual to compute t than F in these circumstances.)

3. The regression approach to the comparison of means is used when it is necessary to partial out the effect of some nuisance variable prior to evaluating the comparison. This is the problem addressed by the analysis of covariance. In this book this is viewed as an instance of stepwise regression. The baseline deviance is the deviance for the regression on the nuisance variable. The current model is the regression on the nuisance variable with the predictor, group. An F ratio is computed which tests the significance of the difference between the groups on a dependent variable which has been 'corrected' by partialling out the effect of the nuisance variable.

4. It is only possible to attribute causality in an experiment where there is a true manipulation, e.g. where two groups are randomly sampled from the same population and one of them treated in some way. The type of statistical test used has no bearing on whether causality can be attributed or not.

WORK SHEETS

MINITAB

Minitab commands introduced in this chapter: copy, dealing with missing data.

Comparing means in a regression analysis
Retrieve the data from the experiment on the effect of temperature on typing performance from Chapter 6. Name the columns, if you have not already done so, and print them out.

> **name c1 'Errors' c2 'Temp_grp'**
> **print c1 c2**

The print command will give a display of the form

```
ROW   Errors   Temp_grp

  1      28         1
  2      24         1
  3      47         1
  4      30         1
  5      45         1
  6      37         1
  7      30         1
  8      28         1
  9      25         1
 10      11         1
 11      26         1
 12      13         1
 13      34         2
 14      31         2
 15      40         2
 16      25         2
 17      52         2
 18      31         2
 19      39         2
 20      48         2
 21      42         2
 22      40         2
 23      30         2
 24      36         2
```

The first 12 values in the column are the warm group and the last twelve the normal group. The second column contains a 1 for all the warm group and a 2 for all the normal group. In Chapter 6 these data were subjected to a t-test. Examine the distribution of scores with a box plot and then compute a t-test. Write down the means and t value obtained.

> **boxplots 'Errors';**
> **by 'Temp_grp'.**
> **twot c1 c2;**
> **pooled.**

We cannot regress Errors onto Temp_grp as it stands as the groups have been coded as 1 and 2. They need to be recoded as 0 and 1. This can be achieved by using the let command to subtract 1 from each code.

> **name c3 'New_tg'**
> **let 'New_tg' = 'Temp_grp' - 1**
> **print 'Errors' 'Temp_grp' 'New_tg'**

We can now compute the regression - Errors is the predicted or dependent variable, New_tg is the predictor.

> **regr 'Errors' 1 'New_tg'**

This gives the following output

```
The regression equation is
Errors = 28.7 + 8.67 New_tg

Predictor         Coef        Stdev      t-ratio          p
Constant        28.667        2.713        10.57      0.000
New_tg           8.667        3.837         2.26      0.034

s = 9.399        R-sq = 18.8%      R-sq(adj) = 15.1%

Analysis of Variance

SOURCE           DF            SS           MS          F          p
Regression        1        450.67       450.67       5.10      0.034
Error            22       1943.33        88.33
Total            23       2394.00

Unusual Observations
Obs.  New_tg     Errors       Fit Stdev.Fit   Residual
St.Resid
   3     0.00      47.00     28.67      2.71      18.33
2.04R

R denotes an obs. with a large st. resid.
```

Testing

Find the F ratio which evaluates the difference between the two groups in this display. Is it significant at the .05 level? Check that the t value obtained with the twot command is indeed the square root of this F ratio (there may be small discrepancies due to rounding error). Use the regression equation to work out the mean for each group (New_tg = 0 for the warm group and 1 for the normal group). Check that these means are the same as those obtained using twot.

Analysis of covariance

Box 9.1 provides a general procedure for performing analysis of covariance. The example used to illustrate this procedure is the playgroup experiment from the introduction. Work through the example referring back to the introduction where necessary.

Box 9.1   Step by step procedure for analysis of covariance

Step 1—Tabulate the data with one row for each subject and two columns, one for the dependent variable and one for the nuisance variable. This means that the scores for both groups appear in the same column. The scores for one group will follow on from the scores for the other.

e.g.

The dependent variable is social adjustment rating (SA), the nuisance variable is age. The data are tabulated as follows, the first six subjects did not attend playgroup, the second six did.

Subject	SA	Months	
1	21	57	Not attending
3	23	58	
5	18	61	
7	17	53	
9	15	50	
11	24	55	
2	25	65	Attending
4	26	67	
6	24	69	
8	29	73	
10	23	62	
12	28	63	

Step 2—Enter the data into Minitab with an additional column containing a code, 0 for one group and 1 for the other (NOT 1 for one group and 2 for the other).

e.g.

name c1 'SA' c2 'Months' c3 'Group'

read 'SA' 'Months' 'Group'

21 57 0

23 58 0

18 61 0

17 53 0

15 50 0

24 55 0

```
25 65 1
26 67 1
24 69 1
29 73 1
23 62 1
28 63 1
end
```

Step 3—Check the data and correct any mistakes.
e.g.

print 'SA' 'Months' 'Group'

Step 4—Compute descriptive statistics and correlations. The corr command will give the correlation between the dependent and nuisance variables and point biserial correlations between group and the dependent and nuisance variables. Mean scores for the dependent and nuisance variables for the two groups cannot be obtained with desc as both groups are in the same column. Instead use the twot command. Copy down these results.
e.g.

corr 'SA' 'Months' 'Group'

gives

```
                SA      Months
Months      0.787
Group       0.747      0.830
```

The point biserial correlation between group and SA is .75.

The point biserial correlation between group and Months is .83.

The correlation between SA and Months is .79.

twot 'SA' 'Group'
twot 'Months' 'Group'

The latter command gives

```
TWOSAMPLE T FOR Months
Group   N       MEAN        STDEV       SE MEAN
0       6       55.67       3.88        1.58
1       6       66.50       4.09        1.67

95 PCT CI FOR MU 0 - MU 1: (-16.04, -5.627)

TTEST MU 0 = MU 1 (VS NE): T= -4.71   P=0.0011   DF=    9
```

(See Table 9.2 for means etc. t = 4.71, p<.05)

Step 5—Draw up a blank analysis of variance table to be filled in as the computation proceeds. Write the headings d.f., SS, MS, F and p. The rows should be headed as follows: the first as 'Reduction in deviance', the second as nuisance and group and the last as nuisance alone.

e.g.

	DF	SS	MS	F	p
Reduction in deviance	...	...	...	...	...
Months & Group	...	...	...		
Months	...	...			

Step 6—Use the regress command to compute the baseline deviance; that is the regression of the dependent variable on the nuisance variable. The predicted variable is specified first, then '1' then the nuisance variable.

e.g.

regr 'SA' 1 'Months'

The results will be as follows

```
The regression equation is
SA = - 7.65 + 0.498 Months

Predictor        Coef         Stdev      t-ratio          p
Constant       -7.647         7.577        -1.01      0.337
Months         0.4976         0.1233        4.03      0.002

s = 2.788        R-sq = 61.9%      R-sq(adj) = 58.1%

Analysis of Variance

SOURCE         DF           SS          MS         F          p
Regression      1       126.52      126.52     16.28      0.002
Error          10        77.73        7.77
Total          11       204.25
```

Step 7—Write the 'Error SS' from this computation and its d.f. into the bottom row of the blank analysis of variance table.

e.g.

	DF	SS	MS	F	p
Reduction in deviance	...	...	...	...	...
Months & Group	...	...	...		
Months	10	77.73			

Step 8—Use the regress command to compute the deviance for the full model, that is the regression of the predicted variable on the nuisance variable with group. The predicted variable is specified first, then '2', then the nuisance variable and group.

e.g.

regr 'SA' 2 'Months' 'Group'

The display will be as follows

```
The regression equation is
SA = 0.8 + 0.339 Months + 2.49 Group

Predictor        Coef        Stdev      t-ratio          p
Constant         0.80        12.54        0.06       0.951
Months         0.3389       0.2243        1.51       0.165
Group           2.495        2.927        0.85       0.416

s = 2.827        R-sq = 64.8%      R-sq(adj) = 57.0%

Analysis of Variance

SOURCE          DF          SS         MS        F          p
Regression       2      132.329     66.165     8.28      0.009
Error            9       71.921      7.991
Total           11      204.250

SOURCE          DF      SEQ SS
Months           1      126.524
Group            1        5.805
```

Step 9—Write the 'Error SS', MS and its d.f. into the middle row of the blank analysis of variance table.

e.g.

	DF	SS	MS	F	p
Reduction in deviance	...	...	...	...	...
Months & Group	9	71.921	7.991		
Months	10	77.73			

Step 10—Complete the analysis of variance table. d.f. and SS for the reduction in deviance are obtained by subtraction. MS is obtained by dividing SS by d.f.. F is obtained by dividing the MS for the reduction in deviance by the MS for the full model.

e.g.

77.73 − 71.921 = 5.809
10 − 9 = 1
5.809 / 1 = 5.809

71.921 / 9 = 7.991
5.809 / 7.991 is less than 1

	DF	SS	MS	F	p
Reduction in deviance	1	5.809	5.809	<1	n.s.
Months & Group	9	71.921	7.991		
Months	10	77.73			

Step 11—Use the cdf command to compute a p value for F. The subcommand specifies 'F' and the degrees of freedom for the two mean squares. The degrees of freedom for the reduction in deviance are given first. The probability given by Minitab must be subtracted from 1.000 to get the p value. Copy this into the analysis of variance table. If the p value is less than .05 then the difference between means is significant at the .05 level, even when the nuisance variable is statistically controlled.

e.g.

F is less than 1 so it cannot be significant. (See Box 8.4 for an example of the use of cdf.)

Missing data

Minitab has facilities for dealing with missing data. Missing values are coded as * and then Minitab deals with them accordingly. Let us say that the children were rated again for social adjustment one year later. Subject 7 (not attending group) and subject 11 (attending group) had by then left the school and could not be rated.

```
name c4 'SA2'
set 'SA2'
10 13 8 * 11 13 9 7 6 8 * 10
end
print 'SA' SA2' 'Months' 'Group'
```

If you ask Minitab for means etc. with the desc command you will note that it does the sensible thing and that the N given does not include the missing data.

```
desc 'SA' 'SA2' 'Months'
```

N* is the number of missing values in a column.

```
corr 'SA' 'SA2' 'Months'
regr 'SA' 1 'SA2'
```

Note that regr warns you when there are missing values but corr does not.

Selecting data with the copy command

With large data sets you may want to select some particular rows on the basis of the values in one column. You can do this with the copy command with the use subcommand:

```
name c5 'SAexp'
copy 'SA' 'SAexp';
    use 'Group'=1.
print 'Group' 'SAexp'
```

Testing

Use this command to put the data in a format suitable for performing a Mann–Whitney U test to evaluate the difference in age between the two groups. Apply the Mann–Whitney U test, $p = .0131$.

ASSIGNMENT

1. Retrieve the data used in Assignment 2 in Chapter 8. The first ten subjects are male, the second ten female and there are scores for speech rate, confidence and extraversion. Speech rate is the dependent variable. Extraversion is a nuisance variable. Compare the speech rate of males and females when the nuisance variable extraversion is statistically controlled using an analysis of covariance.

2. This assignment is to show how a t value can be computed using only the let and ssq commands. You will never have to do these computations again. My reason for including them is simply to give you some insight into the rationale behind the comparison of means when it is viewed as a problem of regression.

Retrieve the data on warm and cold typists used at the start of the work sheet and recompute New_tg if it was not saved.

(a) Regress Errors onto New_tg, copy down the analysis of variance summary table. We will first demonstrate that this table could be constructed just using let and ssq.

(b) Write down the commands needed to compute the deviance of the mean (make a new column containing deviations from the mean of all the scores and then use ssq on this column). If you have done this correctly you will get the same value as is given as 'Total SS' in the results of the regression (there may be some small difference due to rounding error).

Create another column containing the group mean for each subject (28.7 for the warm group and 37.33 for the normal group). This is Model 1. Doing this with set can be rather tedious, so the following command will do it more easily. Check it has worked with print. 'Temp_Grp' must have the codes 1 and 2 for the group in it. 'Grp_Mean' is the new column.

   code (1) 28.7 (2) 37.33 'Temp_Grp' 'Grp_Mean'

(c) what is the command needed to create another column with the deviations from Model 1? Using ssq on this column will give the deviance ('Error' SS in the analysis of variance table).

Since 'Regression' in the analysis of variance table is the difference between these two deviances you have now effectively reconstructed the whole table.

(d) Write down the square root of F. Write down t computed using the twot command (use the pooled subcommand). The values should be very similar.

3. This question is designed to test your knowledge of a variety of statistical tests, including tests from other chapters. Answer the questions set below using whatever analyses you think are appropriate. Briefly outline the procedure you used (a list of Minitab commands will usually suffice) as well as the results you got and the conclusions you draw.

Appendix B, Tables B.1 and B.2, contains some real data collected by a student at York and first used in Chapter 4. Children were asked to repeat back 40 non-words such as 'bomat'. A score out 40 is recorded, depending on how many non-words they repeat back accurately. Previous research predicts that their ability to do this should correlate with their ability to learn new words and so the size of their vocabulary. This is because both abilities depend on being able to perceive and remember briefly new combinations of sound.

The childrens' vocabulary is measured with the British Picture Vocabulary Scale (BPVS). This requires the child to name objects depicted with pictures. In addition there are two measures of general intellectual ability: the British Ability Scale (BAS) and a raw score from Raven's Matrices non-verbal intelligence test.

(a) Describe these four variables and the correlations between them.

(b) Is the student's hypothesis supported by these data? (Does the non-word pronunciation task predict BPVS when general ability is statistically controlled?)

(c) The 48 children are divided into two age groups. Group 1 consists of 4 and 5 year olds, Group 2 is 6 and 7 year olds. Compute mean scores for these two groups on each of the four variables.

(d) Are the differences in non-word pronunciation in the two groups still significant when general intellectual ability is statistically controlled?

(e) Appendix B, Table B.2, contains the detailed results of the non-word pronunciation task. If the word was pronounced correctly then there is a 1, if it was not a 0. Compute the split-half reliability of the non-word pronunciation score.

SUMMARY OF DCL COMMANDS
See end of Chapter 5

SUMMARY OF MSDOS COMMANDS
See end of Chapter 5

SUMMARY OF MINITAB COMMANDS

set   (indicate you have come to the end of the data with end, missing data is entered as *)

read (ditto)	**erase**
print	**save** 'name'
let	**retrieve** (**retr**) 'name'
describe (**desc**)	**outfile** 'name'
mean	**nooutfile**
stdev	
sum	**regress** (**regr**)
table	(e.g. **regr c1 1 c2**)
histogram (**hist**)	**correlation** (**corr**)
stem-and-leaf	
boxplots	
plot	
name	**copy c2 c3;**
info	**use** c1=value.

cdf value ;   (value is the number of subjects in the smaller category,
  binomial N .5 .   N is the total number of subjects. The p value is obtained by doubling the probability obtained.)

cdf value;   (value is the F ratio to be assessed. df1 is the d.f. for the
  f df1 df2 .   reduction in deviance, df2 is the d.f. for the other MS. The p value is obtained by subtracting the probability obtained from 1.000.)

twot c1 c2   (between subjects t-test, c1 gives data, c2 specifies the group)

twos c1 c2   (ditto, c1 gives data for group 1, c2 data for group 2)

mann c1 c2   (Mann–Whitney U test, data as for twos. p value specified as 'is significant at'. The mean rank for c1 is W/n_1, the mean rank for c2 is $(N(N+1)/2 - W)/n_2$, where n_1 is the number of subjects in c1, n_2 the number in c2 and $N=n_1+n_2$. Alternatively use the command   **mann** c2 c1, the mean rank for c2 is then W/n_2)

ttest c1   (within subjects t-test on difference scores)

wtest c1   (Wilcoxon matched-pairs signed ranks test on difference scores)

chisq c1 c2   (chi squared test for 2 by 2 contingency table. Critical value 3.84)

help commands

stop

APPENDIX A
CRITICAL VALUES OF R

TABLE A.1

If the observed correlation is equal to or greater than the critical value it is significant at the .05 level (two-tailed). N is the number of subjects; subtract 1 from N when assessing the significance of a partial correlation.

N	r
3	0.997
4	0.950
5	0.878
6	0.811
7	0.754
8	0.707
9	0.666
10	0.632
11	0.602
12	0.576
13	0.553
14	0.532
15	0.514
16	0.497
17	0.482
18	0.468
19	0.456
20	0.444
21	0.433
22	0.423
23	0.413
24	0.404
25	0.396
26	0.388

27	0.381
28	0.374
29	0.367
30	0.361
31	0.355
32	0.349
37	0.325
42	0.304
47	0.288
52	0.273
62	0.250
72	0.232
82	0.217
92	0.205
102	0.195

APPENDIX B
DATA SETS

TABLE B.1

Data for Assignment 2 (Chapter 4), Assignement 1 (Chapter 8) and Assignment 3 (Chapter 9)

The five columns are:

1: Non-word pronunciation (out of 40)

2: Age group

3: British Ability Scale

4: British Picture Vocabulary Scale

5: Ravens matrices, non-verbal intelligence test

There are 48 subjects.

These data are saved in the file ....

23	1	0	10	10	35	1	2	12	11	34	2	16	12	12
33	1	0	8	8	33	1	0	13	11	34	2	2	17	14
27	1	0	7	11	30	2	0	11	6	36	2	9	12	16
16	1	0	11	8	34	1	0	14	16	39	2	38	19	23
26	1	0	8	5	35	2	14	17	14	39	2	21	15	21
17	1	0	8	10	26	2	6	12	14	36	2	9	16	15
23	1	0	9	13	32	2	0	15	14	36	2	1	16	14
24	1	0	14	10	32	1	0	6	9	33	2	0	14	16
19	1	0	11	10	23	1	0	8	17	34	2	1	14	14
20	1	0	8	8	29	2	0	8	0	38	2	0	16	16
25	1	0	9	10	20	2	0	11	12	36	2	0	18	23
21	1	0	11	9	30	1	0	11	11	33	2	0	15	20
22	1	0	8	9	32	2	0	13	8	33	2	33	17	18
24	1	0	6	9	26	2	0	11	10	35	2	0	16	19
29	1	0	7	12	20	1	0	13	11	27	2	6	14	14
27	1	0	12	10	31	2	0	9	12	36	2	2	15	20

TABLE B.2

Data for Assignment 3 (Chapter 9), word pronunciation task, item data

Each data point indicates whether the word was correctly pronounced or not. There are 40 words (columns) and 48 subjects (rows).

These data are saved in the file ....

```
1111001011110111111110001100110010000100
1111111111110110111100011111011110111011111
1111111011010111110100011011101100011100
1110001001100111001001101000010000000100
1011101011111111011000011011111110000100
1110001010010110101000001100010111000100
0100101011100011101110001101111101001101
0110111001110111101110001001101100011100
1111011011010111100000011000100010000100
1111011001110010100011001100101101000100
1111001111111111111110001100010100001100
1111011011100110110010001100110100011000
0111101001010011111111001100010011100100
1110011011110111101110001111101000000100
0111111111011111111110011100110011001101
1111111011110111110100011011101100010100
1111111111101111111111001101111111110111
1111011111111111101110011011111111111100
1110011111111111111110010101110111011100
1111111111111111111110011011110110011101
1111101111111111111000110111111111111111
1111101111010110111100011001101110011100
1110111111111111111110001101110111110110
1111011111111111101101011011110110111100
1111001011011010111000011011101100000110
1111111011111111111100001101110011010101
1001101011010110101100011100010110011000
1111101011001111111110001100111111111110
```

1101101111111111101110011111111110011110
1101001111111111011000011011010110111100
1111100000100010111100001101110111000100
1111111011111111111101011011101101101011 00
1111111011011101111101101101111111011111
1111001111111111111110111011111110011111
1111111011111111111101111111111110011111
1111111111111111111111011111111111111111
1111111111111111111111111111111111111101
1111111111111111111111101111111110011110
1111111111111111111110111110111110011111
1111111111111111111110001110010111111110
1111111111111111111111011101101101110011 10
1111111111111111111111111101111110111111
1111111111111111111110011011111110111111
1111111011111111111100111111111010100
1111111111111111111100011011111010101
1111111111111111111110110011111110110
1111011011101111111000110111010101 00
1111111111111111111000110111111111111

TABLE B.3

Data for Assignment 3 (Chapter 4), arithmetic test, item data

Each data point is the mark out of 5 for the arithmetic problem. There are 20 problems (columns) and 48 subjects (rows).

These data are saved in the file ....

2 4 3 3 3 4 2 2 5 3 1 3 3 2 4 1 3 3 2 0
2 4 5 4 3 4 2 2 4 3 1 3 3 4 3 3 4 4 4 4
2 4 5 3 3 3 2 2 5 2 1 3 3 3 4 2 3 4 4 0
2 2 3 3 2 3 2 2 4 2 0 5 2 2 3 1 2 3 2 0
1 4 4 3 3 4 3 2 4 3 0 3 3 3 4 3 4 3 2 0

```
2 2 3 3 2 3 2 1 4 2 0 3 3 2 3 2 4 3 2 0
1 0 4 3 3 3 1 2 4 3 1 3 3 3 4 3 3 3 4 2
1 2 5 3 2 4 2 2 4 3 1 3 2 3 4 2 3 4 4 0
2 4 4 3 3 3 2 2 5 1 0 3 3 2 3 1 3 3 2 0
2 4 4 3 2 4 1 1 4 1 2 3 3 2 3 3 3 3 2 0
2 4 3 4 3 4 3 2 5 3 1 3 3 2 3 2 2 3 4 0
2 4 4 3 3 3 2 1 5 1 1 3 3 2 4 2 2 4 2 0
1 4 4 3 2 3 1 2 5 3 2 3 3 2 3 1 4 4 2 0
2 2 4 3 3 4 2 2 4 3 1 3 3 4 4 2 2 3 2 0
1 4 5 4 3 3 3 2 5 3 1 4 3 2 4 1 4 3 4 2
2 4 5 3 3 4 2 2 5 2 1 3 3 3 4 2 3 4 2 0
2 4 5 4 3 3 3 2 5 3 2 3 3 3 4 3 4 5 2 4
2 4 4 4 3 4 3 2 4 3 2 3 3 3 4 3 4 5 4 0
2 2 4 4 3 4 3 2 5 3 1 4 2 3 4 2 4 4 4 0
2 4 5 4 3 4 3 2 5 3 2 3 3 3 4 3 3 4 4 2
2 4 4 4 3 4 3 2 5 3 1 3 3 3 4 3 4 5 4 4
2 4 4 4 3 3 2 1 5 3 1 3 3 2 4 2 4 3 4 0
2 2 5 4 3 4 3 2 5 3 1 3 3 3 4 2 4 5 2 2
2 4 4 4 3 4 3 2 4 3 1 4 3 3 4 2 4 4 4 2
2 4 3 3 3 3 2 1 5 3 0 3 3 3 4 2 3 3 2 2
2 4 5 3 3 4 3 2 5 3 0 3 3 3 4 1 4 4 2 2
1 2 4 3 3 3 2 1 4 3 0 4 3 2 3 2 3 4 2 0
2 4 4 3 3 2 3 2 5 3 1 3 3 2 4 3 4 5 4 2
2 2 4 4 3 4 3 2 4 3 2 3 3 4 4 3 3 4 4 2
2 2 3 4 3 4 3 2 4 3 0 3 3 3 3 2 4 4 4 0
2 4 4 2 1 3 1 1 5 3 0 3 3 3 4 2 4 3 2 0
2 4 5 3 3 4 3 2 5 3 1 4 3 3 4 2 3 4 4 0
2 4 5 3 3 3 3 1 5 3 2 4 3 3 4 3 4 4 4 4
2 4 3 4 3 4 3 2 5 3 2 4 3 3 4 3 3 4 4 4
2 4 5 3 3 4 3 2 5 3 1 5 3 4 4 3 3 4 4 4
2 4 5 4 3 4 3 2 5 3 2 4 3 4 4 3 4 5 4 4
2 4 5 4 3 4 3 2 5 3 2 5 3 4 4 3 4 5 4 2
2 4 5 4 3 4 3 2 5 3 2 4 3 4 4 3 3 4 4 2
2 4 5 4 3 4 3 2 5 3 1 5 3 3 4 3 3 4 4 4
2 4 5 4 3 4 3 2 5 3 1 3 3 3 3 2 4 5 4 2
```

2 4 5 4 3 4 3 2 5 3 2 4 3 3 4 2 4 3 4 2
2 4 5 4 3 4 3 2 5 3 2 5 3 3 4 3 3 5 4 4
2 4 5 4 3 4 3 2 5 3 2 3 3 3 4 3 4 4 4 4
2 4 5 3 3 4 3 2 5 3 1 4 3 4 4 3 4 4 2 0
2 4 5 4 3 4 3 2 5 3 1 3 3 3 4 3 4 4 2 2
2 4 5 4 3 4 3 2 5 3 2 4 3 2 4 3 4 5 2 2
2 4 4 3 3 4 2 2 5 3 1 3 3 3 4 2 3 4 2 0
2 4 5 4 3 4 3 2 5 3 1 3 3 3 4 3 4 5 4 4

TABLE B.4

Data used in Chapter 8

The four columns are:

1: Recall (out of 35)

2: Age in months

3: Time taken to learn the list

4: IQ

These data are saved in the file ....

20	61	21	100
23	65	15	160
21	59	16	92
25	74	25	105
30	83	25	96
26	69	13	124
22	61	11	109
23	64	13	118
27	68	10	132
29	71	11	90

INDEX

^S
  DCL 126
  MSDOS 128
% in file specification, DCL 97
* in file specification
  DCL 97
  MSDOS 98
^Q, DCL 126
^A, DCL 125
.LIS files 72
.MAI files, DCL 98
.MTW files 72
<F3>, MSDOS 127
<insert>, MSDOS 128
χ^2 163

alternate forms reliability 91
analysis of covariance 213
average 28

between-subjects designs 157
  advantages and disadvantages 161
binomial test 111, 123
booting the system, MSDOS 18
box-plots 33, 47
boxplots command, Minitab 146

causality 220

cdf command, Minitab 124, 201
ceiling effects 142
chi squared 163
chisq command, Minitab 173
choosing a test 167
columns in Minitab 40, 44
commands
  DCL 14
  MSDOS 18
comparing means 135, 149
  in a regression analysis 214, 223
  with a correlation coefficient 218
computing
  analysis of covariance 225
  chi squared 174
  correlation matrices 118, 120
  Mann–Whitney U 147, 149
  multiple correlations 199
  r 118, 120
  significance of F 201
  stepwise regression
    descriptive use 205
    statistical control 201
  t (between subjects) 146, 149
  t (within subjects) 170
  Wilcoxon tests 170
contingency tables 25, 38, 163
continuous variable 11

copy command
  DCL 65
  Minitab 230
  MSDOS 69
corr command, Minitab 96, 118
correcting mistakes, Minitab 41
correlated-sample design 159
correlation 85
correlation coefficient, r 85
correlation matrices 181
covariate 216
critical values of r 113
cumulative frequency 60

date command, MSDOS 19
DCL 13
degrees of freedom 185
delete command
  DCL 65
  MSDOS 69
delete key
  DCL 16
  Minitab 41
  MSDOS 19
dependent variable 8, 12
describe command, Minitab 39
designing your own experiments 161
deviance 79, 184
deviance from the mean 83
deviation 79
dir command
  DCL 63
  MSDOS 67
directories
  DCL 63

MSDOS 66
dividing columns 230

erase command, Minitab 41
expected frequencies 164
experimental control 9
experimental manipulation 220

F ratio 186
file
  extension, DCL 64
  extension, MSDOS 67
  name, DCL 64
  name, MSDOS 67
  protection, DCL 97
files
  DCL 63, 97
  MSDOS 66, 98
fixed effect 10
floor effects 142
floppy disks 20
formulae 54
frequency histogram 29

Gaussian distribution function 136
graphs 54

help command
  DCL 16
  Minitab 72
histogram command, Minitab 45

independent variable 8, 12
  levels of 8, 12
independent-samples design 159

info command, Minitab 93
inter-quartile range 32, 38
intercept 57
interval measures 11

least squares solution 82
leaving Minitab 43
leaving the system
  DCL 17
  MSDOS 20
let command, Minitab 41, 42
levels of an independent variable 12
linear equations as models 184
linear functions 56
linear regression 82
LIS files 72
logging in 14
  for the first time ever 14
  normally 22
logging out 15
logout command, DCL 15, 17

mail command, DCL 17, 127
mann command, Minitab 147
Mann–Whitney U test 141, 147
matched-samples design 160
mean 28, 38
  command, Minitab 43
  standard error of 35
mean rank 143, 148
measures
  of central tendency 28, 38
  of dispersion 38
  of variation 32

ratio, interval, ordinal and
  nominal 11
median 28, 38, 62, 144
missing data, Minitab 229
mode 29, 38
more than one predictor 190
MS 186
MSDOS 13
MTW files 72
multiple correlation coefficient, R 183
multiple regression 181

name command, Minitab 93
nominal data 11, 163
nominal measures 11
nominal variable 8, 11, 25
nooutfile command, Minitab 70
normal distribution 136
  violation of assumptions 138
nuisance variable 188, 213
  several 190
null hypothesis 110, 136

one-sample test 159
one-tailed tests 115, 143
order effects 162
ordinal measures 11
outfile command, Minitab 70
outliers 31, 47, 142

p value 110
parametric tests 138
partial correlation 188
  formula for 196
password 14

Pearson's product-moment
  correlation, r 85
percentile point 62
plot command, Minitab 70
point biserial correlation 218
populations and samples 35
power efficiency 141
practice effects 162
preference rating 7
print command
  DCL and MSDOS 71
  Minitab 39
probability 26, 38
prompt
  DCL 14
  MSDOS 18, 66

quartile 32, 62

r 85, 89, 115, 118, 120
  critical values of 113
  significance of 113
  strength of 114
R-sq 94
r² 87, 95
random effect 10
randomisation 162
range 32
  inter-quartile 32
ratio measures 11
read command, Minitab 45
regress command, Minitab 94, 120, 199
regression 79
  degrees of freedom 185

multiple 181
stepwise 184
  predictive use 190
  significance testing 189, 192
  statistical control 187
regression equation 82
reliability of a psychometric test 89
reporting
  analysis of covariance 217
  binomial tests 116
  Chi squared 167
  correlations 115
  F 195
  Mann–Whitney U tests 143
  multiple regression 192
  stepwise regression 192
  t-tests (between subjects) 143
  t-tests (within subjects) 166
  Wilcoxon tests 166
retrieve command, Minitab 44
return key
  DCL 14
  MSDOS 19

sample 10, 35
sampling bias 163
sampling from a population 35
save command, Minitab 43
scattergram 58, 62, 115
self selection 163
semi-inter-quartile range 38
set command, Minitab 39
sign test 111
significance 109
  levels 110

of F 201
of r 113
skew 31, 138
slope 56
Spearman-Brown formula 91
split-half reliability 91
SS 186
ssq command, Minitab 93
standard deviation 33, 38
standard error of the mean 35
standardisation sample 60
statistical inference 105, 187
statistics using ranks 140
stdev command, Minitab 43
stem and leaf display 45
stepwise regression 184
   descriptive use 190, 205
   significance testing 189, 192
   statistical control 187, 201
stop command, Minitab 48
Student's t distribution 138
sub-commands in Minitab 122
subject variables 9, 12
subjects 9
sum command, Minitab 43
switching off
   DCL 17
   MSDOS 20
switching on, MSDOS 18

t-test
   between subjects 138
   within subjects 160
table command, Minitab 45

tables and graphs 53
test-retest reliability 89
trend in a scattergram 58, 79
ttest command, Minitab 170
two-sample test 147
two-tailed tests 115, 143
twos command, Minitab 147, 160
twot command, Minitab 146
type command, DCL and MSDOS 70
types of measurement 11

up arrow key, DCL 124
user name 14

variables
   continuous 8, 11
   dependent 8, 12
   independent 8, 12
   nominal 8, 11
   subject 9
variance 34, 38
version number, DCL 64, 66

whois command, DCL 15
Wilcoxon matched-pairs signed-ranks
   test 161
wildcards
   DCL 97
   MSDOS 98
within and between subjects designs
   157
within subjects designs 171
   advantages and disadvantages 161
wtest command, Minitab 170